MY LIFE IN HIM

I HAVE STORED UP YOUR WORD IN MY HEART, THAT I MIGHT NOT SIN AGAINST YOU.

ISBN: 9798554042485

Published by:
The Jenkins Institute
thejenkinsinstitute.com

Professional Editing:
Kathy Jarrell

Logo & Cover Design:
Andrew Jenkins

Interior Layout:
Joey Sparks

Order additional copies of this resource at:

thejenkinsinstitute.com/shop

or

tji@thejenkinsinstitute.com

Dedication

One of the great treasures of life is when you find someone who does with excellence what you cannot do. The Jenkins Institute has now published a healthy shelve full of books. All of these have come in the last 10 years or less. For over 30 years we have both been writers.

What changed that has caused us to now have so many volumes available? One thing stands out. Well, actually two. Our expert editor, Kathy Jarrell has read, reviewed, encouraged, and corrected hundreds of thousands of words for us. She has been the church secretary for the church of Christ in Green Hills for roughly two decades, prior to that she edited in the dissertation office at Vanderbilt. She is kind and caring even in her careful work of correcting. We turn anything we have written over to her with confidence.

We said two things stand out. The other is Joey Sparks. Joey, like Kathy, brings a unique set of skills to the work he does with The Jenkins Institute. He is brilliant, dedicated, and efficient. Joey puts up with hard deadlines and continual changes and frequent check-ins for updates with kindness and grace. We trust not only his skill but his faithfulness.

Without these two dear friends you would not be able to see the books we have written. They both make us better and we love them for it. It is with the deepest of appreciation that we dedicate this book to Kathy Jarrell and Joey Sparks.

CONTENTS

FOREWORD

My life in Christ reflects Christ's life in me. Paul, in chains in Philippi, says, "For me to live is Christ and to die is gain" (Philippians 1:11). For Paul "to live is Christ" means his aim in life is the same as Christ's, which is to save as many lost people as possible. For that reason, Paul is able to rejoice in his imprisonment. "I want you to know, brothers, that what has happened to me has really served to advance the gospel, so that it has become known throughout the whole imperial guard and to all the rest that my imprisonment is for Christ" (Philippians 1:12-13). Paul was chained, day and night, to Roman soldiers. Sometimes the soldiers must have wondered who was whose prisoner. Paul had a "captive audience" for his gospel message.

 When we become so enthralled with Christ's stated purpose that we can rejoice at our own personal misfortune when it furthers that purpose, we can say with Paul, "for me to live is Christ."

Paul also said, "I have been crucified with Christ. It is no longer I who live, but Christ who lives in me. And the life I now live in the flesh I live by faith in the Son of God, who loved me and gave himself for me" (Galatians 2:20). In Christ, we break the chains that hold us in bondage to sin. We die to sin. We crucify the old man we once were. "Therefore, if anyone is in Christ, he is a new creation. The old has passed away, behold, the new has come" (1 Corinthians 5:17).

This is a powerful book. Each day, you will explore how, in a different setting, a different relationship, when wrestling with a negative attitude or problem, and in a triumphant life lived in the Spirit, Christ in you blesses and helps you. By faith you know Jesus Christ lives in you and you in him as you live your physical life. This book will cause you to start each day with that uplifting truth in mind.

Don't miss that blessing. Start every day centering on this truth, "My life...In Him."

Cecil May, Jr.
Dean Emeritus, Biblical Studies
Faulkner University
Montgomery, AL

My Family

MARCUS M^cKEE

KNOW ABOUT HIM OR KNOW HIM?

TODAY'S SCRIPTURE: John 14:1-7

There is a difference between knowing about Jesus and knowing Him.

I may know a lot about Jesus, but how well do I know Him? Jesus challenges His disciples with the statement: "If you had known me, you would have known my Father also" John 14:7. Perhaps something that often hampers our walk with Jesus is that we know a lot about Him, but we don't know Him.

Make no mistake, we can't know Jesus unless we first get to know about Him (Romans 10:14). It is my responsibility as a husband and a father to ensure my family knows about Jesus and continues to learn more and more about Him (Deuteronomy 6:7). It is also my responsibility to model a relationship with Jesus and to help each member of my family develop their own personal relationship with Him (Ephesians 6:4). A relationship with Jesus is what will determine my family's eternal future because knowledge of someone does not change hearts and lives – knowing them does! For example, you may know who my wife is but that probably doesn't inspire you to make sure you don't ever wake her up unexpectedly, but because I know her, I will sleep on the floor if it means not waking her up!

Has knowing Jesus ever caused me to sleep on the floor? When we get to know Jesus, we begin to love Him, and that love motivates and causes us to give our discretionary efforts to His cause, not our minimal effort, because to know Jesus is to give up everything for Him (Matthew 10:37-39). Knowing Jesus, not just knowing about Him, means that we don't have to be worried about hearing Jesus' words: "I never knew you; depart from me, you workers of lawlessness" (Matthew 7:23).

Today, I will...assess my relationship with Jesus to determine if I am modeling a relationship with Him or only have a knowledge of Him.

TREASURES HERE OR THERE?
TODAY'S SCRIPTURE: Matthew 6:19-21

Am I helping my family know Jesus and lay-up treasures in heaven?

When kids go off to college, most parents know whether or not their child will do well, because they have spent over 30 hours a week for the last 13 years preparing them, and they have seen how they have done. However, many of those same parents are very concerned about their child's faith in college because "so many of the youth from church over the last several years aren't faithful Christians anymore." As parents we always have a reason why such as: "There were not many opportunities for Johnny to get involved because he just didn't have anything in common with the other kids." "They didn't teach enough about developing your faith to the young people." These very well may be true; however, if we are honest with ourselves, we might see that too often as parents we have focused on success in one area to the detriment of another. We expect our young people to spend a minimum of 30 hours a week to prepare to move to the next grade level, but only 1 ½ hours a week in Bible study to prepare for eternity.

Home is where it starts! It is my responsibility as a father to make sure that Jesus is the top priority in my child's schedule and my behavior will model the way. Do my children see me studying my Bible or more often do they see me watching a ball game? Am I more likely to help them understand Common Core Math and leave the Bible stuff to the ministers and Bible class teachers? Jesus said: "Do not lay up for yourselves treasures on earth...but lay up for yourselves treasures in heaven..." (Matthew 6:19-20). 1 ½ hours a week is not helping our children lay-up treasures in heaven.

Today, I will... evaluate priorities to make sure that Jesus is first and ensure that I'm helping my family seek the things above (Colossians 3:1-2).

WHAT MY POSTS SAY ABOUT MY VALUES

TODAY'S SCRIPTURE: Matthew 6:19-21

What message am I sending my family with my posts?

The things which parents recognize and upon which they brag are those things on which children will focus and often use to determine their self-worth.

When I post on social media how proud I am of Mary because she sacrificed all of her Saturdays and Sundays to make the A team, I am telling her that I value her being on the team more than her being at worship. When her mom posts pictures at 9:00am on Sunday telling how everything they had to give up this year was worth it because they are in the finals with a chance to redeem themselves for finishing 2nd last year, it tells her that being in the championship game is the most important event of the year! While many parents would claim that God is their number one priority, they swell up with pride when their child makes the game winning play during a Sunday morning tournament but fail to notice that he can't find 1 Peter without looking at the index in the Bible. No one can serve the master of championship success and Jesus at the same time (Matthew 6:24).

Paul consistently demonstrates his values through the recognition given others. He tells Timothy that he longs to see him and is reminded of his sincere faith (2 Timothy 1:4-7). No doubt Timothy understood that not only was he important to Paul, but that his faith was also important to Paul. If I want my child to develop a strong faith, I must show her that it is very important to me. One of the most effective ways I can do that is by recognizing and praising spiritual accomplishments and values more than secular ones.

Today, I will... recognize and praise a member or all members of my family when they are like Jesus.

TREATING THE FAMILY LIKE MY FAMILY

TODAY'S SCRIPTURE: Colossians 3:12-17

Do I treat fellow Christians as my Family? Do I extend the same grace towards them?

Ever notice how we tend to make exceptions for the mistakes of our family members and closest friends? This is something I have definitely done because I will focus on their positive traits which leads me to minimize anything negative about them. As I think about this, I don't so much wonder if it is a good or bad thing, but ask myself: "Self – why don't you do this for all your brothers and sisters? Aren't all Christians your family? Aren't Christians, told to put on compassionate hearts, kindness, humility, meekness, and patience, bearing with one another and, if one has a complaint against another, forgiving each other (Colossians 3:12-13)? Yes! Self – I am to love my neighbor as myself (Galatians 5:14)."

Think about that for a minute, when it comes to my interactions with other Christians, I am to be: compassionate even if it was Brother Grouchy's fault that he lost job; kind although Sister Better-than-you complains about my prayer, reading, or most probably my singing; humble and not get upset when Brother Look-at-me took all the credit for the VBS decorations; gentle when dealing with Sister Porcupine and her pew; patient with Brother and Sister New-to-church who don't quite understand why and continue to ask the same questions.

Paul goes on to say that "above all of these, we are to put on love which binds everything together in perfect harmony" (Colossians 3:14). Love binds everything together because when I react out of love, I will respond in the way Christ wants and not how I want or think the other person deserves. When I react out of love, I treat all family like family. I look for and find everyone's positive traits.

Today, I will...look for the good in all my brothers and sisters and focus on each person's positive qualities and treat all the family like my family.

MAKING PEACE

TODAY'S SCRIPTURE: Romans 12:18

It depends on me to live peaceably with others.

Have you ever had a situation where you were at odds with someone and you tried to resolve it, but the other person wasn't having it? You went "the extra mile" in your mind to make amends, but it wasn't enough. Maybe it even reached the point where you said something like: "I've done all I can do; the ball is in their court now".

Paul tells us: "Repay no one evil for evil but give thought to do what is honorable in the sight of all. If possible, so far as depends on you, live peaceably with all" (Romans 12:17-18). Many times, I have taken this verse to justify why I stopped making an effort to mend a relationship I had broken. It would make me feel good about myself. After all, I had apologized, repented, paid back the money, paid for the repairs, and written a letter to the elders, what more could I do? Instead of wondering if I had done everything that others would think is reasonable or everything I was told to do, I had to ask if I had done everything that depended on me? A lot of times the answer was: "No, I hadn't."

If I truly let the peace of Christ rule my heart (Colossians 3:15), you know the peace that did not revile nor threaten when mocked, beaten, and killed but trusted in God (1 Peter 2:23), if that peace rules my heart then I understand there is a lot more that depends on me when it comes to lively peaceably with all (Romans 12:18). Instead of looking for a reason why I don't have to make peace or can to quit trying to, I will find any reason at all to forgive and make peace, especially when it comes to family, my whole family.

Today, I will...pray that God softens my heart to forgive and make peace with someone or maybe even make peace with a situation.

WEEK 2

The Church

TRAVIS BOOKOUT

BABEL TO PENTECOST

TODAY'S SCRIPTURE: Acts 2

The Tower of Babel story in Genesis 11 is a wild ride. Babel (a.k.a Babylon) is the epicenter of all the wicked kingdoms of the earth. In this account, the whole earth was unified in word and language. They developed new building technologies, developed a city, and colluded to construct a massive tower to "make a name for ourselves." They feared being scattered throughout the earth (Genesis 11:3-4).

God abruptly ends this project. When He sees the great power of their unity, He notes "nothing that they propose to do will now be impossible for them" (Genesis 11:6). There is tremendous power in a unified people, so God divides, scatters, and confuses their languages.

One of the major themes throughout the rest of Scripture is how to undo the terrible events of Babel. In the next chapter, God begins a plan to bless "all the families of the earth" (Genesis 12:2-3). The Bible contains glimpses and promises of a time when "all peoples, nations, and languages" will serve together in God's kingdom (Daniel 7:14; Revelation 7:9-10).

This backstory is essential for understanding the church as God's united community. The central mystery of the gospel is the unification of Jew, Gentile, and every nation on earth into one family (Ephesians 3:6ff).

The project to reverse Babel is vividly described when the church begins on Pentecost. "Men from every nation under heaven" are gathered together again in one city (Acts 2:5). Their diverse languages are united as "each one was hearing them speak in his own language" (Acts 2:6). In Acts 2, however, they are glorifying God and Christ rather than themselves.

There is still tremendous power in a unified people. The church is the divine community of God that unites into one family those of every nation, tribe, and language. In the church you play a role in reversing Babel and bringing unity to our hurt and divided world.

Today, I will…make my mission to bring unity, rather than division, into God's world.

FOREVER FAMILY

TODAY'S SCRIPTURE: Mark 10:28-31

Jesus was radical in so much of what He said and did. His kingdom challenges nearly everything we consider to be the norm. Mark 10 is perhaps the most challenging chapter in the Bible. Jesus challenges the way we practice marriage (Mark 10:5-11), wealth (Mark 10:21-25), and authority (Mark 10:42-45). But tucked away in the middle of these challenges is one of the greatest blessings we have in this life.

"Truly, I say to you, there is no one who has left house or brothers or sisters or mother or father or children or lands, for My sake and for the gospel, who will not receive a hundredfold now in this time, houses and brothers and sisters and mothers and children and lands, with persecutions, and in the age to come eternal life. But many who are first will be last, and the last first" (Mark 10:28-31).

Jesus' response is an incredible reassurance to those who have sacrificed for the kingdom. Even if following Jesus has cost you family, God cares and gives you more family. Even if you lose your house, you'll receive many more. This new way of thinking about family depends upon the definition of family given by Jesus in Mark 3:35: "Whoever does the will of God, he is my brother and sister and mother." In the church you receive a new and larger family. You receive more houses, lands, parents, and children.

Years ago there was a flood in our city that damaged our house. My wife was pregnant with our first child and we had to leave our home as water was filling up our living room. Neither of us had any family that lived near us. But in a very real way, we had family that lived near us. We had so many houses open to us and families to welcome us. The church proved to be our family in a time of need. That's what the church is called to be.

Today, I will...treat the church as my true family.

LOVE ONE ANOTHER

TODAY'S SCRIPTURE: John 13:34-35

John 13 records stirring, emotional, and convicting details about the life of Jesus. It's in this chapter that Jesus lowers Himself and washes His disciple's feet and gives His disciples a "new commandment" to love another. Jesus loved His disciples and showed it by washing their feet (John 13:1). He wants them to imitate Him and "wash one another's feet" (John 13:14). He also wants them to imitate Him, saying, "you love one another: just as I have loved you, you also love one another. By this all men will know that you are my disciples, if you have love for one another" (John 13:34-35).

The defining characteristic of Christian discipleship is love. The greatest way to show love to one another is service. Jesus embodies both love and service and calls us to imitate Him. This is how the world knows that we follow Him; His love and service continue through our attitudes, words, and action.

John 13 also contains other events. It is in John 13 that Judas, with freshly washed feet, walks away from the Lord to betray Him (John 13:30). It is also here where Jesus predicts that Peter will deny Him three times (John 13:38). John 13 reminds us of powerful, self sacrificial love of Jesus, but it also reminds us of the disciple's failure to live up to it. Yet Jesus loves anyway.

This chapter looks so much like the church. We have been served and washed by Jesus, stand in awe of His goodness, we are called to imitate Him, we strive to show the depth of His love and service towards one another, but we fail so often. Yet Jesus loves us anyway. And even in our failures, the brightness of God's love shines through. I've never felt or experienced the love of God more closely than when I'm among His people, trying, failing, and trying again.

Today, I will...show the love and service of Jesus to my church family.

PILLAR OF TRUTH

TODAY'S SCRIPTURE: 1 Timothy 3:14-15

Among my favorite passages in the Bible are the "purpose statements." These are the passages that tell you the purpose of a writing. A great example is 1 Timothy 3:14-15: "I hope to come to you soon, but I am writing these things to you so that, if I delay, you may know how one ought to behave in the household of God, which is the church of the living God, the pillar and buttress of the truth."

You no longer need to wonder why Paul wrote 1 Timothy or why it is in our Bible. It was written so we know how to behave in God's house, the church. There are some powerful descriptions of the church in this passage. The church is called the "household of God" and the "pillar and buttress of the truth." If you want to live in God's house, there are some matters of truth that need to be upheld.

Being a support for the truth is one of the greatest vocations of the church. God has charged us with caring about, living by, and upholding truth. This means if you want to learn about God and learn eternal truth, the church is a great place to go. One should be able to go to the church and find the truth. The church should rely on Scripture for truth alongside one another's encouragement in it.

You do not have to discover all the truth entirely on your own. You do not have to learn the Bible on your own. You do not have to learn everything about Jesus alone. The church has teachers, preachers, elders, mature Christians who have spent years studying Scripture, practicing the faith, growing in wisdom, and imitating Jesus. There are minds other than your own that can help you. You can learn truth from these people. The church is a wonderful resource for study, learning, guidance, and truth.

Today, I will...use my church family as a resource in my spiritual journey and search for truth.

CHURCH MATTERS

TODAY'S SCRIPTURE: Ephesians 1:22-23

God did not call us to do Christianity alone. Jesus did not die for us to be Christians by ourselves. The Bible does emphasize a "personal relationship" with Jesus. The Bible also emphasizes a communal relationship with Jesus. Jesus gave His life for His community of disciples. God wants us to do Christianity with the help, support, and encouragement of a community of followers.

Westerners live in a dangerously individualistic world. We like our privacy. We believe we can pull ourselves up by our own bootstraps and we don't need anybody else telling us what to do or how to live. We are in charge of our own lives. Even spiritually we like to individualize the gospel and personalize our discipleship to meet our specific needs. The great problem with this is that it's not what Jesus asked for and it leaves little room for His church.

The church is bigger than me. The church was predestined in the mind of God before creation (Ephesians 1:3-14). The church is the family of God, the culmination of a plan long established to bring peace, unity, and reconciliation to God's world (Ephesians 2:11-3:21). Jesus died to be the Savior of the church because He loves her, and wants to sanctify, cleanse, wash, and present her in all her glory, being blameless and without blemish (Ephesians 5:25-27). Jesus is the head, not only of the church (Colossians 1:18), but head "over all things to the church" (Ephesians 1:22). To the church, Jesus is the head of every single thing, because we are His body (Ephesians 1:23).

The church matters to God. He wants us to be reconciled to Him in the church, to be part of a new family, to show the world a new depth of love and service, to live with, learn from, and rely upon one another. The call of the gospel is about "us" and not just "me."

Today, I will...commit myself to being part of a community of Christians that is greater than myself.

Spiritual Growth

STEVE LUSK

JESUS GREW

TODAY'S SCRIPTURE: Luke 2:52

Human growth and development is the study of how people grow. When our children or grandchildren aren't growing and developing in all areas of life as they should, we become concerned!

Jesus took on human form even though He was the Son of God (See Philippians 2:5-10). While we do not know much about his early life, Luke gives us glimpses of Jesus as a baby (Luke 2:1-7) and as a growing boy. Luke 2:52 states "And Jesus increased in wisdom and in stature and in favor with God and man."

The four-fold nature of Jesus' growth shows us how a healthy individual will grow. His ability to use the knowledge He was acquiring was seen as He increased in wisdom. He grew physically taller and stronger as He increased in stature. He learned to relate well to other people as He grew in favor with man. He grew spiritually as He increased in favor with God.

Jesus' example shows us that we must be growing spiritually in order to be healthy individuals. What did that growth entail? The context of Luke 2 gives us insight into the spiritual development of Jesus.

Jesus' family observed the religious festivals of Judaism (Luke 2:41-42). Getting in the habit of being with God's people to celebrate and worship Him will enhance our spiritual growth.

Jesus was interested in learning from those who could teach Him (Luke 2:46-47). The very Son of God was listening and asking questions of the Temple teachers. One trait of an individual who wants to grow spiritually is his or her willingness to listen, ask questions, and learn.

Jesus was aware of the importance of doing His Father's will as He said, "I must be in my Father's house" (Luke 2:49). Putting the Father's business before all else is essential to our spiritual growth and development.

Jesus was submissive to His parents (Luke 2:51). Learning to be obedient to the voice of authority is vitally important if we desire spiritual growth.

Today, I will... make growing in favor with God a top priority in my life.

14

I NEED MILK!

TODAY'S SCRIPTURE: 1 Peter 2:1-3

Erma Bombeck, my mother's favorite humorist, once wrote an essay entitled, "Why Don't You Grow Up," about a mother who was frustrated by her children's immaturity. When a child doesn't develop physically, we become concerned. When that child fails to mature in other ways, deeper problems can result.

We can relate to the apostle Peter because he struggled with immaturity. He spoke up when he should have been listening. He made promises that he could not keep. Failing to listen and being undependable are signs of immaturity.

After Peter gained a measure of maturity in Christ he wrote about spiritual growth. "So put away all malice and all deceit and hypocrisy and envy and all slander. Like newborn infants, long for the pure spiritual milk, that by it you may grow up into salvation—if indeed you have tasted that the Lord is good" (1 Peter 2:1-3).

Peter understood that growing babies need milk. Infants cannot tolerate solid food until their digestive systems mature. Spiritual babies need the milk of the Word. Certain things shouldn't be in our diet—malice, deceit, hypocrisy, envy, and slander.

We need the milk of the Word in order to grow, but milk is not enough to sustain growth. Peter continued to grow as manifested in numerous ways:

> ...boldly preached the first Gospel sermon on the day of Pentecost (Acts 2).
> ...was imprisoned and beaten for proclaiming the resurrected Christ (Acts 4:2-3; 5:40-42). ...overcame prejudice and taught the first Gentile convert, Cornelius (Acts 10:47-48).
> ...wrote to Christians facing persecution encouraging them to endure (1 & 2 Peter).

Peter's life is a case study in spiritual growth from infantile behavior to mature steadfastness. As he closed his second letter, he wrote, "But grow in the grace and knowledge of our Lord and Savior Jesus Christ. To him be the glory both now and to the day of eternity. Amen" (2 Peter 3:18).

Today, I will... acknowledge the need for spiritual growth in my life by feeding on the milk of the Word and continuing to grow in the grace and knowledge of Jesus Christ.

SOWING AND REAPING

TODAY'S SCRIPTURE: 1 Corinthians 3:1-7

More Americans are growing their own food. "According to the National Gardening Association, 35 percent of households in the US grow food either at home or in a community garden" (farmerfoodshare.org). Many Americans are learning what farmers have always known—God has ordained the principles of sowing and reaping (Genesis 1:11-12).

Sowing and reaping also applies to our spiritual growth. In 1 Corinthians 3, Paul addressed Christians who needed to understand that failure to sow the Word of God into their lives was stunting their growth. He called them "infants in Christ" and said they were not ready for "solid food." They had not grown because they were "people of the flesh" instead of spiritual people. They needed to understand that their growth was not dependent on Paul or Apollos, but on God! Paul and Apollos were merely "gardeners" who planted and watered the seed. God made it grow.

In Matthew 13 Jesus told a parable about a farmer who went out to sow seed. Some seed fell along the well-worn pathway and could not take root. Some seed fell on ground that was not deep enough to sustain growth. Some seed was sown on ground that was encumbered with thorns that choked out the good plants. And some seed fell on good ground and produced the desired result—a bountiful harvest.

Jesus explained this parable by saying that some are hard-hearted and will not allow the seed (Word of God) to begin to grow. Others are not sincere in accepting the Word and fall away when persecution comes. Still others allow the cares and riches of the world to choke out the Word. Thankfully, some produce fruit by hearing and understanding the Word.

Let's clean out the thorns, dig out the rocks, and allow the Word of God to be planted in our hearts, take root, and grow. God has promised that good fruit will be produced in our lives. That is spiritual growth!

Today, I will... allow the Word of God to take root in my heart so that I can produce spiritual fruit in my life.

BECOMING MATURE IN CHRIST

TODAY'S SCRIPTURE: Ephesians 4:11-16

One day after baseball practice a father asked his son how practice had gone. One of the boy's teammates had scolded him for something he was doing wrong. Instead of pouting or becoming angry, the boy thanked his teammate for the advice. As a result, the boy improved and the team was strengthened. This father expressed appreciation to his son for the maturity he had shown.

Dr. Tim Elmore has identified "Seven Marks of a Mature Person" (Generation iY: Our Last Chance to Save Their Future). One of those characteristics is the "ability to be unshaken by flattery or criticism." Instruction and correction is needed during every stage of our lives. The ability to take direction and criticism is a critical part of maturation. Maturity is also needed when we receive commendation for a job well done.

Paul wrote to the church at Ephesus from prison in order to urge them to "walk in a manner worthy" of the Lord. He was addressing their need to be spiritually mature. He encouraged them to love one another and stay united in Christ (See Ephesians 4:1-6).

He reminded the Ephesians that Christ has given apostles, prophets, evangelists, shepherds, and teachers in order to equip us for works of service so that His body, the church, could be built up. He stated that maturity will be manifested in unity with each other and knowledge of the Son of God. Infants (immature Christians) will be fickle because they are susceptible to deceitful teaching schemes and crafty individuals. Deceit is defeated by "truth in love" which produces maturity in Christ.

When I demonstrate the ability to listen and respond to truth and speak truth to others out of love for them, I am walking in a manner worthy of the Lord and showing spiritual maturity.

Today, I will... develop spiritual maturity in my life by listening to the truth and showing love to others.

YOU WHO ARE SPIRITUAL

TODAY'S SCRIPTURE: *Galatians 6:1-2*

"Help! I've fallen and I can't get up!" is a line advertising a device that people who live alone can use to call for help if they get in a helpless situation.

Maybe you haven't fallen with no one to help you regain your feet, but most of us have experienced a "fall." Maybe your fall had to do with something you messed up at work, or a relationship issue, or perhaps a moral failure. Most of us have fallen.

Paul prescribes what should happen when someone falls. "Brothers, if anyone is caught in any transgression, you who are spiritual should restore him in a spirit of gentleness. Keep watch on yourself, lest you too be tempted. Bear one another's burdens, and so fulfill the law of Christ" (Galatians 6:1-2).

Those "who are spiritual" should help those who have fallen. Spiritually minded people seek to restore (mend) those who have transgressed.

The spiritual person understands that "anyone" can get caught in a transgression. "All have sinned and fall short of the glory of God" (Romans 3:23). Sixteenth century preacher John Bradford is said to have watched a criminal being led to execution and exclaimed, "There, but for the grace of God, goes John Bradford." Understanding this spiritual truth changes our perspective on the one who has transgressed.

A spiritually minded person will restore the transgressor "in a spirit of gentleness." We demonstrate spiritual growth when we are kind and considerate toward those who have sinned. In Ephesians 4:32, Paul wrote, "Be kind to one another, tenderhearted, forgiving one another, as God in Christ forgave you." Because Christ loves us enough to forgive, we should forgive each other.

Carrying the burdens of fellow strugglers is a sign of spiritual maturity. We "fulfill the law of Christ" in so doing. Jesus said, "So whatever you wish that others would do to you, do also to them, for this is the Law and the Prophets" (Matthew 7:12). Golden Rule living is a sign of spiritual growth.

Today, I will... show spiritual maturity in my life by gently helping someone who has fallen.

Parenting

DALE JENKINS

PARENTING

TODAY'S SCRIPTURE: *Joshua 24:14-15*

This week we are going to focus on how to make our families godlier and thereby stronger as parents, Today we start with the 30,000 foot view.

The world says the family is finished. They have allowed the evil one to spread suspicion and distrust, to paint the family with a brush of confusion, to become so busy and distracted that when the smallest upheaval comes families don't have the fortification to sustain. Just as individuals have differing strengths and weaknesses, no two families are alike. And, there are times and challenges that arise that make it where the ideal cannot exist, but the fact remains, God has an established plan for families. That plan includes a dad who is to be the head of the household, who has an unequivocal love for his wife, a love so deep that only death would cause him to leave her, a mom who with amazing skill is an encourager to all in the family and works in and/or out of the house to bring order and a deft compassion to that family.

The Children obey and bring an amazing joy, hope, and life to that unit. Each strives to live for God and to encourage each, the other, in that mission. The home is to be a haven for happiness, a life raft in choppy waters of culture, work, school, a launching pad for success, a refueling station for encouragement. I know that doesn't always happen, and I know that no family does family perfectly, but sometimes we should step back from the lies that satan fuels and remember how beautiful the family, as God designed it, can be.

Sometimes we need to allow each other to push the reset button and return to God's blueprint. It can be that way. We can begin anew. We can do it God's way. And this idyllic, some would say utopia-istic haven can happen if you will each allow it to be. You can go back.

Today, I will... write out a plan of my dreams for my family.

YOU CAN DO THIS

TODAY'S SCRIPTURE: Deuteronomy 6:1-3

We rolled around on the floor. I rode him around like I was a pony. I tickled him and gave him zerpels and we laughed and laughed. And he fell asleep laying on the carpet beside me watching cartoons. He was five and the next morning he would be going to school for the first time. I've never thought of myself as a deep thinker and seldom do I reflect on the past. But I remember that night from 30+ years ago like it was yesterday.

As I watched him smoothly breathe as he slept. I thought tomorrow life changes for me and for him. Up until this night, Melanie and I have been his life. Yes, he had his little friends and there were his class teachers at church and parents who were friends of ours. But these were controlled environments, safe places. Tomorrow that all changes. Tomorrow there will be teachers we don't know as well, students who don't come from families where the language is clean and morals are high. Tomorrow I will no longer be the one influence in his young life.

Little by little, others will have influence over your children. That is why it is vital that as a young parent you start proactively planning the most significant lessons you want to ingrain in them. Over the next few months, we began to make a list of what was important to us. Things we did not want them to leave home without. Yes, this parenting thing is a daunting task. If you do it right, at times it will probably seem overwhelming. I want to say to all parents out there, "you can do this." God and His People are on your side. Seek help from both. If you have children, I hope you have moments like that fun afternoon with your children, and I want to assure you the moments you'll get to enjoy them when they are grown and you are older, will be even more delightful.

Today, I will...begin my own list of imperatives I want to instill in my children.

HANNAH HAD IT RIGHT

TODAY'S SCRIPTURE: 1 Samuel 1-2

Humanism devalues life.
Abortion devalues children.

Roll back the clock a couple of hundred years and the live birth of a child was a precious and valued thing. According to OurWorldInData.org, in 1800 the global average child mortality rate (percentage of children who do not reach one year of age) was 43.3%. By 2019 that rate had fallen to 3.4% globally and .7% in the United States. Go to an old grave yard and you will often see a small tombstone inscribed with something like this, "Infant Child of Bob and Bev Smith born April 3, 1873, died April 6, 1873." The reason it reads "Infant Child of" is simply that often because of the high death rate of infants children would not be given a name until they were 6 months to one year old.

As our culture has become more secular the value of a life has decreased. If the motivating determiner for your world view does not include God, then there is no true compelling reason to value any life other than your own. Perhaps that would explain so much of the lack of consideration for others, the anger, self-serving actions, and angst presently manifesting itself in our culture.

God says: "Behold, children are a heritage from the LORD" (Psalm 127:3).

The world sound-bytes that no child should be left behind and then hides behind its politics. I think Hannah had it right and that each of us needs to be reminded of, and emulate her decisions: Hannah "prayed to the Lord and wept bitterly. And she vowed a vow and said, 'O Lord of hosts, if you will indeed look on the affliction of your servant and remember me and not forget your servant, but will give to your servant a son, then I will give him to the Lord all the days of his life...'" (1 Samuel 1:11).

Do you want to know the secret to great parenting (Genesis 18:19)? Want to have well adjusted children in a maladjusted world (Ephesians 6:4)? Want to aid in the assurance of stability for your family Proverbs 1:8-9)? Want to give your children the best opportunity to launch successfully (Isaiah 54:13)? Want to give them the very best? Give them to the Lord.

Today, I will...pray for all the children of the world and if I still have children in my house, I will rededicate myself to giving them to God.

I'M GONNA BE LIKE YOU, Pt 1

TODAY'S SCRIPTURE: John 8:38-44

Before you go further, read Today's Scripture. These are some of the Lord's most difficult words to hear. He is speaking to some of the Jews who believed in him, note especially verses 38 and 44.

Admit it. If you are a parent or ever think you might be one you've said these words about some issue: "When I have kids, I'll never be like my parents..." And, then you are. You'll catch yourself and realize that what you just said/did was just like your mom or dad. The fact is, it takes a lot of effort to not be like our parents. And, while it's the traits you don't desire that get attention, our emulating our parents runs the gauntlet of the good and the not so desirable.

Rather than dissect the why's and how's of this, may I direct your attention to your own parenting methods?

I've worked with local churches now for over 40 years. In those years I've seen thousands of parents. I've watched their levels of commitment, their involvement in good works, their activity in worship, their attitudes, their levels of maturity and I have something to say.

Your children are going to be like you.

So, if your speech is filled with negativity, get ready to raise some kids who will have a negative bent on life. If your speech is filled with gossip or criticism get ready for that to come back to you. If you are always involved in drama, it's coming home. If you jump into every fight ready to fight, it's doubtful you'll raise a peacemaker. If your commitment to the Lord lacks follow though, be prepared for your kids commitment to probably even be less. You may sing "Oh, how I love Jesus," but your kids will know. You may talk about loving the church but if you are continually critical of the elders, the preacher, the song leaders, the deacons, the teachers, etc...well, I think you get it.

Your children are going to be like you. What are you modeling?

Today, I will...examine my attitudes, words, and actions to consider if they are of the nature I want to pass along to the next generation. If not, I will ask God to forgive me and I will begin to work with Him to change.

I'M GONNA BE LIKE YOU, Pt 2
TODAY'S SCRIPTURE: 1 Corinthians 16:15

The writer of Hebrews had his list of heroes, Abraham, Moses, Noah, Gideon, etc. Paul had a list in Romans 16 that one preacher used to form a lesson he styled "When the Roll is Called Down Here." I've got mine too: Heffington, Ryan, Moore, Hunter, Owsley, Cashion, Mayhall, Senn, Birdyshaw, and there are too many other to list.

In a letter that addresses a lot of contentious people in a congregation that was on the verge of becoming toxic, Paul recognizes one family that stands in contrast. He says of the household of Stephanas that they "have devoted themselves to the service of the saints" (1 Corinthians 16:15).Yesterday we talked about many of the negatives that can come about when we model unhealthy or sinful attitudes or actions in front of our children. But here in the noxious environment in Corinth is a family who modeled service to God's people. You know how impressive that is? The impact that makes on a local church? The example that spreads within a community when that is the template? The impression that makes on a city when that is the reputation of the church set by even one exemplary family? I've seen it. My list above, that's who they are. They are people who so devoted their lives (the KJV says "addicted themselves") to be servants that their very names became synonymous with caring, constant, and continuous service. When a need is there, they are the first to sign up, the first to show up, and the last to leave.

My experience is that this becomes contagious within a family. Just as negative actions are imitated, so are positives. I know of families who don't miss their favorite college teams games, or whose children play every sport, or are heavily invested in some other extracurricular activity, and those children grow up disconnected from the Kingdom. You want to raise faithful, fruit-bearing children. Be that as a parent.

Today, I will...examine my activities and see if there is more I can do to serve the saints with my family.

Marriage

BILL WATKINS

SUBMITTING ISN'T EASY

TODAY'S SCRIPTURE: Ephesians 5:21-33

Submitting isn't easy. What does it mean?

The idea of a wife submitting to her husband doesn't go down well with many these days. It conjures up visions of dominance, cruelty, fear, abuse, and low self-esteem.

Yet the Scriptures are clear: "Wives, submit to your own husbands, as to the Lord" (Ephesians 5:22). Does this mean that a wife must always obey her husband? Does it mean that her thoughts and opinions cannot be as important as her husband's?

The Greek word that is used for submit is a military word that means to stand under. The private is under the sergeant, the sergeant is under the captain, and so on. In the military, each soldier is obligated to follow the orders of those who are above him in the chain of command.

While that is what the word generally means, it is not the way Paul uses the word here.

Two verses make that clear. The first is verse 21: "submitting to one another out of reverence for Christ." If submitting means that the one underneath has to always do what the one above says, how do we submit to one another?

The second is verse 33: "However, let each one of you love his wife as himself, and let the wife see that she respects her husband." Paul practically defines what he means by "submit" by substituting the word "respect."

It's still not easy. The word used here in every other case speaks of the reverence that humans are to have toward God.

Submitting does not mean becoming a doormat or parking your brain at the wedding ceremony. It doesn't mean that we can't disagree or have arguments. It DOES mean that when we do, we'll always respect one another.

Today, I will... show respect to my spouse regardless of circumstances.

LOVING LIKE CHRIST

TODAY'S SCRIPTURE: Ephesians 5:25-33

Loving like Christ means sacrificing like Him.

When Jesus gave the defining marks of discipleship, the first requirement was love. "A new commandment I give to you, that you love one another: just as I have loved you, you also are to love one another. By this all people will know that you are my disciples, if you have love for one another" (John 13:34-35).

What's true in discipleship is equally true in marriage. "Husbands, love your wives, as Christ loved the church and gave himself up for her, that he might sanctify her, having cleansed her by the washing of water with the word, so that he might present the church to himself in splendor, without spot or wrinkle or any such thing, that she might be holy and without blemish. In the same way husbands should love their wives as their own bodies. He who loves his wife loves himself" (Ephesians 5:25-28).

No husband has the right from God to be a tyrant in his family. No husband has the right to make his wife be submissive. His responsibility to his family is to love them like Christ loves the church.

Christ loved the church enough that He not only died for it – He lived for it. Every action He took every day was to make the church more beautiful.

Every husband wants to know that his wife respects him. Every wife wants to know that she is the most important person on earth to her husband. When these two things occur, your marriage will be happier and fruitful in all good things.

Christ's love is sacrificial, constant, purifying and beautifying. How about yours?

Today, I will... love my wife like Christ loved the church and know that loving her blesses us both.

DON'T DEPRIVE ONE ANOTHER

TODAY'S SCRIPTURE: 1 Corinthians 7:1-5

Sexual activity in marriage is a gift we give to each other. Never use it as a control mechanism.

Paul starts the passage with a startling statement: "It is good for a man not to have sexual relations with a woman" (1 Corinthians 7:1). It appears that he is contradicting God's plan for man from the beginning. God said at creation, "It is not good that the man should be alone; I will make him a helper fit for him" (Genesis 2:18).

There is no contradiction. Paul is saying, "I think that in view of the present distress it is good for a person to remain as he is" (1 Corinthians 7:26). Persecution was arising and it would become worse. A married person or a couple with children would face hardships that a single person would not.

But he said that there was something worse that those hardships: "But because of the temptation to sexual immorality, each man should have his own wife and each woman her own husband... For it is better to marry than to burn with passion" (1 Corinthians 7:2, 9). At its lowest common denominator, marriage keeps me from sexual sin and sexual sin is worse than suffering persecution.

So God says to never withhold sexual activity in marriage. He says that we gave ourselves to one another when we married and we must not take that gift back.

But He also recognizes that there may be times when withholding ourselves from sexual activity may be necessary, so He gives us guidelines for those times in verse 5. It must be by mutual consent – it must be for an agreed upon interval – we must devote ourselves to prayer – and we must come together again at the end of that time, so that sexual temptation does not become overwhelming.

Today, I will... love my spouse and not hold back what I have already given.

SHOWING HONOR

TODAY'S SCRIPTURE: 1 Peter 3:1-7

Honoring one another honors God. Never criticize your spouse to others.

Much of what Peter writes about husbands and wives reflects what we have seen from Paul in Ephesians 5:22-33. He speaks of the need for the wife to stay focused on respect and for the husband to care for the wife.

He encourages the wife to put more emphasis on inner beauty that on the things which enhance her outer beauty. He's not opposed to taking care of yourself physically, but makes it clear that outward loveliness without inner beauty is a vain thing.

He says that Sarah honored Abraham by calling him "Lord." My wife has never called me Lord, and I'm pretty sure she never will. In Peter's day, however, calling a person "lord" could mean no more that a respectful way to greet people on the street. My wife doesn't call me lord, but she does love and respect me – and that's what Peter is talking about.

Pay close attention to God's word to husbands in verse 7: "Likewise, husbands, live with your wives in an understanding way, showing honor to the woman as the weaker vessel, since they are heirs with you of the grace of life, so that your prayers may not be hindered."

He calls the wife "the weaker vessel" not because she is weaker biologically (Wives tend to live longer than their husbands!), nor because she is weaker intellectually (I know I married above myself!), but because the husband tends to be physically stronger.

This means that the husband must not use his strength to dominate his wife or force her to do what she doesn't want to do. It means he uses his strength to protect her. Husbands when you force your wife to do something because you are stronger, God quits listening to your prayers!

Today, I will... honor my spouse and I will not manipulate or force her/him.

MARRIAGE IS FOR LIFE!

TODAY'S SCRIPTURE: Matthew 19:3-9

Given today's climate, it feels out of touch to demand that marriage be for life. It felt that way in Jesus' day too.

Marriage was cheap in the first century and divorce, even among God's people, was rampant. There was much debate on what constituted grounds for divorce. Rabbi's pontificated on the minutiae of Moses' law and argued extensively.

Since they had arguments for both sides, and since they really wanted to trap Jesus, they asked him if it was lawful to divorce for just any cause. They knew that no matter what position he took, they could argue the other side.

He shocked them when He said: "Have you not read that he who created them from the beginning made them male and female, and said, 'Therefore a man shall leave his father and his mother and hold fast to his wife, and the two shall become one flesh'? So they are no longer two but one flesh. What therefore God has joined together, let not man separate" (Matthew 19:4-6).

Jesus answer skipped over the hundreds of years of intellectual squabbling and went right to the very beginning of man's creation. He said that in the beginning God had a plan for marriage and that it had never changed. Marriage is for life and divorce should not happen.

Shocked, they asked about Moses' law. Jesus said that Moses allowed divorce because of their hard hearts, but he never commanded it. He then said that the only grounds for divorce and remarriage was fornication, and that was not honorable.

When you contemplate marriage, remember that it's for life. If you can't live with that, don't ever marry. If you are married, every problem and obstacle can be overcome if you both are willing to dig deep and trust God

Today, I will... renew my commitment to my spouse and work through difficult times.

Work

ISAAC BOURNE

WORK IS A BLESSING

TODAY'S SCRIPTURE: Genesis 2:15

Do you see work as a burden of life or a gift from God?

It is common for us to see the hardships that are associated with our work. There are difficult days, deadlines, and disappointments. Perhaps there are times when you wish you would have chosen a different profession or a different employer. These hardships and feelings are not uncommon. If persistent, they might be an indication that you do need a change of some kind. For many, the first change needs to be in how they perceive work. All of us have something that we would rather be doing than our "9-5." If we are not careful that can cast a negative perception on work.

Work is a gift from God, as foreign as that might sound. God is the giver of every good and perfect gift (James 1:17). Jesus explained to the Pharisees that God gave the Sabbath to man for his benefit and rest (Mark 2:27). Like the Sabbath, work was meant to be a blessing for man to develop skill, find purpose, create, invent, and make a difference. Work is not a negative consequence of our fallen state. God gave work to man before the fall, "The Lord God took the man and put him in the Garden of Eden to work it and keep it" (Genesis 2:15).

Work is meant to be a blessing. It gives us an avenue to be challenged and grow. It gives us the ability to see to our physical needs and the physical needs of others (Ephesians 4:28). But unfortunately, man in many ways can make it into a curse. If we let work consume our lives and burn us out then we have failed to accept it as God's gift. If we pour ourselves into work but lose ourselves emotionally and spiritually then we have once again turned work into an unnecessary burden.

Today, I will... Take a moment to appreciate the blessing of work and the opportunity it provides me to make a difference in my life and in the lives of others.

CHRISTIAN WORK ETHIC
TODAY'S SCRIPTURE: Colossians 3:23-24

"The best place to pray for potatoes is at the end of a hoe handle."
– N.B. Hardeman

There is no substitute for good work ethic. If you want to stand out from others at work, all you have to do in most cases is simply work. Sadly, most people at work are looking to put in the smallest effort possible in order to continue to receive a paycheck. As Christians, we have been called to a higher standard of living in every facet of life--including our work ethic.

Scripture commands us not only to work but to work diligently. Paul instructed the Christians in Colossae, "Whatever you do, work heartily, as for the Lord and not for men, knowing that from the Lord you will receive the inheritance as your reward. You are serving the Lord Christ" (Colossians 4:23-24).

Wise King Solomon also stressed the importance of work ethic nearly 1,000 years earlier, "Whatever your hand finds to do, do it with your might, for there is no work or thought or knowledge or wisdom in Sheol, to which you are going" (Ecclesiastes 9:10).

Our work ethic is a reflection of our character and our Christianity--and how seriously we take these commands from Scripture. We work hard and diligently not because the manager might be watching but because we know that Jesus is watching!

Strong work ethic is something that seems to be diminishing in our society and is lamented by managers and employers across all fields. As Christians we are striving to fulfill the commands of God by exhibiting a strong work ethic because we realize that ultimately, we are not working for a salary but instead we are working for a crown (2 Timothy 4:8).

Today, I will... Be honest in evaluating my work ethic and what I can do to be more diligent in my work.

SHINING AT WORK

TODAY'S SCRIPTURE: Matthew 5:14-16

How bright does your Christian light shine at work?

Jesus, in his Sermon on the Mount, told us that we need to make sure that we are shining our lights wherever we go. That means in our homes, the ballfield, on vacation, and it certainly includes work. Shining our Christian lights before others is not an attempt of personal promotion to glorify ourselves. Our intention is that when others see our good works they are directed to our Heavenly Father and His glory. Light stands out and makes a drastic difference in darkness, and we are indeed living in a dark world full of sin and broken people.

We need to shine the light of Christ with our smiles, kind words, helpful attitude, and willingness to aid our coworkers in their daily duties. The workplace is not a time to dim our lights but to make them illuminate those around us who are in need of Jesus, the light of the world: "Again Jesus spoke to them, saying, "I am the light of the world. Whoever follows me will not walk in darkness, but will have the light of life" (John 8:12).

By shining our lights at work we can serve others and lead them to Jesus. Paul's trade as a tentmaker or leatherworker did not define his identity. It was a tool that allowed him to fulfill his work in Christ. Our trades/professions are certainly an important part of our lives and take up a great deal of our time, but they do not define our identity. Your life has been hidden in "Christ who is your life" (Colossians 3:4). Our occupation is not a separate compartment that stands independent of our Christianity. That ought to change how we view our purpose at work.

Today, I will... Think of a specific way(s) in which I can shine the light of Christ at work so that others will see it and glorify God.

BEING MISSION-MINDED AT WORK

TODAY'S SCRIPTURE: John 4:35

Lost souls are all around us - even at work. Being mission-minded at work is so important in advancing the borders of the Kingdom.

In our congregation, we have a man, Jim, who is continually setting up Bible studies with his coworkers. He realizes the importance and the opportunity that is before him at work. He knows it very well and takes it personally because that used to be him. Jim was exposed to the gospel at work by Cecil, one of our deacons. Initially, Jim was not interested and was perfectly content in his denominational church. Cecil continued to talk and ask questions--questions that Jim did not have the answers for. Jim studied, searched, argued, and wrestled with the Scriptures until he could not argue anymore. Jim was baptized and then converted his wife. Additionally, after two years of continuous study, Jim converted his mother. Jim continues to study and lead people to Christ through the power of the gospel (Romans 1:16).

It all began because Cecil recognized his 10-hour shift was ripe for the harvest. This was not the first time Cecil had evangelized at work. In fact, Cecil does it regularly and has for years. The majority of the time, people are simply not interested. But to his credit, those negative responses do not keep Cecil from speaking to someone else. Through the years, Jim and others have obeyed the gospel because someone was mission-minded at work.

Jesus' words are still poignantly true for us today: "Look, I tell you, lift up your eyes, and see that the fields are white for harvest" (John 4:35). Those fields are all around us--even at work! Will we look up from the laborious task for which we are paid and see before us the spiritual task for which we have been called?

Today, I will... Pray that the Lord will open my eyes to see the harvest of souls that is before me at work. I will pray for the courage and wisdom needed to help lead people to Jesus and his gospel while at work.

A JOB WELL DONE

TODAY'S SCRIPTURE: Revelation 14:13

There is something refreshing about wrapping up a project and knowing that it was a job "well done." In order for that to take place, there are many steps necessary in completing a project: deciding what the end result is going to be, devising a plan to reach the desired goal, overcoming difficulties and unforeseen obstacles that arise, and making adjustments to initial plans as the end becomes clearer.

This beautifully corresponds to the time when our work will end and we will receive a heavenly reward for a job "well done." We must first decide that heaven, the land of rest, is our ultimate goal. Then we must understand the plan given to us in Scripture for how we can reach that goal. During this lifelong project there will be difficulties and unforeseen obstacles. As we mature in the faith, things become clearer, and we will continue to make adjustments to our lives in order to walk with Christ each day.

In both cases, there has to be perseverance and an unwavering faith that the end result is worth the time and sacrifice. One day our work on earth will come to end. May we live and work so that our lives have been a job "well done."

"His master said to him, 'Well done, good and faithful servant. You have been faithful over a little; I will set you over much. Enter into the joy of your master'" (Matthew 25:23)

"And I heard a voice from heaven saying, 'Write this: Blessed are the dead who die in the Lord from now on.' 'Blessed indeed,' says the Spirit, 'that they may rest from their labors, for their deeds follow them'" (Revelation 14:13)!

Today, I will... Thank God for the promise of sweet heavenly rest through the blood of Christ.

WEEK 7

Finances

DALE HUBBERT

FINANCES 101

TODAY'S SCRIPTURE: Psalm 24:1

We live in a society where it is essential that we deal with money and finances. The Psalmist was correct in Psalms 24:1 when he stated that "the earth is the Lord's and the fullness thereof." That includes the money and other financial instruments that we interact with often on a daily basis. The money system we operate under is becoming more and more complex. A few basic principles will enable us to be good stewards and enjoy our blessings.

It is valuable to remember that it all belongs to God and our role with money is to be wise stewards and caretakers. Faithful stewardship is required as noted in 1 Corinthians 4:2 but it also should be desired. We are taught to honor the Lord with the first fruits of our wealth (Proverbs 3:9). Of all that we receive we are to liberally and cheerfully give to God His portion first.

It is important to spend less than we make. That seems like such a simple and common sense goal but for many the failure to do this becomes troublesome and problematic. The failure to do this impacts our ability to give to God and others and often impacts our mental state as well. Money issues are one of the major causes of divorce,

Learning to save is critical to good financial health. After our monetary commitment to God we need to make a monetary commitment to ourselves to save and prepare for the future as well as the unexpected. Learning about investments and relying on others in this area is helpful.

We live under a financial system that is strongly impacted by the use of insurance. Properly funding health, life, homeowners, automobile, and possibly long term care insurance is vital to good stewardship.

Today, I will... remember that everything, including our money, belongs to God and review my financial plan to make sure it reflects my desired walk with God.

LEARNING TO DO BETTER

TODAY'S SCRIPTURE: *1 Corinthians 4:2*

Every area of our spiritual life offers the potential for growth and improvement. The late Brother Gus Nichols was fond of saying the he believed that God's people will do better when they learn better. I have found that to be true. Hosea the prophet said that a lack of knowledge would destroy God's people (Hosea 4:6). In the financial realm there is certainly room for all of us to grow as individuals and congregations.

One of my favorite preachers was the late Brother VP Black. A well know evangelist, Brother Black spent a considerable amount of time and energy speaking on financial stewardship. His messages have greatly blessed the church of our Lord. He wrote a number of books that have been read and studied by individuals and used effectively in bible classes. His books include: Giving vs Getting, My God And My Money, The Proof Of Your Love, Lord Teach Us How To Give, Rust As A Witness, Giving Our Way To Prosperity, and Growing In Stewardship.

These books are still in print and I recommend them for individual and group study. There are other men and materials in the brotherhood that provide great opportunities to learn in matters of finance. The question is: Do I want to do better?

Handling my finances in a wise and spiritually acceptable way is always a challenge. There will always be changes and temptations that may even come in the form of complacency. Financial stewardship requires faithfulness (1 Corinthians 4:2).

How can I learn to do better? 1) Pray fervently that God will help me to be a good financial steward. 2) Read and listen to material that will encourage and challenge me in this field. 3) Observe others that are good with finances and ask for their help 4) Use a budget to develop a godly game plan and frequently measure the budget to my spending to utilize accountability

Today, I will... commit to learning how to be a better financial servant.

THE PURPOSE OF WORK

TODAY'S SCRIPTURE: Ephesians 4:28

The Bible often tells us what NOT to do and then reveals what TO do regarding a particular matter. Such is the case in the letter to the Ephesians: "Let the thief no longer steal, but rather let him labor, doing honest work with his own hands, so that he may have something to share with anyone in need." (Ephesians 4:28). There are at least three lessons to derive from this directive.

This passage is often referenced in the prohibition against stealing. This type behavior is condemned in both testaments. But why do people steal? Sometimes the answer is because they do not have the money to buy what they need or want. We may be able to say that we are obedient to this command not to steal but have we dug deeper to see what is also stated in the same sentence?

This same passage says that in lieu of stealing we are to do honest work laboring with our hands. Not all work is honorable and our aim is to be employed in a way that brings honor to God and provides a good example to others. God is noted as working (Genesis 2:2) and he intends for us to work. If we are not willing to do honest labor the message is clear: "If anyone is not willing to work, let him not eat" (2 Thessalonians 3:10). We are to participate in honest work to provide for ourselves and our families financially.

The third segment in this verse discloses a second reason we work – to share with those that have needs. What a beautiful concept! We do not have to steal because we are working to provide financially for our families and ourselves. We also use some of what we earn to help people who are not as fortunate.

Today, I will... not steal but do honest to work to provide for our needs and the needs of others.

TWELVE BASKETS FULL

TODAY'S SCRIPTURE: John 6:4-14

Jesus gave considerable to attention to finances and possessions. Almost half the parables Jesus rendered involved money or possessions. The Bible speaks freely of finances and our stewardship in that arena. There are about 500 verses that deal with prayer and over 2,000 that involve money and possessions. While that does not mean that money is four times as important as prayer it does declare the emphasis God places upon financial accountability.

The miracles of Jesus are amazing and numerous. There are very obvious observations found in the miracles but sometimes there are smaller details that we can learn from, as in the miracle found in the 6th chapter of John. Jesus fed about 5,000 with five loaves and two small fish. A detail that can easily be over-looked is the instruction of Jesus in verse 12. After feeding all these people until they were full, Jesus told the disciples to gather up the "leftovers". He further explained that "nothing may be lost".

Jesus did not want anything to go to waste. We live in a wasteful society. We generate over 230 million tons of trash annually. As much as 40% of food produced in our country is never eaten. Annual food loss in the United State is estimated at over $200 billion dollars.

Financially it is easy for us to waste money or at the least not use it in a way that reflects our understanding of the truth that God owns it all. The more we have, the easier it is to be less careful than we should be when it comes to using our finances wisely and to the glory of God. Jesus did not want anything to go to waste. I want to be like Jesus!

Today, I will... seek to avoid wasting when it comes to my finances and be a better financial steward

NOTHING PLUS SOMETHING EQUALS NOTHING

TODAY'S SCRIPTURE: 1 Timothy 6:6-12

Paul's words to Timothy in the 6th chapter of his first letter to him state that "we brought nothing into this world and it is certain we can take nothing out of the world" (1 Timothy 6:7). We are born with a financial net worth of zero and immediately go back to that number when we die. A lot happens in between birth and death financially, but we know the ending financial net worth – zero!

This section of inspired writing highlights the fact that godliness with contentment is great gain. It further urges contentment if we have food and clothing. That is quite a challenge in our time. We are served well if we can learn true contentment and don't feel a strong urge to have the latest phone, vehicle, technology tool or "toy."

We along with Timothy are warned that the desire to be rich is dangerous and provides temptation that can lead to pain as well as spiritual and financial ruin. Riches and money are not evil but the desire for riches and the love of money are a toxic combination that leads to self-inflicted pain.

Paul warns that we should "flee" from the pursuit of riches and love of money. He explains that our focus in life including the use of our finances is to use these blessings to pursue righteousness, godliness, faith, love, steadfastness, and gentleness. Fighting the good fight of faith and taking hold of eternal life should lay the foundation of how we handle our finances.

We start with nothing financially. We are blessed and entrusted with an amazing amount of money if we take the time to add it up. God wants us to be good caretakers and stewards as he has given us all things richly to enjoy (1 Timothy 6:17).

Today, I will... reflect upon my net worth when I leave the walks of this life and determine to be a wise financial steward.

Prayer Life

JEFF JENKINS

HE HEARS EVERY WORD

TODAY'S SCRIPTURE: Hebrews 4:14-16

The days following June 20, 2019 my prayer life changed drastically. Please don't misunderstand. We were taught to pray from our earliest days and pray has always been an integral part of every aspect of life.

These days it has taken on new meaning, and new life. The place where we laid my sweet wife's body is in a serene cemetery not far from one of our nation's largest cities. It is under a beautiful tree where friends have come to hang chimes, banners, and other sentiments of love.

I go there often. In fact, every day that I'm in town, even after fifteen months. Some days, it is a short visit. Other days I sit for an hour or more. Some might think it strange, but I always talk to Laura. I tell her how much she is missed by her family, our Church family, and everyone who knew her. I tell her how much I miss her smile, her voice, her beauty inside & out, her wise counsel, and her laughter. I don't know if she can hear me or not. My preference is to believe she can.

While there, I also talk to my Heavenly Father about everything in life. There is no doubt in my mind that He can hear me. He tells us in His Word that we are to talk to Him about everything. "Do not be anxious about anything, but in everything by prayer and supplication with thanksgiving let your requests be made known to God" (Philippians 4:6) He tells us to pray all the time. "Pray without ceasing" (1 Thessalonians 5:17). He invites us to come before His throne at any time. (Hebrews 4:14-16)

I'm not sure if Laura can hear me, but I know my Father can. I hope and pray it isn't presumptuous, but sometimes I ask Him to relay messages to her. That's how much faith we can have because we know He hears every word!

Today, I will...remember that my loving Father hears every word I pray and that He cares deeply about whatever is on my heart.

THE MASTER'S SCHOOL OF PRAYER, Pt 1

TODAY'S SCRIPTURE: Luke 11:1-2

One thing was abundantly clear.

They had heard Him pray. They listened to Him pray early in the morning and late into the evening. They heard Him pray before meals. They heard Him pray at crucial crossroads in His life. They hear Him pray before He made big decisions. So, naturally, they came to Him and said, "Lord, teach us to pray" (Luke 11:1). During the moments they made this request of the Master, He was praying.

Once again, as He always did, Jesus graciously answers their request. In the next words of our Lord, He not only taught these men who He loved how to pray, He taught all of us to pray. He taught me to pray. Every wise follower of the Master will do well to master the concepts found in this prayer.

"Father, Hallowed be Your Name." Let that sink in for just a moment. The Creator of the world and all of life desires that those of us who He created call Him "Father." John beautifully describes this relationship. "See what kind of love the Father has given to us, that we should be called children of God; and so we are" (1 John 3:1).

Every Father (and Mother) knows the sweet blessing of hearing a small voice say, "Mommy" or "Daddy." Our Heavenly Father longs to hear the voice of His children as well. It isn't because God is lonely, or because He has some innate need that we fill. It's because of His great love for us. He wants us near Him, communicating with Him, pouring out our heart to Him, about every need that arises. "Let us then with confidence draw near to the throne of grace, that we may receive mercy and find grace to help in time of need" (Hebrews 4:16).

Today, I will...remember that my Heavenly Father longs to hear from His children, just as we long to hear from ours. I will reverence His Name because of all He is and all He does.

THE MASTER'S SCHOOL OF PRAYER, Pt 2

TODAY'S SCRIPTURE: Luke 11:2

Of course, we can pray about anything! Yet, there are some concerns about which we should pray regularly, even every day.

There will no doubt, be times in life when prayer becomes an emergency. Those crisis moments when we find ourselves, as the old spiritual goes, "Standin' in the need of prayer."

However, a child of God should have the kind of prayer life that even these "crisis moment" prayers do not seem awkward. When the disciples asked Jesus to teach them to pray, our Savior indicated that daily prayer should be as natural as daily food.

Whether or not Jesus would want us to say the exact words recorded in this "model prayer," might be up for discussion. It does seem that He would want us to pray with these concepts in mind as we approach the Father's Throne each day.

We should pray about the Kingdom. It is true that in our day the Kingdom has come, but we can pray that the Kingdom would grow and that it will come into the lives of those who are yet to become children of God. We should pray that the Will of God would be accomplished on earth just as it is in Heaven. The Church is where we are most well-equipped to see that God's Will is done on earth.

The importance of Jesus instructing His disciples to ask God to give us our daily bread is a reminder that our God is concerned about our physical needs. It helps us understand that there is nothing wrong with our asking our Father to help us with these needs. When Jesus said, "all of these things will be added to you," "these things," speak of the physical necessities of life (Matthew 6:33).

If God is concerned about our physical needs, He is even more aware of our spiritual needs. Our next lesson will address how crucial it is for us to spend time praying about our walk with our Father.

Today, I will...pray about the Kingdom of our Lord, that many who have yet to become citizens of Kingdom will have opportunity to do so.

THE MASTER'S SCHOOL OF PRAYER, Pt 3

TODAY'S SCRIPTURE: Luke 11:4

During more than forty years of preaching, as every preacher would understand, I've been asked enough questions to fill a book or more. One of the most often asked questions has been, "Does the Bible teach that we have to forgive someone who has wronged us, even if they refuse to ask for forgiveness?"

I've spoken with numerous preachers and Bible professors about this question. As you would probably guess, there are many differing answers. Here's what we can know for certain. Jesus told His disciples to pray, "...And forgive us our debts, as we have forgiven our debtors" (Matthew 6:12). Our Savior is telling us that the forgiveness we receive from God, is directly related to how willing we are to forgive those who have sinned against us!

Here's one more thought that is a certainty. If we refuse to forgive those who have wronged us, regardless of the sin, it will not likely hurt the person who has sinned against us. However, it will cause great pain, guilt, and even resentment in our life if we fail to release the wrong that has been done to us.

Anger can wail up in our heart if we hang on to wrongs committed. Mark Twain once said, "Anger is an acid that can do more harm to the vessel in which it is stored than to anything on which it is poured." The writer of Hebrews reminds us, "See to it that no one comes short of the grace of God; that no root of bitterness springing up causes trouble, and by it many be defiled" (Hebrews 12:15)

Our willingness to forgive not only releases the one who has sinned, it also releases us from harboring ill-will toward others. May God help us to learn forgiveness from our Master.

Today, I will...make a conscientious choice to forgive those who have wronged me, even as I ask God to forgive me for the many times, I have sinned against Him.

FRIDAY

THE MASTER'S SCHOOL OF PRAYER, Pt 4

TODAY'S SCRIPTURE: Matthew 6:13

When I go visit my grandchildren, I always stay in a hotel. One of the main reasons for this is so that they can swim in a pool and so that their parents can have a night off. We always stay on the tenth floor. The kids love riding the elevators all the way up, then down, and they love pushing all the buttons. My precious grandchildren believe that I own the hotel! They have told friends of theirs that they are going to spend the night in Pop's hotel. They often say, "Pops, come see us so we can stay in your hotel." Eventually, I'll tell them differently, but it is rather fun letting them think they have an extremely well-connected Pops!

The last section of the prayer our Lord taught His disciples says, "And do not lead us into temptation, but deliver us from evil. For Yours is the kingdom and the power and the glory forever. Amen." The confidence the Master gave to the followers, that God could deliver them from evil, was the assurance that our Father possesses the kingdom, the power, and the glory, forever.

No wonder James said, "Every good thing given and every perfect gift is from above, coming down from the Father of lights, with whom there is no variation or shifting shadow" (James 1:17). Every Christian should cherish these words from God, "For every beast of the forest is Mine, the cattle on a thousand hills. I know every bird of the mountains, and everything that moves in the field is Mine. If I were hungry, I would not tell you, for the world is Mine, and all it contains" (Psalm 50:10-12). We are blessed to be able to be called children by the God who owns it all.

Today, I will...remember that I am blessed by a Father in Heaven who owns everything and who pours out blessings upon me because of His Goodness.

WEEK 9

Bible Study

MICHAEL COX

DILIGENTLY TEACH YOUR CHILDREN

TODAY'S SCRIPTURE: Deuteronomy 6:6-7

While about 60 years has passed, it seems like yesterday to me. Climbing up onto my mother's lap, at the close of day, to hear her read that night's Bible story was the way we ended each day on our farm. Looking back, I have often said that my mother worked as hard or perhaps harder than my dad on the farm but being too tired was never mentioned when it came time for the nightly Bible story. It was the time of day that I looked forward to the most.

The Bible my mom used was a Children's Hardback King James Version with artist renderings of the stories. As she read the words, I would gaze at the pictures and place myself in the story, imaging what it was like to be there with Daniel in the lion's den, David as he faced down Goliath or Jesus on the cross. As the years passed, I could almost recite the words of each story along with her but still I enjoyed hearing her voice and feeling the warmth of her caress.

That same hardback Bible, along with a generous amount of duct tape to hold it together, was shared with my own children as they grew up, and now it has been shared with my son's children. I hope one day it will be shared with my great-grandchildren.

My love for God's Word started there on my mother's lap. She motivated me to have a passion for the Bible! In the Old Testament, regarding inspiring a devotion for the Bible, God's children were instructed thus: "And these words that I command you today shall be on your heart. You shall teach them diligently to your children, and shall talk of them when you sit in your house, and when you walk by the way, and when you lie down, and when you rise" (Deuteronomy 6:6-7).

Today, I will...not pass up an opportunity to instill a deep and abiding love for God's Word in the heart of a child.

THE WEAPON AGAINST TEMPTATION

TODAY'S SCRIPTURE: Matthew 4:1-11

In 1789 Benjamin Franklin, in a letter to Jean-Baptiste Le Roy, said, "Our new Constitution is now established, and has an appearance that promises permanency; but in this world nothing can be said to be certain, EXCEPT DEATH AND TAXES." To Mr. Franklin's statement may I add the guarantee of TEMPTATIONS.

Temptations are a sure-fire thing as one passes from the age of innocence of a child to the stage of a more maturing individual who knows right from wrong. Temptations take three main forms; "For all that is in the world—the DESIRES OF THE FLESH and the DESIRES OF THE EYES and PRIDE OF LIFE - is not from the Father but is from the world" (I John 2:16). Temptations will come knocking on the door; so, what should a Christian do? Take a cue from Jesus!

Jesus faced all three forms of temptations. When, at the end of His forty day fast, the devil approached Him in the wilderness (which reminds us that the devil most often attacks during our weakest point). Jesus answered every temptation with the strength we should rely on...God's Word.

For example: "And the tempter came and said to him, "If you are the Son of God, command these stones to become loaves of bread." But He answered, "It is written, "'Man shall not live by bread alone, but by every word that comes from the mouth of God.'" (Matthew 4:3-4).

When one tries to rely on personal strength, self-confidence, or the foolish notion that temptations won't draw one away, that person will eventually fail. Only when the Christian takes refuge in the Bible, will one be able to withstand the tricks of the devil.

God's Word is our weapon against Satan. Paul wrote to the Ephesians, "And take the helmet of salvation, and the sword of the Spirit, which is the word of God" (Ephesians 6:17).

Today, I will...turn to God's Word every time the devil tries to trap me with his tricks.

KNOW, THEN APPLY

TODAY'S SCRIPTURE: 2 Timothy 3:16-17

Ok, I will confess, I'm a book-a-holic. I read several books each month, mostly books in the field of Christianity but I do have a few non-religious books in my library. For example, I have my DIET COOKBOOKS.

My diet cookbooks are all about healthy eating. I have vegan diet books, cookbooks for diabetics since that issue is in my family history, low sodium diet cookbooks, and diet cookbooks about using foods to lower blood pressure, another health problem in my bloodline. Presently I have a total of 12 diet cookbooks.

Still, with all the many diet books I have, I am currently 34 pounds over the optimal weight my physician would prefer. Why am I overweight? It's all a matter of application. I know what I should be eating but I fail to apply that knowledge.

As a Christian, it's not really an issue of knowing that I need to be a better student of God's Word; it's a matter of studying God's Word and applying that knowledge.

The Psalmist wrote, "Your word is a lamp to my feet and a light to my path." (Psalm 119:105). A flashlight tucked away in a drawer is useless when the power goes out, unless it is turned on and used. The Bible becomes useless if it remains on the bookshelf, gathering dust like my diet cookbooks.

The Bible needs to be applied to the life of the Christian. Paul reminded Timothy, "All Scripture is breathed out by God and profitable for teaching, for reproof, for correction, and for training in righteousness, that the man of God may be complete, equipped for every good work" (II Timothy 3:16-17).

The Bible does a superb job at teaching, reproving, correcting, and training in righteousness but ONLY IF it is applied. Like the medication in the bottle, the Bible works only if it is brought out and used.

Today, I will...make an effort to apply at least one principle I have learned from the Bible to my life and I will continue to do that daily.

IT TAKES EFFORT

TODAY'S SCRIPTURE: Ephesians 5:16

I was mesmerized as a little boy. I grew up attending one of two congregations my ancestors helped to start, one in the early 1840s and the other in the late 1880s. At that congregation started in the 1880s, the third Sunday in July always meant one thing...it was the first day of the annual gospel meeting.

For most of those gospel meetings the elders would invite a preacher from the area to be the guest speaker. These capable men all had one common denominator...they were bi-vocational ministers meaning they had full time jobs that supported their families while they preached on the weekends.

One year the elders invited a man who was a full-time preacher. As he stepped up to the podium that Sunday, I noticed he ONLY had a Bible. He didn't have the folder of notes other preachers always used while speaking. As he continued through the week of lessons, he still only had the Bible with him, even though he never opened it.

As he quoted verse after verse, I tried my best to double check his quotations. While I was unable to keep up with the dozens and dozens of verses he recited, the ones I was able to check were quoted perfectly.

I had to know HOW he was able to do this amazing feat. After the close of worship, while I waited for the line of adults to thin out, I was finally next. His answer was short and simple. "I study each and every day a minimum of 2 hours." The old saying, "No pain, no gain" is true. It takes EFFORT.

To become a good student of the Bible I must put in the time, but so often, time is something I fail to manage well. I waste time in focusing on things that are not important. Paul wrote, making the best use of the time, because the days are evil" (Ephesians 5:16).

Today, I will...make the effort to achieve better use of my time as I devote more of my free time to studying God's Word.

REWARDS OF BIBLE STUDY

TODAY'S SCRIPTURE: Philippians 4:8

God blessed us with two great children, a son and a daughter. As my wife and I raised our children we often used REWARDS to help motivate the behavior, quality, or trait we were trying to instill in our child. For example, we wanted our children to be courteous and kind to each other, so when we caught them being good to each other, we would heap on generous amounts of praise and give them a reward. Perhaps an extra 30-minutes of playtime before bed or their selection of the main course for that night's dinner.

REWARDS are something we, as adults, are accustomed to receiving. For those of us who have a job, the paycheck is our reward for our labor. For those of us with a green thumb, the beautiful flowers and garden are our rewards.

God has REWARDS built into His plan of salvation. Of course, there's the reward of heaven for the faithful Christian but His rewards are not limited to only heaven.

Becoming a better student of the Bible REWARDS us with a better outlook on life itself. We can overcome the hardships and troubles of the world by leaning on God's Word.

Becoming a better student of the Bible REWARDS us with better relationships, from our marriage to friends in general.

Becoming a better student of the Bible REWARDS us with a better and deeper understanding of the Creator.

Becoming a better student of the Bible REWARDS us with better priorities in life. Paul wrote, "Finally, brothers, whatever is true, whatever is honorable, whatever is just, whatever is pure, whatever is lovely, whatever is commendable, if there is any excellence, if there is anything worthy of praise, think about these things" (Philippians 4:8).

Truly with God's Word, we can accomplish any task. "I can do all things through him who strengthens me" (Philippians 4:13).

Today, I will... remind myself of the many REWARDS God's Word brings into my life.

Evangelism

DAN JENKINS

EVANGELISM WAS HIS PURPOSE

TODAY'S SCRIPTURE: Luke 19:10

The decision about our highest priority must come from a realization that when Immanuel lived on this earth He left us the prime example of what must be the highest priority. The Son of God has shown us what is truly important.

Obviously, He came to save the world with His blood, but look at how He described His purpose in coming. "For the Son of Man came to seek and to save the lost" (Luke 19:10). He came to save the world by telling them about salvation. Without evangelism the cross is meaningless.

Before He entered the world, He said, "A body You have prepared for Me...Behold, I have come to do Your will, O God" (Hebrews 10:5, 9). God prepared His body and Jesus used that body to seek the lost. He also prepared our bodies to do His will and that is to seek the lost.

When we became Christians, we became God's possession. He owns us. Paul reminded the Corinthians of this vital truth. "Or do you not know that your body is a temple of the Holy Spirit within you, whom you have from God. You are not your own for you were bought with a price. So glorify God in your body" (1 Corinthians 6:19-20). We understand that when we were saved we gave our heart, mind, soul and strength to Him. However, there is more. He purchased even more—He purchased our bodies!

"How beautiful are the feet of those who preach the good news" (Romans 10:18). Your feet are not yours, He prepared them for His work. How sweet are the lips He prepared for us to say to the lost, "Come and see." How blessed are the eyes which are uplifted and see the harvest around them. Our eyes, our feet, our lips are His!

Today, I will... use the members of my body (which actually are His) to touch the lost.

EVANGELISM OFTEN COMES UNEXPECTEDLY

TODAY'S SCRIPTURE: Matthew 28:18-20

The life of Jesus was filled with unplanned and unexpected opportunities to teach others. We sometimes evangelize in these words. "I have arranged a study with my neighbor on Friday, so this week I have one day I can reach the lost." This is not the Bible view of how we teach the lost.

We read the Great Commission and so easily can misunderstand it. Jesus said, "Go therefore and make disciples of all the nations" (Matthew 28:19). The Greek literally says, "As you are going teach the lost." Biblical evangelism does not begin after we arrive at the place of study. It happens in our lives repeatedly as we are going.

The life of Jesus shows us that some of best opportunities can come unexpectedly in our lives. Jesus met the Samaritan woman at the well (John 4). That study was not a "prearranged planned study on a Friday." It just happened as he was going through that land. He did not prearrange the study with the short man in the tree. It just happened as he passed through Jericho. He had not planned to teach the adulterous woman who was brought to Him by those who planned to stone her (John 8). He taught Nicodemus who came to Jesus by night (John 3). He taught the rich young ruler who came seeking salvation (Matthew 19). In His trials, He talked to Pilate about His kingdom which unlike the kingdoms on this earth (John 18). Even as He died, He used the door opened before Him to teach the dying thief (Luke 23). We think of our lives as having periods of evangelism. Jesus saw His life as being evangelism. Think about this.

Today, I will... watch for lives I can touch and uses these opportunities given to me by God to teach those who unexpectedly come into my life.

DO NOT PICK YOUR PROSPECTS
TODAY'S SCRIPTURE: Luke 8:11-15

One mistake we make in evangelism is that we often eliminate individuals before we have ever approached them. The life of Jesus shows how He saw all around Him as potential followers and never prejudged their responses. In the parable the sower Jesus shows us that as we sow the seed, every kind of soil deserves the seed equally—even the wayside soil. He sent us as sowers, not as soil inspectors. He does not give us the right to prejudge others on the basis of "they are not interested" or "I know they will reject what I say and I cannot deal with that rejection." Jesus never did this and we are called to mimic His life.

Would you have seen the woman who had five failed marriages and was living with another man as a prospect? Jesus did. He changed her life and she brought the entire city to sit at His feet (John 4:18-19, 39-40). Would you have seen that thief who was blaspheming you as a prospect? Jesus did and the thief will be in heaven with us (Mark 15:32; Luke 23:42-43). Would you have seen Mary Magdalene, a woman possessed with seven demons, as a prospect? Jesus did. Her life was changed and she became part of that group of holy women who followed him and financially supported Him (Luke 8:2-3). Would you have seen Paul, the man at the forefront of the massive persecution of the church as it began, as a prospect? Jesus did and he soon was at the forefront of leading Gentiles to serve the Lord. The truth is that Jesus saw every person He met as a prospect. He did not ignore hearts like wayside soil, shallow soil with stones underneath, soil filled with thorns of cares, riches and pleasure, or even good soil. He made no distinction. When we do, we have not seen how the life of Jesus can impact our lives.

Today, I will... look at those I meet throughout this day and see them as Jesus does.

EVANGELIZING LITTLE CHILDREN

TODAY'S SCRIPTURE: Matthew 18:1-11

One group of people we easily overlook in evangelism is little children. Many may have not reached an age of personal accountability, but in those younger years we can sow the seeds which, as they mature, will lead to their salvation. Jesus did not ignore children when He came to open the doors of heaven for all mankind.

As He traveled with the apostles to Capernaum, the apostles were arguing over which one of them would be the greatest in the coming kingdom. When they arrived in the city Jesus taught them that the greatest in the kingdom would be those who served. How did He do this? He brought a little child and sat that child in the midst of them and said, "Unless you turn and become like children you will never enter the kingdom of heaven" (Matt. 18:5). He did more than that for He took that little child in His arms! He told them that receiving both the Father and Himself was determined by how they received a little child.

He then said, "Whoever causes one of these little one who believes in Me to sin, it would be better for him to have a great millstone fastened around his neck and to be drowned in the depth of the sea" (Matthew 18:6). Look at the implication and application of these words. Think of how blessed those are who teach little children to keep them from sin. Jesus evangelized little children and we must be like Him.

He said even more. "See that you do not despise one of these little ones. For I tell you that in heaven their angels always see the face of My Father who is in heaven" (Matthew 18:10). God will know those who destroy the faith of little children and those who create faith in them. Evangelism involves teaching small children!

Today, I will... be part of building faith in my children or if I have no children to build faith in, the hearts of the children where I worship.

TOOLS OF EVANGELISM

TODAY'S SCRIPTURE: Psalm 19:1-3

Far too often we think the only way to begin reaching out to others is to begin by opening our Bible as a starting place. The life of Jesus shows us that such is not usually how evangelism happens. Remember how often men were first brought to Jesus because someone said to them, "Come and see." We may not be those who are able to teach, but everyone one of us can say, "Come and see."

We have failed to see how the Model Teacher used such diverse items to open the door to talk about spiritual matters. What He used and the way He used it, shows us how the most unusual items can lead to spiritual truth. Look at all He used.

Jesus used the birds which God feeds every day even though they neither sow nor reap; the well in Samaria when He was thirsty; the lilies of the valley which are so beautifully clothed by God; the axe laid at the root of the unfruitful tree which was about to be cut down; the winnowing fan which separated the wheat from the chaff; the treasures hidden in a field; the leaven used to make bread rise; the fishnet filled with both good and bad fish; a Roman coin and the images on the coin; the stones destined to kill an adulterous woman; a small child; a fishing boat as a stage; various houses where He sat and taught; the perfume used to anoint Him; the casket of the widow's son in Nain; the gravesite of the brother of two grieving sisters; coins that were lost; sheep that were lost; pearls of great price; the hem of His garment—the list is endless. He began teaching others using items around them to start the conversation and so can you!

Today, I will... open my eyes and pray to God he will help me be more like Jesus in seeing not just lost souls, but the items around them I can use to talk to others about God.

Assurance

PAUL SHERO

THE POWER OF GOD

TODAY'S SCRIPTURE: Mark 10:25-27

There is a definite limit on what I can do. I can only lift so much; walk so far, and jump so high. God, on the other hand, has no limit to His power.

When God promises me I can be forgiven of the unforgiveable; escape temptations and be sanctified, those promises are impossible, until you remember who is making them. There are no limits on God. God is the one, the only one who does the impossible.

I know I do not have the strength to overcome sin and Satan. Jesus calls Satan the strong man; well-armed and holding me captive. So with Paul, I cry out "Wretched man that I am! Who will deliver me from this body of death?" (Romans 7:24).

Jesus also says He is the one to overcome the strong man and free his captives. So with Paul, I can answer my own question with "Thanks be to God through Jesus Christ our Lord." (Romans 7:25).

"Thanks be to God through Jesus Christ our Lord." God once asked, "Is anything too hard for God?" Often we make promises we can't keep. Not God! God is able! When the three Hebrew men refused to bow down to Nebuchadnezzar's idol, he was enraged and threatened to throw them into a fiery furnace. He ended his threat with "And who is the god who will deliver you out of my hands?" (Daniel 3:15).

In the next verse, Daniel 3:16, they say, "Our God is able." And He was.

Back to Paul. In Romans 7:25 he repeats this great truth. He says, "Now to him who is able." To the church in Philippi, Paul says, "I can do all things through him who strengthens me" (Philippians 4:13).

We have confidence and assurance because we know the one who makes the promises is able.

We sing "Angels Descending, Bring from Above."

Today, I will... Lean on the power of God who makes promises.

GOD IS ETERNAL

TODAY'S SCRIPTURE: Hebrews 7:25

God has made some great promises to us. We sing "Blessed Assurance, Jesus is mine." We live by promises that have been made. Our response to those promises is faith. In Hebrews 11:1, we learn "Now faith is the assurance of things hoped for, the conviction of things not seen."

How can I have assurance when there is so much that I don't know, so much I haven't seen? How am I going to believe when there is so much I don't know? Well, here is what I do know. The One who makes the promises is alive!

My grandfather told me not to worry about my college expenses. He said he would take care of them. And he meant it, but he died. You see, we make promises based on the thought we will be alive when it is time to deliver. Death is the big reset event, isn't it? All plans stop. This rule does not apply to Jesus. Jesus conquered death. "Since he always lives." In Hebrews 7:24, the Bible says "He continues forever".

Once our grandson Steven came to visit. He was bout four. It was a bad time for him to come. I was going through some 'stuff'. Actually I was wallowing in it. I was depressed and desperate. We were in the office at the house. He wanted to look at a rifle. I didn't want to get up. He said, "I want to see the one that you look through and see that cross like where Jesus died." I said, "What did you say?" He said, "You know, that gun that you look through and see that cross like where Jesus died." I said, "Tell me about that cross and Jesus." And he did. No detail was left out. I started crying. Steven looked surprised and said, "Pa, it is ok. He is alive you know."

Now, I am really crying. I go get Patsy and tell Steven to tell 'Honey' what you told me." And he did. Now, we are both crying and that little guy says, "It's ok. He is alive, you know. Nothing can stop Jesus." I knew that but I forgot. The one who makes promises is alive forever more. "Oh, What a foretaste of glory divine."

Today, I will...remember Jesus is alive.

GOD IS EVERYWHERE

TODAY'S SCRIPTURE: Psalm 139:5-10

When the girls were little, I often told them I would protect them and I would never let anything bad happen to them. And I meant it, but I was wrong.

Once we went out to the country for a campout. The cabin was primitive but dry. There was a mountain to climb, a river to cross (on a cable bridge) and woods to explore. Our spirits were up for a great adventure. At the end of the day, we were heading back from the mountain. It was getting dark and a winter storm was coming. No problem! We were not far from the cabin and I had everything under control. Jennifer said she wanted to go ahead of us. I could see the top of the bridge. It wasn't far so I said, "Go ahead, but wait at the bridge."

When we got to the bridge, she wasn't there. The wind started to blow and it started to sleet. I couldn't find my daughter! I ran here and there calling her name. I could barely hear her call back, "Daddy, I'm over here." Well, in what seemed like forever, Patsy found her at the camp.

Unlike me, God is everywhere at once. There is no dark place where he cannot see; no locked room he cannot enter. Even in death, he does not leave us. Our uncertainty is rooted in our limitations.

That is why we are afraid. But when our confidence is in God and not us, our fear evaporates because his promises are not limited by geography. So, whether we are in the assembly or in a whale's belly; whether we are here or there, God is with us. Daniel would remind us that whether we are in Jerusalem or a lion's den, God is not far away.

Can I believe this? Can I put all my weight down on God's promises? The answer is yes! But the real question is, will I? I should! I must! My faith and God's grace allows me to be in his presence even when I'm in a bad place. We are here and now, but we are also with him. So I can sing, "Oh what a foretaste of glory divine. This is my story, this is my song, praising my savior, all the day long."

Today, I will... Cling to the fact that there is no where I can be that you, O Lord, are not there.

GOD KNOWS EVERYTHING

TODAY'S SCRIPTURE: Isaiah 48:5-6

We live in nervous times. We soon realize we cannot cover all our bases. We don't even know where the bases are! If we prepare for a fire and have a flood, we are sunk. The bigger the threats and the faster they come, the more desperate we are. Assurance is not a word we use often. Maybe we will say "I am absolutely sure disaster is coming." Even promises from God must be accepted by faith. But how can I put my whole weight down on something that hasn't happened yet? We think this way because we don't know everything. It's hard to believe that anyone can. So, we worry!

Is there enough trust in the promises of God to react with "Assurance of things not seen?" Can we sing, "Blessed Assurance, Jesus is mine. O What a foretaste of glory divine?" This is where the promises of the scriptures really help build assurance.

How could anyone know hundreds and hundreds of years before the promised event happened? Who could give such precise details? Even naming names of people that would be born! We can't even tell what the weather will be like tomorrow or what the Stock Market will do next month. This is what it is like being human.

This, however, is not the reality of God. He knows everything! From how many hairs on your head to what is going to happen on the last day and even when the last day will be. This is demonstrated by the many prophesies in the Old Testament. No one is like God. He said it would happen and it did. This should give us confidence (assurance) in the promises he makes. We think we know. He knows. We think we see where things are going. He is already there.

I can put my whole weight on the promises of God because he has all power, is everywhere, is eternal, and knows everything. I can believe his promises.

Today, I will... Thank God for his promises.

THE LOVE OF GOD

TODAY'S SCRIPTURE: John 3:16 & 15:13

The nature of God produces assurance in our hearts because God is alive forever more; because Jesus rose from the grave; because God knows everything and because he has all power. All of these truths would not, by themselves, assure our hearts if it were not for the fact that "God is Love". Without the love of God, these qualities could terrify us.

God has all power. You can never defeat him. God is everywhere; you can never hide from him. God knows everything; you can never trick him. God is eternal; you cannot out last him. If he hated us, we would be done for. But wonder of wonders—HE LOVES US.

He loves us. He proves it. No one ever paid more to save us. The cost of his son and the patience he has shown prove it. The willingness of Jesus to die cannot be overlooked. He loves us. Only love causes this kind of sacrifice. When we see it, we know.

When a father eats a stale sandwich everyday so he can afford braces for his daughter, we see love. When a person gives a kidney to a relative, we see love. When a friend risks his life to save a friend, we see love. When a mother does work she doesn't want to do so her son can go to college, we see love.

We know the great definition of love in I Corinthians 13. Paul called it "The more excellent way." We have love defined, explained, and commanded; but when we look at the cross, we have it demonstrated. He loves us. So, we trust his promises, obey his commands and have full assurance in him.

We sing "Watching and waiting, looking above, filled with his goodness, LOST IN HIS LOVE."

Today, I will... Wrap myself in the warm blanket of God's love. Today, I will sing "this is my story!"

Friendship

BILLY SMITH

JESUS IS MY FRIEND

TODAY'S SCRIPTURE: John 13:34-35; 15:12-17

Like you, I cherish friendship. My life has been blessed with so many friends that I cannot imagine life without them, nor would I wish upon anyone the absence of this special relationship, a gift from the very heart of God. Emerson had to be thinking of Solomon (Proverbs 18:24a) when he said, "The only way to have a friend is to be one."

One hundred and three titles are ascribed to Jesus in Scripture, but the most personal one has to be friend. Imagine how the apostles felt in the Upper Room when He assured them, "No longer do I call you servants . . . but I have called you friends" (John 15:16). He demonstrates that friendship by the way He loved them, and us.

First, Jesus loved His friends selflessly. Absolutely no one can be more unselfish than Jesus and His Father, who sent Him into the world to die for our sins and those of the whole world. In leaving the glories of heaven, He became one of us, taking the form of a servant, humbling Himself by becoming obedient to the point of death, even death on a cross (Philippians 2:7-8)!

Second, Jesus loved His friends sacrificially. Forever underscored in the Christian's life are these words, "Greater love has no one than this, that someone lay down his life for his friends" (John 15:13). It is one thing to talk sacrifice, but another thing to be sacrificial; that's when you know you have a true friend. Paul adds that the Lord's sacrifice was made while we were still sinners" (Romans 5:8)!

Third, Jesus loved His friends sympathetically. While Judas was betraying the Lord, Peter, James, and John could not stay awake while He was praying, in agony, in Gethsemane. At His arrest, they all ran with fear. While on trial, Peter denied Him with a swear and a curse. Yet, the Lord understood and looked upon them with the deepest sympathy the world will ever know. He knew what they would, by the grace of God, become. That is how Jesus, our greatest Friend, also loves us!

Today, I will... be a friend to Jesus by sharing His friendship with people generally, and brethren specifically, with *selflessness, sacrifice,* and *sympathy.*

FRIENDSHIP: BE THANKFUL

TODAY'S SCRIPTURE: 1 Samuel 18

There is a significant difference between an *acquaintance* and a *friend*. An acquaintance may know *about* us, but a true friend knows *us*. They know our strengths and weaknesses, our loves and likes, our successes and failures. They may like us *because* of, but they love us *in spite* of, "warts and all."

The Bible speaks to every setting and situation in life, or at least provides principles and examples for whatever circumstance we may face. One such example of genuine friendship is that shared by David and Jonathan, who could not have been closer if they had been brothers (Proverbs 18:24b). They were joined at the heart, one soul living in two bodies. Time and again they would demonstrate their willingness to give their life for each other.

Though Jonathan had every right to expect he would succeed his father Saul as king, when he met David after the monumental defeat of Goliath (1 Samuel 17), he "loved him as his own soul" (18:1, 3). Incredibly, he made a covenant with David and gave him his own royal robe, his armor, his sword, bow, and belt. So thankful was he for David's character, courage, and conviction that he basically provided him a coronation as the next king, pledging his lifelong support. Most young men in Jonathan's place of privilege would be insanely jealous of such a rival, but not Jonathan; he was filled with gratitude that God had sent David into his life.

When the Lord blesses us with friends that mean more to us than life itself, we understand how rich we are without money. We love each other, long to see each other, weep and rejoice with each other, and share the great moments of life together. The Lord's church is designed to be God's family, where we enjoy relationships with fathers and mothers, brothers and sisters, and children that we come to love as our own. We share the life of faith, hope, and love; we enjoy the beauty of worship, the joy of fellowship, and spiritual growth in doing the Lord's work. How richly blessed we are, knowing the best is yet to come in that land that is fairer than day.

Today, I will... praise God for His gift of friendship; especially, for all the relationships we enjoy in Christ Jesus our Lord and His church.

FRIENDSHIP: BE TRUE

TODAY'S SCRIPTURE: 1 Samuel 19

Life reveals there are friends, and there are true friends. This reality brought the following observation from Henry Adams: "One [true] friend in a lifetime is much; two are many; three are hardly possible." A member of the world may well identify with these words, but the one who is in Christ and a member of His church will find his life blessed with an abundance of genuine friends who will prove to be true no matter what life may bring.

David had such a friend in Jonathan. When it became obvious Saul was determined to kill David, "Jonathan, Saul's son, delighted much in David" (1 Samuel 19:1) and commended him to his evil father: "Let not the king sin against his servant David, because he has not sinned against you, and because his deeds have brought good to you" (19:4). Jonathan would have made a good and godly king had David not been God's anointed successor to Saul, and his devoted friend could not have been happier with that divine appointment.

Jonathan was not only true to David instead of his father, he also told David the truth, warning him of his impending danger: "Saul my father seeks to kill you . . . if I learn anything I will tell you" (19:2-3). The truth may hurt on occasion but it also saves. We do no one, not even our closest friend, a favor when we withhold from them the truth. Imagine how this news filled David with fear, but it is precisely what he needed to hear in order to survive and fulfill the plans God had made for him.

I did not appreciate these words at the time, but in a critical moment a cardiologist said to me after an extended visit, "I know I have not told you what you wanted to hear, but I have told you what you needed to hear." In the years since, I could not be more grateful for his prognosis. He helped me, and in our ministry, that is exactly what we need to say to those who most need it. A genuine friend, therefore, is not only one who proves to be true to us, but one who tells us the truth at all times, even when it hurts.

Today, I will... prove to be true to my friends, and in doing so, I will always be truthful.

FRIENDSHIP: BE THOUGHTFUL

TODAY'S SCRIPTURE: 1 Samuel 20

My best friend growing up is still my best friend as we both approach another birthday. We were born three weeks apart and neither of us remembers a time when we did not have each other and love each other. We did everything together, to the point people thought we were brothers, sharing the same last name. The elders of our home congregation asked that we both preach our first sermons, at age sixteen, on the same Sunday; I spoke in the morning and he in the evening. He served as my Best Man, and his wedding, three weeks after my own, was the first I was honored to perform.

The night before I left home to attend Freed-Hardeman, he was the last person I was with to say "goodbye for now." We had never been apart and it was a difficult, emotional farewell. I have never forgotten that neither of us knew what to do, what to say; eventually, we collapsed into each other's arms in the midst of tears. We have shared many life experiences in the years since; yet, I miss his physical presence every day, though he is always just a call, an email, a text, or a three-hour trip away.

The day came when David and Jonathan had to say goodbye. Here is the emotional exchange between them: "David fell on his face to the ground and bowed three times. And they kissed one another and wept with one another, David weeping the most. Then Jonathan said to David, 'Go in peace, because we have sworn both of us in the name of the Lord, saying, The Lord shall be between me and you, and between my offspring and your offspring, forever'" (20:41-42).

It is significant that "David wept the most." He knew that Jonathan had risked his life for him and that he had chosen David over his murderous father. His eyes filled with tears of love and gratitude for the careful thoughtfulness of his one true friend who saved his life. He also knew he was about to miss the encouraging presence of Jonathan for the indefinite future. David would never forget Jonathan's devotion.

Blessed is the person who has such a friend, or as members of the church, many such friends. It has been said, "Value a friend who, for you, finds time on his calendar; but cherish the friend who, for you, does not even consult his calendar."

Today, I will...be a faithful companion to the friend who needs me, who will never leave my thoughts, my heart, and my prayers.

FRIENDSHIP: BE TRUSTWORTHY

TODAY'S SCRIPTURE: 2 Samuel 9

A true friend is one who over a period of time has won your trust and is therefore trustworthy. You have every confidence in such a friend, to the point you can share anything and everything; you know what they will say and not say, what they will do and not do, where they will go and not go. You, too, have proven your trust, time and again, to that friend. Your friendship, therefore, is for life.

David and Jonathan enjoyed that kind of friendship, though Jonathan's life was cut much too short due to the foolishness of his father Saul. King David would never forget him and all the kindness Jonathan afforded him; nor would the young king forget the commitment he made to care for Jonathan's descendants.

Today's Scripture reading provides the touching story of David's compassion: "Is there still anyone left of the house of Saul, that I may show him kindness for Jonathan's sake" (2 Samuel 9:1)? When he learned Jonathan had a crippled son named Mephibosheth, he called for him to be brought to the king immediately, saying, "Mephibosheth! Do not fear, for I will show you kindness for the sake of your father Jonathan, and I will restore to you all the land of Saul your father, and you shall eat at my table always" (9:6-7).

David kept his word, and that is what it means to be trustworthy, worthy of trust. We cannot earn the trust of anyone until our "yes means yes," and our "no means no," constantly and consistently. True friends are those you can count on, who are going to rush to your side when you most need them, whose presence means performance, not just promises. Their words fill you with hope, their prayers go right to the heart of God, and their love is unending.

This series began with the everlasting example of our ultimate friend, Jesus. To Him we cling and to Him we would bring the whole world if only they would listen, trust, and obey. We close with the beautiful words of Will L. Thompson:

> *Jesus is all the world to me: I want no better friend;*
> *I trust Him now, I'll trust Him when life's fleeting days shall end.*
> *Beautiful life with such a friend, beautiful life that has no end.*
> *Eternal life, eternal joy: He's my Friend.*

Today, I will... endeavor to be worthy of my friends' trust, keeping my word even as I am kept by the Word.

Love One Another

CHRIS McCURLEY

BEAUTY FOR BEASTS

TODAY'S SCRIPTURE: Romans 5:6-8

Beauty and the Beast is about a poor peasant gentleman who steals food from the grounds of a large castle inhabited by a beast. The beast catches him and says, "I'm going to put you in my dungeon, and you will be my prisoner forever, unless you send your beautiful daughter to live with me." To make a long story short, the daughter decides to save her father by going to the castle and living with the beast. Of course, unbeknownst to anyone else, the beast is really a handsome prince who had been turned into a hideous beast by a fairy after he refused to let her in from the rain. The only way for the curse to be broken is for the prince to find true love. As the story comes to a close, the beast lies dying from a wound inflicted by his enemy, Gaston. Belle, the beauty, confesses her love for the beast and gives him a kiss that breaks the curse. The simple yet profound message is this: the beast had to be loved as a beast before he could return to being a handsome prince. Someone treated like an animal will likely become an animal. But someone treated with value, dignity, and beauty will likely become more.

We tend to love the beautiful and despise the beastly. However, we forget something very vital in our assessments—we are beastly.

For while we were still weak, at the right time Christ died for the ungodly. For one will scarcely die for a righteous person—though perhaps for a good person one would dare even to die—but God shows his love for us in that while we were still sinners, Christ died for us (Romans 5:6-8).

Before becoming a Christian, there was nothing beautiful about us. We were stained with the ugliness of sin. We were the beasts. But that's the beauty of God's love. It's not based on who we are. It's based on who He is.

Some people can be beastly. Why should I love them? Because God does. If you love God, you will love like God. You will love those who are rude, mean, insensitive, malicious, thoughtless, and uncaring. You will love them because you want them to see the love that God has for them.

Today, I will...search for the beauty in the people I come across.

SEEK THE SOURCE

TODAY'S SCRIPTURE: 1 John 4:7-9

In 1991, the Japanese government sought a way to attract endangered albatrosses to the Izu islands in the hope that the birds would reproduce and replenish their diminishing population. So, 100 wooden decoys were placed in the water to help attract the birds to the islands. And the project worked...for the most part. The endangered birds began breeding and the population increased. However, there was one five-year-old albatross who refused to play by the rules. He was given the name Deko. And for two years, Deko tried to woo the love of his life. He built fancy nests. He fought off rival suitors. He spent countless days standing faithfully by her side. But he was unable to win the affection of his one and only. And do you know why? Yes. Because the love of his life is a decoy. And despite the blank stares and wooden personality, Deko never caught on. Deko's infatuation with a fake bird is keeping him from meeting a real mate. He seems to have no desire to date real birds.** All too often we humans do the same thing. We become so infatuated with the decoys that we miss out on genuine love. If we want to experience authentic love, then we must go to the source.

John writes:
Beloved, let us love one another, for love is from God, and whoever loves has been born of God and knows God. Anyone who does not love does not know God, because God is love. In this the love of God was made manifest among us, that God sent his only Son into the world, so that we might live through him (1 John 4:7-9)

Love didn't start with us. God is the source. Jesus is the manifestation of God's love. Christ embodied love. That is why He hung out with sinners and why He hung on a cross for sinners.

Too many people are looking for love in all the wrong places. Seek the sources, not a decoy!

Today, I will...make love a priority and display Christ-like love to those around me.

**https://www.sermonillustrator.org/illustrator/sermon12/dont_settle_for_idols.htm

TOUGH LOVE

TODAY'S SCRIPTURE: Luke 10:25-37

Have you ever heard the phrase "tough love?" Do you know what "tough love" is? Do you know how you define "tough love?" Exactly the way Jesus did—"You shall love your neighbor as yourself" (Mark 12:31). That's tough love, isn't it? Not always. There are some "neighbors" that we have no problem loving. But some "neighbors" are tough to love. Some we even go to church with. What makes Jesus' commandment tough is that it forces us to remove all boundaries. We all have limits to our love. All of us have certain stipulations, disclaimers, and conditions when it comes to sharing our love. And rightfully so, in some cases. Some people are undeserving of our love. Some people abuse our love and take it for granted. However, Jesus' command comes with zero stipulations, disclaimers, or conditions. There's no but, unless, or except—only a period.

In Luke's gospel we find an expert in Jewish law asking Jesus a follow up question to our Lord's command to "love your neighbor as yourself." The lawyer asks, "And who is my neighbor" (Luke 10:29). This is a boundary question. This expert in Jewish law wanted a precise definition of who qualified as his neighbor because, after all, he didn't want to be careless with his love. To love a fellow Jew was certainly a neighborly thing to do, but that's where his neighborliness reached its limit. The lawyer's question was the wrong question because the issue is not defining who your neighbor is. The issue is being a neighbor. That is why Jesus responded to the man's question with a parable in which a hated Samaritan becomes the hero (Luke 10:30-37).

What the expert in Jewish law needed to comprehend, and what we all need to understand is this: When it comes to loving others, you don't start with the "other." You don't start with yourself. You start with God. He's the standard. That's how we love even the most unlovable. We are even commanded to love our enemies. How do we do that? Not by starting with your enemy. Not by starting with our emotions. We start with God. We love our neighbor best when we love God first.

Today, I will...seek to make amends with someone I am at odds with.

WHAT'S YOUR THREE-LEGGED CHICKEN?

TODAY'S SCRIPTURE: Mark 12:28-31

One day a man was driving down a country road when he noticed a chicken running ahead of him. He glanced at his speedometer and couldn't believe his eyes: he was topping 50 miles-per-hour, and the chicken was outrunning the car! The man increased his speed to 60, then 70 miles-per-hour and still the chicken was increasing its lead. Suddenly, the bird made a right turn onto a small farm and disappeared behind a small chicken coop. Amazed by the chicken's performance, the driver pulled over and walked to the farmhouse door. When the owner appeared, the man asked excitedly, "Sir, do you know that chicken of yours can run over seventy miles an hour?" The farmer chuckled, "Oh you must mean our three-legged chicken. Yep, he sure is fast. You see, I live here with my wife and son and when it comes to eating chicken, we all love drumsticks. So, we decided to breed three-legged chickens." "That's amazing," the visitor said. "How did that turn out? Does a three-legged chicken taste good?" With a sigh of disappointment, the farmer replied, "I don't know. We haven't caught one yet."

What's your three-legged chicken? We all have at least one three-legged chicken in our lives. It's whatever we love most, and whatever we love most is what we'll spend our time pursuing. Jesus said that the most important commandment is to "love the Lord your God with all your heart and with all your soul and with all your mind and with all your strength" (Mark 12:30). "The second greatest commandment," He said, is to "love your neighbor as yourself" (Mark 12:31).

What I hear Jesus saying is, "Love God more." Start with God. The most loving thing we can do for others is to love God more than we love them. There's a reason why Jesus said that the second is like the first. The two go hand in hand. If you love God the most, you will love your neighbor best.

Today, I will...examine my priorities and strive to put God first.

OUR IDENTIFYING MARK

TODAY'S SCRIPTURE: John 13:34-35

When I was a kid, I spent a lot of time with my grandfather. We had a ritual that involved my grandfather unrolling the newspaper and me sitting in the recliner with him as we read "The Funny Papers," as he called them. My grandfather always believed in reading the comics first because that would set the tone for reading all the bad news that was printed. In the "Comics" section of The Paragould Daily Press, Peanuts was the first comic strip. I remember one particular cartoon that had Lucy demanding that Linus change the channel on the T.V.; threatening him with her fist if he didn't. Linus says, "What makes you think you can walk right in here and take over?" To which Lucy replies, "These five fingers." She goes on to say, "Individually they're nothing but when I curl them together like this into a single unit, they form a weapon that is terrible to behold." Somewhat dejected, Linus responds with, "What channel do you want?" Then he turns away, looks at his fingers and says, "Why can't you guys get organized like that?"

We need to get organized like that. Like a fist, the church needs to come together individually to form a weapon that is terrible for the devil to behold.

In John 13:35 Jesus stated these words:
By this all people will know that you are my disciples, if you have love for one another."

"By this all men will know that you are My disciples..."

> By your political views.
> By your debating skills.
> By the memes you post on social media.
> By how many arguments you win.

Nope. Nope. Nope. The love we display to those around us is our identifying mark. As disciples of Jesus Christ, the one thing that should give us away is our love; our love for God and our love for our fellowman. This type of love dispels hatred, division, bitterness, etc.; all things the devil uses to conquer the hearts of individuals. So, we fight our most formidable foe with our most formidable weapon—LOVE.

Today, I will...refrain from promoting things that harm my identity as a Christian.

Bear One Another's Burdens

BO SHERO

LIVING CHRIST'S VICTORY

TODAY'S SCRIPTURE: 1 Peter 3:1-9

There is a famous photograph of a sailor bending a nurse backward as he plants a kiss on her lips. That picture came to express the euphoria of this country when it heard that World War II had ended. We've heard stories of huge street celebrations in Europe as the allies liberated towns. Imagine their joy that the oppressive enemy was gone, and they had survived to start a new life.

God uses many terms to describe the salvation that He has brought to us. He says that He redeemed us, which is language of the market place. In language from the court, He justified us. In terms of personal relations, He reconciled us to Him. And from worship experience, He says that He is our sacrifice. But some of the greatest imagery of our salvation is created by God's use of battle field language when He says that He has brought us victory.

"But thanks be to God, who in Christ always leads us in triumphal procession, and through us spreads the fragrance of the knowledge of him everywhere" (2 Corinthians 2:14, ESV).

"He has delivered us from the domain of darkness and transferred us to the kingdom of his beloved Son" (Colossians 1:13, ESV).

Sadly, most people know little of this victory. The media pours out dark news. Fear grips many of the people that we live among. Heroes have become villains. Victories are redefined as oppression of someone or everyone. The burden of living a hopeless life must be overwhelming.

But in Christ, mankind has been redeemed, justified, reconciled, we have a sacrifice, and we have victory. Hopeless people see this victory best as Christians live as those who have overcome through Christ. Just by living as a child of God, you bear part of the burden of living in a dark world.

Today, I will…talk, and act like a child of God who has been saved by Jesus Christ so that others might see the reality of hope and victory in Jesus.

ENDURING GREAT EVIL FOR THE SAVING OF OTHERS

TODAY'S SCRIPTURE: Genesis 50:19-21

Joseph's brothers were the source of great suffering in his life. They rejected him and sold him into slavery, which led to imprisonment. When they arrived in Egypt to buy food from him, many would conclude that it would have been right for him to exact revenge by rejecting their request or even by imprisoning them. Though he tested them, he sold them food. And after revealing who he really was, he treated them like beloved brothers and took care of them.

At their father Jacob's death, Joseph's brothers feared his retaliation. But Joseph consoled his brothers with these words, "As for you, you meant evil against me, but God meant it for good, to bring it about that many people should be kept alive, as they are today." (Genesis 50:20).

As Jesus hung on the cross, those who sought His death believed that they had won a great victory. Satan's forces must have enjoyed the great evil that they had wrought. But Jesus, like Joseph, held no grudge. He said from the cross, "Father, forgive them, for they know not what they do." (Luke 23:34).

Joseph did not die for our sins. Joseph is not our savior. But Joseph certainly endured great evil for the blessing of others and forgave like Jesus.

Bearing great evil, suffering, or difficulty in our lives may not lead to the salvation from starvation as it did with Joseph. It cannot be the once for all sacrifice that saves people from hell. Jesus has accomplished that already. But like Joseph, your bearing great evil while forgiving that evil and looking to a greater good by the hand of God, can help others see the ultimate goodness of the God of the Bible. I see Jesus in Joseph. Maybe others can see Jesus in you.

Today, I will...bear whatever evil, suffering, or hardship that may come to me, forgiving those who brought it and looking to the good that God will bring about through it to the glory of Jesus.

WEDNESDAY

DRIVING TO REPENTANCE

TODAY'S SCRIPTURE: Matthew 7:1-5

I convinced myself that the road construction and the "crazy" drivers were the reason for my bad attitude. Then the little tiny car to my left turned into "my" lane nearly taking my front bumper off. I instantly knew that the driver was an impatient college girl. Where are the police when you need them? She next showed a complete inability to negotiate a four-way stop. She started to go when it was not her turn and failed to go when it was. I thought she needed to repeat driver's education. She repeated her inept performance at the second four-way stop. I growled at her from my truck. At the third, she put her car in park. I knew it was in park because I saw the backup lights flash on as the gear shift passed through reverse. I growled again. Then she took off her seatbelt and started fooling with something in the console. Cars began to back up behind me. I growled louder. Then she opened her door and got out of her car in the middle of traffic, in a construction zone. As her door began to open, I began the loudest growl yet. But that growl was quickly turned to repentance when a little old lady exited the offensive car. She approached my window and told me she was lost in her search for the Heart Hospital. I gave her the directions she needed. Then I told God how sorry I was for my growling.

I don't know why she needed to go to the Heart Hospital, but all my guesses involve serious illness for herself or a loved one. I'm sure her heart was overwhelmed with worry. The confusion of the construction zone, with its temporary stop signs, only added to her burden. As I blame my own bad behavior on circumstance, my Heavenly Father demands that I extend the same exemption to those around me (Matthew 18:21-35).

Today, I will...bear the burdens of others by my patient forgiveness of their mistakes and even their wrongs

BEARING ANOTHER'S BURDEN IN SMALL THINGS

TODAY'S SCRIPTURE: Matthew 25:31-46

When you imagine the judgement scene at the end of time, what does it look like? If there is a discussion during judgement, what is it about? Does the conversation involve doctrine? Do those being judged give an account of their worship or their response to the plan of salvation? Matters of salvation in Jesus Christ, worship, and church organization are no doubt of great importance. But do they become part of the conversation in Jesus' portrayal of the judgement recorded in Matthew 25:31-46?

When you think of pleasing God, what comes to mind? Does one need to preach repentance to the masses as John the baptizer did? Must we lead armies to victory as so many heroes of the Old Testament did? Must we bear the blows of persecution like Paul? Must we personally face evil alone like Elijah on Mount Carmel, or David before Goliath?

In fact, when Jesus describes this great judgment scene in Matthew 25, He commends the saved and convicts the condemned regarding small everyday things in which they bore the burden of another person. There are no grand heroic acts mentioned. Everything in Jesus' list is something that any regular person can do to bless another person. Being a Christian is seldom about going to dark jungles to preach the gospel or dying as a martyr. Being a Christian is in great part the everyday actions of feeding the hungry, clothing the naked, caring for the prisoner and the sick, welcoming the stranger, and a simple drink for the thirsty. These burdens are available every day for each of us who are willing to bear them.

However, while Jesus' list from Matthew 25 may not seem heroic to us, if you are hungry, the one feeding you may well seem heroic to you. One should also note that every act on this list is considered by Jesus to have been done to Himself.

Today, I will...find someone with an everyday burden that I can bear because, and to the glory, of Jesus.

PRAYING ALL NIGHT

TODAY'S SCRIPTURE: Luke 18:1-8

He was scared and upset. He feared that it would be a long hard night and that he would not perform well at the night's tasks. He felt unprepared mentally and physically. I love him, so I wanted to help. But I could not do anything physically for him. Mentally, his task was far beyond my ability. So I was useless to him or so it would seem.

Then I remembered another night that was quite a physical battle for him. That night, like the recent one, I could do nothing physically to help. But that night I prayed and I prayed. I prayed all night. My understanding of prayer grew that night long ago. So I told him to do the best he could and that I would pray for him all night again.

The fearful night turned out to be easy. Others, who were qualified, pitched in to lighten the load. The demands were much less than feared. All in all, it was a pleasant time. And some would say that luck was with him. But I say God was with him. After all, I asked and asked and asked again for over nine hours for God to be with him. When we ask God and receive what we asked for, we must thank God.

I must learn some day that when I cannot help physically, monetarily, or mentally, I can still bear another's burden in prayer. Prayers are better than any other form of help as they call on the most powerful of helpers.

Some would say that God would have done this with or without my prayer. But with my prayer, I am sure that it was God and not luck that brought the blessing. So as for me and my house we will pray and thank God for His blessings.

"In these days he went out to the mountain to pray, and all night he continued in prayer to God." (Luke 6:12, ESV)

Today, I will...find someone in need and bear their burden through my prayers to God.

Honor One Another Above Yourself

TOMMY HAYNES

MORE SIGNIFICANT THAN YOURSELF

TODAY'S SCRIPTURE: Philippians 2:1-10

It is unfortunate that we allow pride and arrogance to convince us that we are better than another person. Racial prejudice stems from this human flaw, and so many other sins as well. Many of us walk into a room and automatically believe that we are the smartest person in the room. The football player walks off the field after one good series with his finger in the air declaring "I am number one" even though the game is not over, and they might not win.

Jesus was completely different. He was the smartest person in every room. He is "The Word" that John writes about who was with God in the beginning and was part of creating the universe (John 1:1ff). Yet He was always humble and helpful. When the mother of James and John came to ask that her sons sit at the right and left hand of Jesus, He replied, "...even as the Son of Man came not to be served but to serve, and give His life as a ransom for many" (Matthew 20:28).

This is why Paul writes, "Do nothing from selfish ambition or conceit, but in humility count others more significant than yourselves" (Philippians 2:3). This is why Jesus would go to Matthews house even though others would accuse Him of eating with publicans and sinners (Luke 15:1-2). This is why Jesus needed to go through Samaria and teach a people most Jews despised (John 4:4-5). When we view other people as more significant than ourselves, we will approach differently, and our honor and respect will show in what we say. "Let your speech always be gracious, seasoned with salt, so that you may know how you ought to answer each person" (Colossians 4:6).

When we align our hearts with the heart of our Lord, we will develop His mind within us (Philippians 4:5), and we will always treat others with honor.

Today, I will...remind myself to look at people the way Jesus would, and express respect and honor in how I treat them.

RENDER TO CAESAR

TODAY'S SCRIPTURE: Matthew 22:15-22

We are living in strange times. The word "anarchist" has rarely been uttered in our society, and now we have an organized movement of anarchists (isn't organization the very thing they detest?). Some who claim to be Christians do not believe in civil government and try to get away with not paying their taxes. This is not what Jesus believed and exemplified.

The leadership of the Jews were trying to trap Jesus any way they could. They thought that perhaps this could be done by revealing how He felt about the Roman Empire. Jesus shocked them by using a Roman coin as an object lesson. "Show the coin for the tax" Jesus said (Matthew 22:19). Then He asked them, "Whose likeness and inscription is this?" They said, "Caesar's." Then He said to them, "Therefore render to Caesar the things that are Caesar's, and to God the things that are God's" (Matthew 22:20-21). This ended the test, and they went away.

Jesus was no anarchist. He believed that you should honor the crown in whatever country you lived. Paul will teach us to be good citizens (Romans 13:1-7). We are to pray for our civil leaders so that we can live a peaceful and quiet life (1 Timothy 2:1-7). This is not being cowardly or placing a government above the Lord. In fact, this opens doors for us to help men come to a knowledge of the truth."

Honoring civil authorities is honoring God. The Lord uses civil governments to protect us, and perhaps even our right to teach others about Jesus. Paul addressed Felix, Festus, and Herod Agrippa with respect (Acts 23:23-26:32). This was so apparent that Felix calls Paul into a private audience to ask him more questions and Paul tries to teach him the gospel (Acts 24:24-26). Not all of the intentions of Felix were honorable, but Paul's demeanor opened a door.

Honoring civil leaders is not compromise.

Today, I will...pray fervently for the leaders of our nation and that I develop more respect for them.

HE MADE NO ANSWER

TODAY'S SCRIPTURE: Luke 23:6-12

Governor Pilate saw an opportunity to gain political favor with King Herod by sending Jesus to him as Jesus was being tried. In fulfillment of prophecy, Jesus said nothing before His accusers (Isaiah 53:7; Luke 23:9). Our Lord knew what was in the hearts of men even before they spoke (Mark 2:8), and there was no point to His defending Himself before such vile men, so He did not speak. By not speaking Jesus was honoring the throne of Herod, for our Lord knew everything about the man and could have pointed out every flaw, but He did not.

When we place others above ourselves, we will not become hyper-critical of them. Even if we know a lot of their flaws, we need to consider whether pointing those flaws out will help or hurt the cause of Christ. We are ambassadors for Christ wherever we go and must always bear this in mind (2 Corinthians 5:20). Just as Jesus emptied Himself to come here as a lowly man and live among us so He could save us, we must empty ourselves of our own pride so we can esteem others better than ourselves (Philippians 2:7).

Defending ourselves seems to be one of our national pastimes. It is not always wrong to defend yourself, but it often does more harm than good to the cause of Christ. Jesus remained silent, and we can learn a lot from His example. Oftentimes, honoring others means saying nothing. James teaches us to listen more than we talk (James 1:19). People who listen well tend to draw us to themselves because we believe they are truly interested in what we have to say. When counseling with a troubled person, we must listen in order to be able to help them, otherwise we cannot know the problem.

Jesus gave no answer to Herod because He knew what He had to do, save us. Perhaps by listening more than we talk, we can save more people than we do.

Today, I will...honor others by listening to them more caringly.

PLACES OF HONOR

TODAY'S SCRIPTURE: Luke 14:7-14

Upon entering the banquet hall, the host ushered the guests to their tables. The purpose of the banquet was to honor several people, but there was no head table. The host was asked why this was the case? He replied, "The people we are honoring would never have honored themselves, so we did not want to put them on display and embarrass them." A wonderful atmosphere and attitude was displayed throughout the evening, probably due mostly to this format.

Jesus entered a prominent Pharisee's home and noticed many who immediately chose the best seats. Jesus gave the parable of not picking the places of honor when you come to a dinner much like what they were attending. He pointed out that you would be embarrassed if the host came and made you move because a person of higher honor needed your seat. He taught that it was best to sit in the lower seats so that if the host came and led you to a higher seat, you would be honored instead of embarrassed.

Jesus went on to teach that it would be better to invite people who would normally not be invited to a dinner at your home, than to invite your close friends. If we invite the poor, crippled, lame, and blind, we will be rewarded (more than if we are invited back to a prominent person's house because they felt obligated). Honor has nothing to do with prominence, it has more to do with valuing another person, even if they are not very valuable to the rest of the world. King Arthur chose a round table because he wanted all to understand they were equal in value.

Jesus died because He placed a high value on our souls. He gave His unique life so that we can live in heaven with Him. There is no high table in heaven, we are all honored guests at His banquet.

Today, I will...honor a person no one else would honor and place a value on his or her soul in the same way Jesus would.

OUTDO ONE ANOTHER

TODAY'S SCRIPTURE: Romans 12:9-13

Sometimes we honor people simply because it is expected. We are to show honor to whom honor is due (Romans 13:7), but we need to make sure we really honor the person in our hearts before extending that honor to them. If we fail to examine our motives, the honor is not genuine.

Learning to honor others is valuable. Paul teaches us to "...outdo one another in showing honor..." (Romans 12:10). What precedes this is that we should love one another with brotherly affection. That means that with such a relationship, we will naturally "out-honor" others because we love them. It will not be forced, cold, and heartless. It will be a great joy for us to honor another person, for we are not seeking honor.

Jesus entered the house of Simon the Pharisee and was given no water for His feet, and no greeting with a kiss. A woman, who was a sinner, came and anointed Jesus with fragrant oil wiping His feet with her tears and hair. Simon was insulted, Jesus was honored. The two hearts revealed what was in them clearly. Simon felt Jesus should be honored to even be in his house, while the woman was honored to have the opportunity to humble herself before Christ.

Which of the two would we be? If we love our brethren we will go out of our way to honor them. A good friend during a gospel meeting was invited to a rich person's home at noon, and a poor person's home that evening. The meal at the wealthy home was sparse, but at the poor man's house was bountiful. Which one honored the preacher?

We will not feel diminished in any way by honoring brethren but will be grateful for the opportunity to let them know how we feel. The humble never expect honor, but are the very ones who deserve it most.

Today, I will...look for an opportunity to praise a brother or sister in Christ, and especially those who would never expect it.

Live In Harmony With One Another

RUSS DYER

TO KNOW, KNOW, KNOW YOU IS TO LOVE, LOVE, LOVE YOU!

TODAY'S SCRIPTURE: John 21:17

It was a hot summer day, about 40 or so years ago. My mother, my younger sister, my wife and I were visiting with my grandparents at Oak Creek Lake, near Blackwell, TX. They had owned a fishing cabin at that lake since the late 1950s. We loved to spend a few days with them in rugged and rural location. One of the reasons we were there was to celebrate their 69th Wedding Anniversary. Anyway, on one of the days we were all going to town to do a little shopping and such. We were all loaded in the car except my grandmother, waiting for her to secure the lock on the back door of the cabin. As she made her way toward the car, my mother asked her 91 year old father a question. She asked, "Daddy, do you still love her?" There was no hesitation as he responded, "More every day, honey; more every day." His words were sweet, but didn't strike me as more than just words, until much later. I had seen their love through the years, but didn't see it for what it was. I had especially noted the way my grandmother would take care of little things for my grandfather. She would fix his cup of coffee, make sure he had bread on his plate, check his clothing, and many other details. He doted on her and was ready to do just about anything she requested. While their interaction may be pretty normal, what needs to be seen is that it takes time to really learn the kind of love that works for nearly seven decades.

In the heart challenging exchange between Jesus and Peter there is an underlying message from Jesus. You can only affirm that you really love me when you have taken the time to know me. For, it is in the knowing that the doing finds its way. Peter came to learn that message, clearly as the years passed. So, I guess seven decades of marriage is a pretty good testimony to that point.

Today, I will...think about the people I love and make the commitment to know them more fully as time goes by.

EBONY AND IVORY

TODAY'S SCRIPTURE: Galatians 2:9

Not one person has it all. Each person has unique talents or abilities. Even Peter and Paul recognized that everyone focusing toward his best ability would lead to greater usefulness to the whole work. Whether we vary by race, history, heritage, geography, education, or any other aspect, when we learn how to use what we have for the Lord in harmony with others, it makes great music.

Several years ago, there was a small town church with a group of members who were learning and practicing songs after a Sunday evening service. There were some talented singers in the group, but most were just your typical shower-time singers. The person directing the practice worked with the female singers who were learning the lead, or melody part of the song. They learned the part, and they sounded good. Then the director called on the rest of the singers to join with their parts. A verse of the song was shared with enthusiasm and smiles. As the verse ended, one of the singers jumped from his seat, and looking at the group said, "Did you hear that difference. The ladies sounded great, but when the other parts were added, it was fantastic." He was right. When it comes to singing, a single voice can be marvelously beautiful. Sill, when the different parts join and blend their voices into a well-matched harmony, the level of beauty increases even more.

The song, Ebony and Ivory, was written by Paul McCartney, and sung as a duet with Stevie Wonder. The metaphoric use of the black and white keys on the keyboard, as the song is sung by men of different color, carries a powerful message. For, it is true that we are valuable as individuals, and from different races. Still, we are so much more when we blend our differences into a harmonic balance. When the cause is unity of song, the music can be amazing.

Today, I will... strive to recognize not only my differences from other people, but how I can blend them with others to serve the Lord in even better ways.

I'M STILL HERE, CHIEF

TODAY'S SCRIPTURE: John 6:67-69

It had to be hard for Jesus, as He watched so many people turn from him. Many of the people who were rejecting Him had been fed, healed, and taught by Him. It had to hurt. Then to turn and ask His closest followers if they would also leave Him, must have seemed overwhelmingly depressive. Peter wanted to reassure the Lord, and let Him know that he and his fellow disciples were not seeking an exit. They were "in" to stay.

Without a doubt, some people are in for the whole show, but far too many find an exit long before the curtain falls. When it came to facing the really tough stuff, even the closest disciples of Jesus finally slipped through the side door. He had said they would. "You will all fall away because of me this night. For it is written, 'I will strike the shepherd, and the sheep of the flock will be scattered'" (Matthew 26:31).

There is an old military saying: "No battle plan survives first contact with the enemy." It is a common mark of self-preservation to shrink from conflict when your life or welfare is acutely in danger. It is hard to know how far a person will go, or how great a risk will be undertaken, until the moment of challenge arrives.

Perhaps there are few greater encouragements in life than to learn that someone is still present, in support of you. In the movie, "Frequency", John Sullivan believes that his father, Frank, died several years earlier. Even with several unusual events taking place, it appears that John is about to die at the hands of a murderer. Instead, a supportive shot is fired. As the smoke clears, his father is seen. Frank looks at John and simply says, "I'm still here, Chief." The support of someone special changes the whole story.

Today, I will...strive to be more of that reliable support who is determined to be where I am needed without fail.

FOR YOU, I WILL

TODAY'S SCRIPTURE: Galatians 6:10

Gene was a great guy, and always ready to do something for the church, when needed. He kept track of the classes, counted the attendance, helped count the contribution, and even kept the church lawn in great shape. He was a very congenial, likeable guy. Still, there was something he had decided not to do for the church. He was not going to drive the van that was assigned to pick-up widows and other adults who needed a ride. The problem was that some of those ladies could get kind of bossy about the driving and the route that was followed. Gene just didn't want to have to deal with it. Not knowing of his decision, I needed a driver for an event. I went to Gene and simply asked him to do the job. He quickly told me of his decision to not to drive the van, and his reason. I was just about to take back my request, when Gene made another statement. He said, "For you I will do it." As far as I know, that was the last time Gene drove the church van.

When choosing to do something, the person or cause for whom we are doing it does make a difference. Common employees "clock-out" at the end of a work day, limiting their work to the required time frame, and nothing more. On the other hand, if that work is for something or someone that is dear to a heart, an "employee" becomes an invested part. Then the clock is just a clock, and what needs to be done becomes the passion of the worker, regardless of how long it takes. Just take a minute, and ask yourself what limits you would place on what you are willing to do for the people you love.

What we do for the Lord, the church, or for family is special. Paul wrote, "And whatever you do, do it heartily, as to the Lord and not to men" (Colossians 3:23). It is all right to say, "For you, I will."

Today, I will... make the extra effort to go the extra mile for the people that are important in my life.

WHAT I HAVE, I GIVE TO YOU

TODAY'S SCRIPTURE: Romans 12:16

He found his way to the church service on Sunday morning. His little daughter was with him. He was greeted, as just about any visitor would be. His clothing and car, spoke of a man who had very limited resources. Being given a card with his address, I took the opportunity to go to his house for a visit. It was a small, very humble house. It happened that he was not home, but his wife and daughter were there. The little girl recognized me, and greeted me. I explained who I was to his wife, and told that her I just wanted to thank him for visiting our services. The next Sunday, all three of the family members were present for worship. In the following days, we studied the Bible together, and he was soon baptized. In the course of one of our conversations, he asked if I wanted to know why he and his family had returned. I said that I did. He told me that they had visited a number of churches in the area, and that I was the only preacher who had taken the time to come by their home for a visit. He was made to feel that they were not seen as important enough for a visit. By a simple visit, they had then been given value.

When Peter and John paused for the lame man at a gate of the temple, he had wanted money. Peter's response was classic and powerful. He said, "I have no silver and gold, but what I do have I give to you. In the name of Jesus Christ of Nazareth, rise up and walk" (Acts 3:6)! The man may have been hoping for money, but it would be hard to say that what was given was less than expected.

We all have gifts to share. It might be money, or it might simply be a kind word. It might be a helping hand, or even a little bit of time. In the broad array of opportunities, giving what you have to share may be more of a gift than what was expected.

Today, I will... keep in mind what I have that I can give to the benefit of another person.

Edify One Another

MATTHEW MORINE

NO NICKNAMES, PLEASE

TODAY'S SCRIPTURE: Romans 15:2

I love to give people nicknames. My friends are called Mayhem, Viper, Wild Boar, Sir Wellington the 3rd, and many others. I also love to use alliteration when I call people on the phone. When someone picks up, I will say, "Is this prominent, powerful, pulpiteer Packer?" And my friend hates this, but I thinkwho would not want to be given a nickname or have a long list of alliterative adjectives used before their name? Sadly, not all people like this. So for this friend, I have to give a boring greeting because these thoughts are about pleasing the other person and not myself.

To edify another person is to think about what is pleasing to the other person. What you like might not be exactly what the other person enjoys. You might love sushi while the other person loathes raw fish. One person might love cold weather, while another would sleep in a dry sauna. Too often, we assume what we like is what everyone likes.

Paul talks about being other-person-minded in Romans 15:1-2, "We who are strong have an obligation to bear with the failings of the weak, and not to please ourselves. Let each of us please his neighbor for his good, to build him up." Humans have the tendency to think that what is best for me is best for you. We justify our selfishness by convincing ourselves that our actions are focused on edifying the other person. Certainly, the wife will love this fly-fishing rod even though she has never tried fly fishing. It is something we can do together, and she is always talking about us doing more together. All people can fall prey to a self-imposed con job.

Instead of building ourselves up, we need to be adamant on acting in a way that builds up the other person. What is best for them should be more important than what is best for me.

Today, I will...meet the needs of the people around me first.

PRAISE FOR PEACE

TODAY'S SCRIPTURE: Romans 14:19

Have you ever had someone say something hurtful to you? Maybe the person was picking at you about some mistake or character weakness. How did you feel? Sometimes we appreciate the honest feedback and acknowledge the mistake that we made. Other times we feel that the person is being a small-minded critic. An interesting reaction takes over the brain at this point. If you feel the criticism is unwarranted, you have a tendency to nitpick them in retaliation. You judge them more harshly. You start looking for stuff to throw back at them. No wonder Jesus said, "Judge not, lest you be judged." Being critical creates a negative vortex. The person is critical, which makes you more critical of them, which makes them more critical of you, and on and on the pattern reproduces.

On the other hand, praise promotes praise. A person that is always praising you, causes you to praise them. Maybe there is a little ego going on in the mind, but certainly someone that appreciates you must be a pretty smart guy. He or she sees a lot of your admirable qualities, which causes you to look for all of the character strengths of the other person. Looking for positive qualities causes other people to see positive qualities. After a while, each person that is praising the other person, creates a wonderful and positive relationship. Good luck trying to dislike your biggest fan in life.

Paul tells the Romans to praise each other. There is tension in Rome between the Jews and Gentiles, and Paul's solution is to praise each other. A Jew could look at the gentiles and pick out all of the qualities that he or she disliked. These Gentiles did not follow the Sabbath, there is no respect for history, and none of them have the Old Testament completely memorized. The Gentiles could look at the Jews and criticize that they are legalistic, harsh, and too judgmental. Each side could attack the difference between them. Instead Paul tells them in Romans 14:19, "So then let us pursue what makes for peace and for mutual upbuilding."

If there is conflict in a relationship, praise the other person. What is the worst that can happen? The person starts thinking that you are too nice? To overcome a lot of tension in a relationship, focus on praising them and see what happens.

Today, I will...praise all of the people I see.

ANNOYING KNOW-IT-ALL

TODAY'S SCRIPTURE: 1 Corinthians 8:1

Imagine yourself on a long journey across the United States. You left New York City to travel to Portland, Oregon. While on the trip you travel through the barren landscape of Kansas which is filled with long stretches of windswept terrain. In one particular expansion of arid high plains land, you have gone for twenty-four hours without water. Your lips are dry and your body is dehydrated. You are becoming incapably weaker. How much would you desire water? All you would think about is water, needing water, where to find water, and how much you long for a drink of water. Water would consume your thoughts. In a situation like this, even imagining something else would seem ridiculous. You would not be hoping for a Subway sandwich, and having a Starbucks coffee would be beyond comprehension. All you would want is water.

Now imagine that all of a sudden there was no air. Are you even thinking about water any longer? Probably not, because in that moment, needing air trumps needing water. Everyone has an order of priorities: water over food, and air over water.

Priorities are what Paul has in his mind when he implores the Christians in Corinth to put love first over knowledge. In the congregation, there are some different feelings over the eating of idol meat. Some of the affluent Christians are accustomed to eating idol meat at the temple and in homes, while the poorer Christians are mostly priced out of the idol meat market. The rich Christians are arguing that freedom in Christ allows them to eat the meat while the other Christians believe that to eat the meat is to engage in idol worship. Both sides want the other side to give in to their mindset. Instead of picking a side, Paul provides a path forward to reconcile everyone. The issue is not about who is right, it is about who is loving.

1 Corinthians 8:1 "Now concerning food offered to idols: we know that 'all of us possess knowledge.' This 'knowledge' puffs up, but love builds up." In some situations, the right thing to do is not to prove your case. Knowledge can create debates, disputes, and hard feelings. There is a mindset that is more important than being right —it is being loving. Like air over water, love supersedes knowledge. People need your love first before they can listen to your knowledge.

Today, I will...hold back what I think, in order to learn more about what someone else thinks.

YOU ARE GREAT

TODAY'S SCRIPTURE: 1 Thessalonians 5:11

Do you ever feel that you are never doing enough? You go to church and each week is about something that you need to be doing better. You've got to read the Bible more, love people more, pray more, and encourage more. "More, more, more!" is a constant drumbeat of a discontented society. In all roles in life, there is room for improvement, but sometimes instead of feeling like you need to be a better dad, mom, Christian, worker, or boss, you need to hear words of affirmation—"You are enough." You are loved for who you are, and the people around you appreciate you for who you are."

God does this to Jesus. Matthew 3:17, "And behold, a voice from heaven said, 'This is my beloved Son, with whom I am **well pleased**.'" Matthew 17:15, "He was still speaking when, behold, a bright cloud overshadowed them, and a voice from the cloud said, 'This is my beloved Son, with whom I am **well pleased**; listen to him.'" Two times, God speaks to his son and those who can hear by letting everyone know that Jesus is pleasing to his father. Jesus is enough. Think about all of the boys and girls that need to hear from their earthly fathers that they are enough, that they are loved for being themselves. Sometimes the command for more needs to be silenced and the affirmation of "enough" has to be shouted.

The event is so powerful that Peter remembers it in 2 Peter 2:17, "For when he received honor and glory from God the Father, and the voice was borne to him by the Majestic Glory, 'This is my beloved Son, with whom I am **well pleased**.'" Everyone likes to know that people are well pleased with them. Edifying is about more than encouraging people to do more. It is communicating contentment with what they are doing. All of us need to hear, "You are a good husband, you are a good father, you are a good Christian." There are times to grow and times to grow in appreciation for one another. Communicate thankfulness for all that people are doing.

Today, I will...accept myself for being me.

PLAY YOUR PART

TODAY'S SCRIPTURE: Ephesians 4:11-12

Years ago, I read about the difference between men and women. In the book it talked about how girls create dyads and boys create teams. Girls will partner up. Boys will be part of a team. Girls will have one close friend and boys can have numerous friends, as long as each boy feels that he is bringing something unique to the team. A girl needs one safe and secure friend in a social situation, and boys need to feel valuable to the group. You have girls that have a BBF for life and boys love being part of a sports team. As long as each boy feels that he has a talent that blesses the team, the team will accept him, and he will feel valuable. Each relationship dynamic is important to each sex.

Everyone has special gifts that can be used for the glory of God and the edification of the Church. No two Christians have the exact same skill set. There are Christians that have the gift of administration and no personality, while other Christians have bubbly personalities, but could not organize a potluck. The beauty about the Church is, that all people are valuable. An arm has a part, the tongue has a role, and even a toe has an important job to do in the building up of the body of Christ (1 Cor. 12:12-31). Everyone is important for the Church to be effective.

Paul notes the need for everyone to serve. "And he gave the apostles, the prophets, the evangelists, the shepherds, and teachers, to equip the saints for the work of ministry, for building up the body of Christ" (Eph. 4:11-12). All of these individuals are gifted in certain areas to equip the saints. Notice the purpose of all of these roles in the congregation—to gain power, to have people praise them, to increase in influence? No! None of these reasons are given. The sole purpose of these roles is to build the body of Christ. Everyone has a part to play in the betterment of the Church.

Today, I will...use my role in the Church to make it stronger.

Admonish One Another

LOGAN CATES

MONDAY

ADMONISH WITH SONG

TODAY'S SCRIPTURE: Colossians 3:16

I can't help but burst into song with my brothers and sisters in Christ! It is such a gift to be able to sing and truly enjoy the sound of God-given voices coming straight from the heart. I know it is right to sing praises to God, using my heart. Do we also comprehend how we can admonish one another with song? Paul said, "Let the word of Christ dwell in you richly, teaching and admonishing one another in all wisdom, singing psalms and hymns and spiritual songs, with thankfulness in your hearts to God" (Colossians 3:16).

Notice we admonish others when the word of Christ is "dwelling in us richly." We admonish others as we sing praises to our God. The admonishing will not stem from some perfect selection of music notes, a great microphone, or any other worldly object. The admonishing comes from within the heart (Ephesians 5:19) and when we are pierced with the word of Christ. When I see the words Jesus spoke, "Seek Ye First the Kingdom of God" and others like them, the words are cutting deep into my heart causing an immediate reaction to burst into song. They are far more powerful than the perfect selection of musical notes or a perfect song leader. Those words not only admonish me, but they will also admonish others as well. I strongly believe, based on the New Testament text, congregational singing has the unique ability to soften people's hearts and sometimes more strongly than a sermon.

Before the Lord's Supper on Sunday, we sing the song, "How Deep the Father's Love For Us," and it is easy for tears to fall. My heart is pierced as I consider the cross and listen to my brothers and sisters sing the same heart-tugging phrases. As the congregation sings, "But I will boast in Jesus Christ, His death and Resurrection," I am admonished. I am challenged. I am warned. I am deeply convicted.

Today, I will... remember to continue to meet with the saints on the Lord's day and admonish one another in song.

ADMONISH YOUR BROTHER

TODAY'S SCRIPTURE: 2 Thessalonians 3:15

Imagine traveling across I-40 on the eastern side of Oklahoma at about 7:45a.m. As vehicles cruise slightly over 70mph, they are unaware of the 580ft section of bridge just destroyed by a barge. However, after eight vehicles and three large trucks drove off the bridge, a man with flares began walking toward the oncoming traffic. He practiced the word "admonish" which means to warn, exhort, or advise. In 2002, fourteen people were killed at Webbers Falls, and there could have been more, had no warnings been given to those on the highway. This has a tremendous application spiritually, as we understand no Christian is exempt from admonishing others as we pass through this life.

The apostle Paul made the statement to the church, "Do not regard him as an enemy, but warn him as a brother" (2 Thessalonians 3:15). The word "warn" here is "admonish." Do we warn our brethren anymore? Would we stand out in the freeway with flares? Would we love at such an elevated degree, to plead with a brother to repent? Have we reached this kind of deep, sacrificial, agape love? Would we help to restore such a one having the spirit of gentleness (Galatians 6:1)? Or has the criticism of hateful judgement silenced any ability to warn? Love rejoices with the truth (I Corinthians 13:6), despite the criticism it may cause. I will, as a Christian, stand to admonish with red flares. This may mean teach, advise, train, or to exhort our own brethren. We were also charged by Paul in the presence of God and Christ Jesus to "preach the word" with "complete patience and teaching" (2 Timothy 4:1) because there will come a time when "people will not endure sound teaching" (2 Timothy 4:2,3). This leaves all Christians no choice but to admonish, and especially our own brethren.

Families are moving toward areas of danger in technology and spiritual complacency. Do we have any "Nathan's" in our proximity telling us "You're the man!"? Is there anyone willing to step out of their comfort zone running at us with red flares?

Today, I will... love in such a way to possibly warn a brother or sister of spiritual dangers ahead.

ADMONISH WITH TEARS

TODAY'S SCRIPTURE: Acts 20:31

Every man of God who stands to deliver the truth to any audience ought to have this scripture on his mind and heart. Paul said, "remembering that for three years I did not cease night or day to admonish every one with tears" (Acts 20:31). Preaching the gospel ought to be more than just reading words on a page and more than just a conveying of monotonous information on Sunday. He ought not to pretend to be something he is not, however the audience ought to see the urgent message of Christ has passed through his heart before it passed onto paper.

Paul is opening his heart and remembering the self-sacrificing devotion he had in preaching the message to the Ephesians. The "fierce wolves" (Acts 20:29) were on the verge of coming in. Men will arise and teach "twisted things" (vs. 30) and "draw the disciples after them." In other words, this message is so serious it demanded Paul passionately pouring out his heart to those he truly cared about.

The church is made of up people, not numbers on an attendance board. Paul clearly reveals how much these souls meant to him. He knew their struggles and he wanted to prepare them for what was coming. I find it easy to care so much for the body of Christ, that it stirs tears, don't you? I find it easy to get connected to people in the same way Paul did. There are those who serve in leadership and guard the flock from harm and do so passionately with tears. The church doesn't need any leadership disconnected from the flock. The church needs Elders and ministers to admonish with tears, spending night and day with the body. The Elders know the flock and the flock also has the responsibility to know the Elders.

Today, I will... show the compassion of Christ, and if there is a need or an opportunity, I will admonish with tears, naturally, because I care so much for the souls of others.

ADMONISH THE IDLE

TODAY'S SCRIPTURE: 1 Thessalonians 5:14

It is difficult to admonish those who don't want to be admonished. The "idle" is an accurate description fitting this category and Paul doesn't exclude them. We have already discussed the critical necessity to admonish others and Paul also said, "And we urge you, brothers, admonish the idle, encourage the fainthearted, help the weak, be patient with them all" (1 Thessalonians 5:14). The Greek word for "idle" describes a people who were undisciplined and insubordinate. Do the undisciplined still deserve to be admonished? What about the insubordinate? We don't have to make that decision, God already did. Everyone deserves to hear the message of Christ. We must not take the place of God, by judging those we think aren't worthy to be taught or warned.

Maybe you can relate to being insubordinate or undisciplined, and someone still used compassion to warn or teach you. Maybe you can relate to the faint-hearted here. They were faint-hearted due to the intense persecution they were facing at this time. They were close to giving up.

Have you ever been gifted with an encourager who helped you navigate through the struggling times of life? Did you happen to take note of the true power of encouragement? In the right gentle spirit, we also have the ability to lovingly warn those who are choosing to live or abide outside of Christ. Paul tried to warn Agrippa. Jonah had to be told twice to go warn Nineveh. Jesus warned the Pharisees and He also warned the seven churches of Asia in the book of Revelation. I remember someone warning me about my own spiritually dislocated attitude in my younger years. I am truly thankful they admonished me.

By admonishing the idle, Paul would help promote peace to the heart of the Christian and also promote peace in the church.

Today, I will... admonish anyone in need with gentleness and kindness, understanding the extreme value of every soul.

RESPECT THOSE WHO ADMONISH YOU

TODAY'S SCRIPTURE: 1 Thessalonians 5:12

You might be thankful for your family, for your friends, for your congregation, but are you thankful for the Elders who may admonish you? In our text, Paul is reminding the church to show deep appreciation to those who labor among them. "We ask you brothers to respect those who labor among you and are over you in the Lord and admonish you, and to esteem them very highly in love because of their work" (I Thessalonians 5:12).

The translation here for "admonish you" means giving instruction (*noutheteo*). Elders have been afforded the responsibility by God to sit down with individuals and admonish. We find no other group of people who would be "over you in the Lord" even though the church was in its early beginning. Think about what Paul is urging the congregation to do.

Here is the urgent, thought-provoking question for today: If Elders have been given the task of "admonishing" and we are given the task of "highly esteeming them," do we respect the Elders when they do admonish us? It may be a rare occasion today to find members humbly and respectfully falling before the Elders who admonish them. It may be a rare occasion to see a respectful, loving response. It might be rare to see someone admonished who wouldn't spread malicious gossip about the church afterward. This is an arduous, troublesome task for an Elder and we as members make it even more difficult. Elders may lose sleep for days and pray diligently before admonishing, but the truth is, there is not a more loving responsibility placed on those godly men.

Brother Earl Edwards once said, "Every Christian is obliged to do everything within his power to promote peace in the congregation of which he is a member" (Truth For Today Commentary, 2008).

Today, I will... remember to respect those who are given the task of admonishing me for the sake of my soul's eternal reward.

Serve One Another

STEVE BAILEY

MONDAY

WHO IS MY NEIGHBOR?

TODAY'S SCRIPTURE: Luke 10:25-37

In November of 2019, Tom Hanks played the lead role in the real life story of Fred Rogers. Mr. Rogers Neighborhood has been viewed by millions of children during the 895 episodes. Mr. Rogers always asked the question "Will You Be My Neighbor?" Rogers is quoted to say: "I feel that those of us in television are chosen to be servants. It doesn't matter what our particular job, we are chosen to help meet the deeper needs of those who watch and listen – day and night!"

The question of "Who is my neighbor?" was asked of our Lord Jesus Christ in Luke 10. The Master Teacher was being tested by an expert in the Mosaic Law by inquiring what he needed to do to inherit eternal life. Our Lord responded by asking the law expert if he knew what was written in the law? Of course he knew the correct answer and had to respond appropriately in Luke 10:27 to the Savior by confirming what the law recorded. The account now takes an interesting turn as the law expert, wanting to justify himself, then asked Jesus a question in return; "Who is my neighbor?"

Perhaps as you are reading, you are asking the same question? How do I get involved with serving my neighbors? Just exactly how much am I to do to fulfill this command?

Maybe we are not asking the right question in regard to this passage? Is it really "how little" I can do? OR perhaps it should be asked this way: Let me see how much "I can do" to show the love of Jesus each and every day! Just imagine what the Church would look like if every Christian actively looked for ways to share the love of Jesus by serving just one person each and every day? Would the light of Jesus shine brighter all over the planet? As Jesus said, "Go and do the same!"

Today, I will...look for an opportunity to do one act of kindness for one person, a family, or a stranger each day this week. Being a servant of Jesus takes devotion each and every day. Soon it will be part of your life.

WHO IS MY NEIGHBOR? Pt 2

TODAY'S SCRIPTURE: Luke 10:25-37

Yesterday we concluded with the question "Who is My Neighbor?" I learned many years ago "to be a friend you have to be friendly!" Would not the same words be true: "To have neighbors you must be neighborly?" How can you do this today?

At the time of this writing, on my way to work one day, I noticed that three houses were for sale on the street where I live. One house in particular, I noticed, had two rental trucks in the drive and another smaller trailer parked on the street. I thought to myself, I need to meet my neighbors...literally...I mean ...stop and have a "meet and greet!" The husband and wife met me on the driveway. As we talked a few minutes, I asked if I could bring lunch to them in a couple of hours and they both agreed that would be nice. So I did...nothing like welcoming some new folks to Texas with a hot steaming bag of "WHATABURGER" hamburgers, fries and ice cold Dr. Pepper! Along with the lunch I also offered an invitation of spiritual food. I handed them my Brown Street Church of Christ business card and asked that they come hear me preach. They were kind and agreed they would indeed consider a visit. Who knows what will come from that one small encounter? Only God really knows as I write. Please pray about that, will you? Paul in one of his letters to the Church in Corinth recorded in 1 Corinthians 3:6-7 "I planted, Apollos watered, but God gave the growth. So neither he who plants nor he who waters is anything, but only God who gives the growth."

Today, I will...look for an opportunity to do one act of kindness for one person, a family, or a stranger each day this week. Being a servant of Jesus takes devotion each and every day. Soon it will be part of your life.

AT WHAT COST DO I RISK SERVING?

TODAY'S SCRIPTURE: Luke 10:25-37

At first glance you may be saying, "That's the wrong motive to be a servant!" Those would be true words. We do not serve with an ulterior motive in mind. We ought to serve those around us because we have been given the example by Jesus Christ to serve one another. This truth is borne out in Matthew 20:28 "even as the Son of Man came not to be served but to serve, (emphasis mine) and to give his life as a ransom for many." This is repeated in Mark 10:45 and John 13:1-17.

Have you ever asked yourself this question? "What if Jesus only demonstrated servanthood when it was convenient for Him?" Most people would likely not find that genuine and even be hypocritical.

Personally, I have a high degree of distrust when I am driving and come to a traffic light and there are two or three people on each corner begging for pocket change. There is usually a sign being held with one hand and the other hand outstretched to my car window expecting me just to hand it all over to them. Honestly, I feel guilty later for not giving my change. I rationalize and say, I don't carry any change these days!" "Obviously, I can't help every person, so therefore I will not help anyone!" We know that is not the answer either. Do you struggle with this as well? Perhaps you do. Others have found the secret of exactly how to deal with this age old question: "At what cost do I risk helping every person in need?" Dr. Ira North wrote a book years ago entitled, "BALANCE" and that has helped me a lot. Perhaps we can "tilt the scales" a bit today to the side of servanthood and help a person in need.

Today, I will...risk...I will use an opportunity to help a person I do not know. I will risk and know that I am doing this deed in Jesus's name, to His honor and glory, not mine. Soon it will be part of your life. Again, as Jesus said in Luke 10:37 (ESV) "... You go, and do likewise."

MAKE ME A SERVANT

TODAY'S SCRIPTURE: Luke 10:25-37

Make Me a Servant, Lord Make Me Like YOU
For You Are a Servant , Make Me One Too

Why is it that when the holidays come around in November and December, that is the time most people think about being a servant? Being a servant can take on many different expressions. The thought of giving is usually one way we think about serving.

At the congregation where I am blessed to preach, 2021 will mark thirty one years of serving "Thanksgiving Day Meal" to our community. Yes you read that right... 31 years of serving turkey dinner with all the trimmings to anyone who needs a hot meal. Praise God! It takes an army of people to make all that happen. We have wonderful deacons who have a start time of 4 A.M. The ovens are pre-heating, pies and vegetables are being prepared. An army of good hearted people from young to old come to serve the meal. Then for those who cannot attend, it takes yet another army to deliver the hot meals to people "shut-in" and cannot drive to the campus. At the end of the day each worker feels exhausted...but it is a good kind of exhaustion! This is repeated year after year...thirty one years to be exact. WHY you ask? Because that is what the Lords Church does...we serve.

Someone maybe asking, yes, but what about the other 364 days of the year? What then?

It is with God and His continued blessings that we serve others with a CARE CENTER known to the county to be a place where you can come and have a good "bill of food" given so the hungry can eat and experience the love of Jesus other days of the year. Gently used clothing that is clean, and ready to wear is also available. All for FREE! Can you serve in a place like that just once this week? Reach out to the opportunities around where you can volunteer for a full day...it is truly the best "kind of tired" in the entire world. YOU served others.

Today, I will...risk...I will use an opportunity to step out of my comfort zone. I will risk and know that I am doing this deed in Jesus's name, to His honor and glory, not mine. Soon it will be part of my life. I will go as Jesus has said in Luke 10:37 (ESV) "... "You go, and do likewise."

MAKE ME LIKE YOU

TODAY'S SCRIPTURE: Luke 10:25-37

In December of 2018 actor Tyler Perry made headlines for taking part in what's become a holiday tradition among some wealthy people; he paid off the layaway accounts of total strangers. Debts were paid at Walmart for 1,500 Atlanta, Georgia area shoppers. The bill totaled $434,000! That was a generous deed. Perry further explained: "I know it's hard times and a lot of people are struggling," Tyler Perry said. "I'm just really, really grateful to be able to be in a situation to do this. So God bless you. Go get your stuff."

If you are like me, I can't come even close to paying off someone's debt like that...not even close. But I can do that for one person or maybe two! Would that make an impact? Not much, but it will certainly be a help to those two families who probably could use that money they would spend to pay a light bill, or to help on the rent that month. It could help make a good holiday for a family.

Paul said in Galatians 6:10 (ESV) "So then, as we have opportunity, let us do good to everyone, and especially to those who are of the household of faith." Is there someone in your church family who needs some additional help with a medical bill, someone having a hard time making ends meet, or is there a struggling young couple that could use some extra financial help anonymously? Maybe you could write an encouraging note to a missionary the congregation helps support. Send a check and write an encouraging note to make their month a little better!

Today, I will...risk...I will use an opportunity to step out of my comfort zone. I will risk and know that I am doing this deed in Jesus's name, to His honor and glory, not mine. Soon it will be part of my life. I will go as Jesus has said in Luke 10:37 (ESV) "... You go, and do likewise."

Forgive One Another

NEAL POLLARD

CAN WE FORGIVE UNREPENTANT OFFENDERS?

TODAY'S SCRIPTURE: Ephesians 4:32

In 2014, Claire Davis' father spoke at a memorial service honoring his daughter, a High School student shot by a classmate who was angry with his debate team coach. Michael Davis said, "My wife and I forgive Karl Pierson for what he did. We would ask all of you here and all of you watching to forgive Karl Pierson. He didn't know what he was doing." Pierson entered the school with a shotgun, 125 shells, a machete and three homemade bombs. He ended his own life. Despite all these facts, Davis says that he forgives Pierson. Is that possible?

Some say Davis had no right to do this. I disagree. Mr. Davis says he forgave Pierson and I have no reason to disbelieve him. His forgiving Pierson cannot effect the young man's eternal destiny. He does not have the power to absolve or wash away Karl's sins. Only Christ's blood can do that. But Mr. Davis' magnanimous step is not only possible, it is vital. Taking the step to forgive someone who has sinned against us is a crucial part of healing our own hearts and preventing ourselves from spiritual struggles like bitterness, anger, hatred, malice, and vindictiveness.

A heart ready to forgive is something that must characterize every Christian. We may be hurt or violated in some way by a person who is impenitent and brazen. While the Bible does not suggest we allow ourselves to be hurt and sinned against repeatedly without recourse or protection, God's child eagerly hopes for the best and stands ready to extend forgiveness to others.

Mr. Davis is to be admired for his gesture. It did not bring his daughter or even that young man back, but it may be key to his own mending. Many who have been sinned against and have stood ready to forgive, have found this to be beneficial to themselves.

The Father in heaven will not forgive those who are not abiding faithfully in His Son, but who doubts that He stands ready to welcome the vilest sinner who truly comes to Him? That disposition could not be more worthy of our adopting. Even in tragedies like that involving Miss Davis, we can be reminded of the power of forgiving!

Today, I will...keep my heart prepared and inclined to release others of their sins against me.

GOD'S BLUEPRINT FOR RESOLVING PROBLEMS WITH EACH OTHER

TODAY'S SCRIPTURE: Matthew 18:15-20

God's blueprint is in Matthew 18:15-20. Jesus gives specific instructions for what to do when a spiritual brother or sister sins. We create trouble when we fail to follow this pattern and follow what seems right or best to us. As we walk through this pattern, we see:

- *Perpetration* (15)--"If your brother sins." It's hard to avoid offending or sinning against each other (Luke 17:1-4). God has a plan for when this happens. It hurts Him deeply when we hurt each other.
- *Correction* (15)--"Go and tell him his fault." There are several action words: "go," "tell," "take," "tell," and "let him be." But, what is first? Go to him! Too often, we rationalize disobeying this command. Jesus didn't say it would be pleasant or easy. He did not say tell others. Address the offender.
- *Discretion* (15)--"In private." Our greatest desire is to protect our spiritual family. We don't want to publicly expose the offender. Private confrontation usually makes one less defensive. Don't we prefer the direct approach over being avoided or treated dishonestly?
- *Aspiration* (15)--"If he listens to you, you have gained your brother." That's the goal! "Restore" (Gal. 6:1) and "turn" and "save" (Jas. 5:20). If they repent, that's the end of it. No one else should ever hear about it! How do you know if he listened? He will repent and return (Luke 17:3-4).
- *Caution* (16-17). They may not listen, no matter how righteously we respond. Pride, shame, guilt, and sinful anger may get in the way, even when a couple or the whole try to reach them. There may not be a happy ending.
- *Repudiation* (17-18). The last step is congregational rejection. For the sake of the offender's soul, we must act. Many texts deal with this (1 Cor. 5; Rom. 16; 2 Th. 3; Ti. 3).

Did you ever fight with siblings growing up? Such didn't indicate a lack of love each other, but the issue had to be worked out. Your parents expected it. If they intervened, it was not pleasant. Likewise, Jesus wants us to work it out, His way! Don't avoid it, gossip, or enable. Follow His pattern! After all, we're family.

Today, I will... be sure that if I've been offended by a brother, I am following Jesus' pattern.

TWO CONSEQUENCES OF A HEART FOR ONE ANOTHER

TODAY'S SCRIPTURE: Colossians 3:1-17

In Colossians 3, Paul tells us to have a compassionate, kind, humble, gentle, and patient heart for each other. Think about these five qualities with which Paul calls for people clothe their hearts. If we sincerely do that, won't it change who we are and how we behave?

This kind of heart bears with one another. We tolerate the annoying and irritating stuff. We put up with each other. "Misophonia" literally means hatred of sound. It was a term proposed about twenty years ago as a condition in which negative emotions, thoughts, and physical reactions are triggered by specific sounds like chewing gum and food, slurping, or whispering. It's a severe sensitivity and causes an immediate extreme reaction. A lot of studies have been done in recent years that suggest that as many as fifteen percent of adults suffer from it.

I wonder how many of us have developed a sort of spiritual form of this—not merely irritation at sounds people make, but an inclination to be aggravated, impatient, and annoyed with others, and quick to display that displeasure. Paul shows us that the way to cure this spiritual condition is to put on a heart that leads to enduring the difficult.

This kind of heart forgives one another. The idea here is of giving freely and graciously as a favor. The New Testament urges this frequently. Isn't that an indication that this is something we struggle with? We live in a society that insists on one's rights and that is increasingly sensitive at the slightest perceived violation. God's family is to actually be the opposite of this, cherishing others' rights and overlooking slights. Paul's inspired counsel is to "be kind to one another, tender-hearted, forgiving each other, just as God in Christ also has forgiven you" (Eph. 4:32, NAS).

Today, I will...practice tolerance and grace with my spiritual family, realizing that is how loving families are supposed to behave.

THE BOY WHO STAYED HOME

TODAY'S SCRIPTURE: Luke 15:11-32

Most of us root for and can relate to the Prodigal Son. We love to read about the father, who represents both the Father but also Jesus (cf. Luke 15:1-2). But, then there's that other character in the parable. How does he strike you? Think about it. His brother has been reckless and irresponsible, and his dad lets him off Scott-free--even throws him a party! His brother has robbed his father blind, and he isn't punished one bit. He represents the religious leaders, and among his flaws was his unforgiving spirit.

His brother had sinned against him, but now he was not willing to forgive him. You see this in how he refers to the prodigal. A servant calls him "your brother" (27). The father calls him "this brother of yours" (32). The only time the older brother refers to him, he tells his father the prodigal is "this son of yours" (30).

I find it interesting that the background of these parables is those religious leaders grumbling against Jesus' receiving sinners. In the first two parables, people go seeking the lost. In the third parable, is it at least implied that the other brother should have gone seeking his lost brother? God implies as early as Cain and Abel that we are our brother's keeper. The New Testament teaches our need of searching for lost brothers (Gal. 6:2; Jas. 5:19-20). But not only did he not search for his brother, now, he won't forgive him.

There's a warning in this for us. "Pay attention to yourselves! If your brother sins, rebuke him, and if he repents, forgive him" (Luke 17:3). "Then Peter came up and said to him, "Lord, how often will my brother sin against me, and I forgive him? As many as seven times?" Jesus said to him, "I do not say to you seven times, but seventy-seven times" (Mat. 18:21-22). It's so easy to harden our hearts and excuse ourselves rather than joyfully welcoming the prodigal brother back home.

All of us may be the prodigal. None of us could be the father. May we avoid being the boy who stayed home.

Today, I will...view my erring brother the way I want my Father to view me.

FRIDAY

I FORGIVE YOU

TODAY'S SCRIPTURE: Matthew 18:35

> *"I forgive you...*
> *...but I won't ever treat you the same."*
> *...but I will make sure you never forget it."*
> *...but I don't think you should serve any more."*
> *...but I will keep my distance from you."*
> *...but I will tell others about your sin."*

The very word "forgive" means to release something from one's presence, to release from moral obligation or consequence (BDAG, 156). That sounds very different from some of the substitute offerings mentioned above. Have we ever considered all the Lord has to say about our forgiving one another?

- But if you do not forgive others, then your Father will not forgive your transgressions (Mt. 6:15).
- If your brother sins, go and show him his fault in private; if he listens to you, you have won your brother (Mt. 18:15).
- Read the moral of the parable of the man forgiven much who refused to forgive the one who owed him little (Mt. 18:34-35).
- Be on your guard! If your brother sins, rebuke him; and if he repents, forgive him. And if he sins against you seven times a day, and returns to you seven times, saying, 'I repent,' forgive him (Luke 17:3-4).
- Be kind to one another, tender-hearted, forgiving each other, just as God in Christ also has forgiven you (Eph. 4:32).
- Bearing with one another, and forgiving each other, whoever has a complaint against anyone; just as the Lord forgave you, so also should you (Col. 3:13).

Perhaps in our zeal to remind offenders that their sin has consequences, we add to those consequences through choices we make in response to their repentance. A penitent sinner is already struggling with guilt and accepting God's forgiveness. The last thing we should do is make it harder for them. When they do try to put their spiritual lives back together again, we should rejoice for them and help them any way we can. Jesus teaches that we can be guilty of sin ourselves by mishandling the challenging discipline of forgiving. May He help us as we strive to do it.

Today, I will..."Forgive from the heart" (Mt. 18:35) and make it easy for someone trying to overcome sin.

Comfort One Another

JOHN MOORE

COMFORT ONE ANOTHER WITH SINGING

TODAY'S SCRIPTURE: Ephesians 5:15-20

We were fighting back tears. His feeble, emaciated body lay nearly lifeless upon the bed. With each passing hour, his breathing became more labored. It was a moment we knew eventually would come, yet one that none of us were ready for. Dad was passing from this life into the next, and our hearts were torn between wanting him to stay and letting him go to a place where his suffering would cease. Waiting for him to die was almost more than we could bear, but among the many things that gave my family comfort and strength was when we gathered around his bed to sing beautiful hymns of praise.

My dad loved to sing, and over the course of his 86 years he had led us in countless hymns. At church assemblies, family reunions, special occasions, and while travelling in our car, singing was a huge part of my life; a blessing of growing up with such a godly man. Singing encouraged Dad, and it encouraged me. My earliest memories of knowing about the love of Jesus and the hope He provides came from the hymns both Dad and my mother sang to me when I was a youth. Even today, when I hear the familiar refrain "Peace, be still," from the well-known hymn Master the Tempest is Raging, I am comforted in knowing the timeless truth learned from my youth that "even the winds and the sea obey him" (Matthew. 8:23f).

Designed by God, singing is meant to shape our thinking and edify our souls (Ephesians 5:19). When words are set to a melodic tune, they are often much more powerful and memorable. Singing awakens our emotions and can soothe our heart during emotionally difficult times (Acts 16:25), and the message of the song tends to stay with us even after its chords have ceased. Like the sound of a harp that continues to vibrate long after its strings are plucked, so is the joy and comfort that remain when music passes the strings of the human heart. Though the sound is gone, its effect remains, just as it did after my father died.

> *In the hours and days that followed our mournful last goodbyes,*
> *my father's earthly passing was seen through heaven's eyes.*
> *The songs we sang while near his side continue with me still,*
> *They calm my heart and soothe my mind wherever I may lie,*
> *I hear them now, they linger on: my dad is "where the soul NEVER dies."*

Today, I will... comfort others and comfort my own heart through singing.

COMFORT ONE ANOTHER BY LISTENING

TODAY'S SCRIPTURE: Galatians 6:1-2

The man just could not understand why his wife didn't see his logic. In efforts to resolve their marital conflict, he continued to explain himself and spent hours arguing his case. He saw himself as a good Christian man who was only trying to do what was right. He went through all the possible scenarios and arrived at a conclusion about their argument. He just knew he was right, and yet his wife's demeanor only appeared to him as evidence of her distress and disagreement. What the husband was failing to see, however, was what he needed to hear. He needed to both hear and listen to his wife's feelings. Sometimes those who are hurting aren't always disagreeing; they might just simply need to be heard.

Failing to listen to others has a detrimental effect on any relationship. When a husband doesn't listen to his wife (or vice-versa), or when parents fail to hear to their children, or when elders refuse to hear the concerns of their flock, people are often left feeling marginalized and insignificant. On the other hand, listening with the intent to understand declares that you care, you love, and that you see the other person as worthy of your time. When we listen, we provide comfort to those who are hurting, confused, or frustrated. Listening empowers and helps others to clarify their feelings. It sends a message to those who are hurting that they are not alone (Galatians 6:1-2; James. 5:16).

Listening to others can be challenging. Our mind can easily wander or become distracted. Sometimes we listen only to refute. Sometimes we are caught up in personal concerns and fail to see the problems of others. However, if we could remember that God is the greatest listener of all, and that we are called to be like Him (Ephesians. 5:1), then listening to the problems and concerns of others will be a must. God listens to those who are hurting and is touched by the feelings of their infirmities (Hebrews 4:15). This is one reason we are so comforted by prayer: we know God listens (1 John 5:14-15).

Today, I will... be like God. I will seek to comfort others by listening.

COMFORT ONE ANOTHER THROUGH POSITIVE TALK

TODAY'S SCRIPTURE: James 3:1-12

Negative, negative, negative. That's how some of us can come across to others. If you look hard enough you can find something wrong with everyone and everything. Have you ever stopped to consider just how draining and psychologically upsetting it can be to others when you or I find fault and complain about so many things? It's difficult when we are exposed to the daily barrage of news stories which regularly report on deaths, riots, debates, and natural disasters, but when we are also subjected to friends or family members who are grim and sour it merely compounds the stress others endure while living in this fallen world.

Positive talk, on the other hand, can be uplifting and extremely comforting. God says that "gracious words are like a honeycomb, sweetness to the soul and health to the body" (Proverbs 16:24). When we speak with a gentle tongue, others will benefit and grow (Proverbs 15:4). As children of light we are called to think on things that are lovely and of good report. What we think about and meditate upon are the things that will "come out" and be displayed in both our speech and psychological posture. So, when we meditate on the goodness and mercy of God, we will find ourselves speaking about it to others as well. Remember, "anxiety in a man's heart weighs it down, but a good word makes it glad" (Proverbs 12:25). As we seek to comfort others, let us always focus on the fact that words are a powerful tool that can either make things better—or worse—for people (James 3:1-12).

As Paul instructed the church at Colossae to speak to one another with grace (Colossians 4:6), may we find complimentary things to say to one another. Look for the good in others and tell them! Remember how they have helped you, no matter how big or small, and give them sincere appreciation. Look for the good in every situation and then talk about it. Positive talk is a leaven in the lives of others. It permeates a family and in turn helps everyone feel comforted.

Today, I will... comfort my family, my church family, and my friends by looking for the good and positive, and then I will express them.

COMFORT ONE ANOTHER WITH PRAYER

TODAY'S SCRIPTURE: Acts 16:25-34

The young preacher had just called on the telephone to ask for help with interpreting a passage. After our discussion, I closed by saying, "Brother, let's pray before we hang up." After praying briefly, we said our goodbyes and ended the call. About a year later, I was blessed to work alongside this same man at a summer youth camp. At some point our conversation turned toward prayer and he confessed to me that when we had prayed together over the phone, it had made him somewhat uncomfortable. Later he realized that his discomfort had stemmed from the fact that praying over the telephone simply wasn't something he was accustomed to. However, once he began to think about prayer in light of scripture, it became a major point of comfort for him to know that even after an ordinary conversation, someone would take the time to pray.

The very act of approaching God on behalf of others will encourage them beyond measure. Obviously, we don't pray to be seen of men (Matthew 6:5-6), but in praying with others we are sending the message that God is our source of strength, and that He is the one who will see us through our trials (Psalm 18:1-6). Just as the apostle Paul received strength and encouragement from the Philippian brethren during his imprisonment at Rome (Philippians 1:19), today we can help others who are imprisoned by worries and pain simply by offering a prayer in their presence.

Over the course of my ministry, I've never had someone turn me down when I offered to pray with them. Most understand the comfort that prayer provides and are often eager to have you pray for them. Prayer is a powerful tool in the hands of the Christian, and when we pray together it's amazing to see what doors the Lord might open (Acts 16:25-27). The fervent prayer of a righteous man accomplishes much (James 5:16).

Today, I will... comfort others by praying with them.

COMFORT ONE ANOTHER WITH "THESE WORDS"

TODAY'S SCRIPTURE: 1 Thessalonians 4:13-18

Only days after we buried her husband, we went to visit and pray with Ruth, a wonderful Christian woman who led many to Christ. "Where do you think my husband is now?" she asked with an inquisitive look. "Well, heaven, of course!" I said in a corrective tone. "Oh, I know that, silly!" she quipped. "I mean, where is paradise, and what might he be doing now?" Her questions were at least as old as the church in Thessalonica, who some 2000 years ago asked similar questions about loved ones passing from this life. The apostle Paul's answer concluded with: "Therefore comfort one another with these words."

While the words of 1 Thessalonians 4:13-18 were directed toward a very specific series of questions about the second coming of Jesus, we must remember that the Bible, overall, was given for our admonition and comfort. The words of God are powerful and will sustain us through hardship and pain. They provide answers, hope, strength, and the message that God loves us unconditionally (2 Timothy 3:16-17; 2 Peter 1:3; Romans 8:24-39; Psalm 119).

When seeking to comfort others, we are often good at praying with and listening to those who are hurting, but how often do we actually open the Bible and simply read to them from God's word? Several years ago in my local ministry, I began making a conscious effort to simply read a chapter or two from the Bible to those with whom I had gone to visit. Whether at the hospital, in the homes of the elderly, in encouraging a wayward member, or in the midst of a counseling session, it is always good to ask if you can read from the Bible to help those who are hurting.

The sword of the Spirit is the word of God (Ephesians 6:17). If God's Spirit, His word, is in us, then we will find comfort and help in time of need (Romans 15:4). The Spirit is called the "comforter" for a very good reason (John 14:26). When we use the Spirit's sword, Christians will find comfort. When they hear the word of God, it will help them to have faith (Romans. 10:17).

Today, I will... comfort others by just reading to them "these words"—the Bible.

Stir Up One Another to Love and Good Works

FERMAN CARPENTER

MEMBERS OF ONE ANOTHER

TODAY'S SCRIPTURE: 1 Corinthians 12:12-27

The most common "one another" command in the Bible is "Love one another". The best way we can love one another is to practice the "one another" commands found in the God's word.

To Christians in Rome, Paul wrote: "so we, though many, are one body in Christ, and individually members one of another" (Romans 12:5). In 1 Corinthians 12:12-27, Paul gives three areas Christians should emphasize to help them be "members of one another."

1) WE MUST EMPHASIZE OUR DEPENDENCY (12:18-21): A Christian is like hand. No matter how useful that hand may be, apart from the body it will never be useful to the body. Paul teaches us that we cannot spiritually survive without the Body, and the body is not made in such a way that it will tolerate independence from its members. Being "members one of another" is much more than being on a church role, we must be dependent on each other.

2) WE MUST EMPHASIZE OUR EQUALITY (12:22-24): No Christian should feel more or less important than any other Christian. God has deliberately made up our bodies so that the less seen parts are vital. In the Lord's church there are lots of people working behind the scenes so that others can serve visibly, but everyone is needed and appreciated. Being "members one of another" is not just being on a role, it is working together.

3) WE MUST EMPHASIZE OUR UNITY (12:12): Paul is very clear that the Body is a unit. God designed our physical bodies to love harmony and hate discord. In the Lord's Body all members must be going in the right direction or there will be problems. There is nothing that will destroy the purpose of the Lord's church faster that division in the Body. Paul says there should be, "no division in the body" (12:25), that's why we should be "eager to maintain the unity of the Spirit in the bond of peace" (Ephesians 4:3).

Today, I will...remember that as a member of the Lord's Body, we are "members one of another."

GREET ONE ANOTHER

TODAY'S SCRIPTURE: Romans 12:10; 16:1-16

The Lord's church is not only a place where God's truth is taught and practiced, but also a place of love and care and attention. In Romans 12:10, the Lord's church is told "Love one another with brotherly affection." In Romans 16:1-16, Paul mentioned 27 people by name; 17 were personal references; and 19 were references of commending and greeting one another. Paul never missed an opportunity to build somebody up. When our vertical relationship with God is right, it is amazing how deep our horizontal relationships become.

Paul gives us three necessities for the Lord's church:
1) WE MUST MAKE ROOM FOR ALL KINDS OF PEOPLE: Paul's list contains men and women; young and old; single and married; wealthy and poor. What kept them close? It was their oneness in Jesus. Ten times in sixteen verses Paul talks about them being "in Christ" or "in the Lord." In the Body of Christ, we have the perfect environment for brotherly love. We have the freedom to be ourselves and yet share the common bond in our commitment to Jesus.

2) WE MUST EXPRESS OUR APPRECIATION FOR EACH OTHER: Paul says, "Love one another with brotherly affection. Outdo one another in showing honor" (Romans 12:10). There are several people that Paul's letter shows honor to because that is how we produce "brotherly affection."

3) WE MUST NEVER TAKE "ONE ANOTHER" FOR GRANTED: It would be hard to imagine Paul coming to worship on Sunday, walking in without talking to anyone; sitting through worship and getting up and seeing how quick he could leave. The more we live in a fallen world, the more refreshing it is to worship and fellowship with other Christians.

Today, I will...ask God to help me love everyone, be friendly, and care enough to say so.

ENCOURAGING ONE ANOTHER

TODAY'S SCRIPTURE: Hebrews 3:12, 13; 10:24, 25

All Christians, as servants of Jesus Christ, need to be encouragers of one another. It is easier to destroy than it is to grow or rebuild, that is why we need more building up to overcome the few who tear down. The word "encourage" is found 109 times in the New Testament, it is always translated "exhort, comfort, encourage." These words have one primary purpose, they describe the functions that helps Christians build up the Body. To become better encouragers let us look at the "who" "when" and "how" of encouraging others.

I. WHO ARE THE ENCOURAGERS?
A. ELDERS (Titus 1:9). Elders are to know the truth and handle it with encouragement to protect and lead the flock. Church leadership that does not encourage, discourages.
B. PREACHERS AND TEACHERS (1 Thessalonians 3:2; 1 Timothy 4:2). Teaching and preaching God's truth is a source of encouragement. When we handle God's truth in a way that stirs the soul, we have encouraged the listeners.
C. THOSE BLESSED WITH THE TALENT OF ENCOURAGING (Romans 12:6-8). If we have the gift of encouragement, then we must use it in the Lord's church.
D. ALL CHRISTIANS (Ephesians 4:29). All of us need to use words that will build each other up. It is not healthy for the Church to be dependent on a few to do all the encouraging.

II. WHEN DO WE ENCOURAGE?
A. AT EVERY ASSEMBLY (Hebrews 10:24,25). Encouragement is one of the great by-products Christians receive when they come to worship. Every time we meet it is incumbent upon all of us to be encouragers.
B. EVERY OPPORTUNITY (Hebrews 3:12, 13)

III. HOW CAN WE BECOME ENCOURAGERS?
A. BY ENCOURAGING OTHERS TO REMEMBER GOD'S PROMISES (1 Thessalonians 4:13-11; Hebrews 13:5; John 9:31; 1 John 1:9; Revelation 21:4; Romans 8:28; etc.)

B. BY ENCOURAGING OTHERS TO REMAIN FAITHFUL (Acts 14:22; Jude 3; Romans 1:11,12).

There is a place in our lives to encourage and to be encouraged to stay faithful. None of us are dart proof. We need to encourage one another.

Today, I will...be an encourager.

LIKE-MINDED TOWARD ONE ANOTHER
TODAY'S SCRIPTURE: Romans 15:1-7

Nothing is uglier than for Christians to argue, fight, or being divisive. Jesus deserves better from His bride. If we are going to be known as The Lord's Church, we must learn to be "like-minded toward one another."

Jesus prayed for unity among His followers (John 17:20-21). Unity is the strategy for evangelism. There are many verses in the book of Acts that talk about this unity, (Acts 2:44-47; 4:32; 6:7). However, in Rome, there were tensions in the Lord's church, not so much over matters of doctrine, but matters of opinion (Romans 14:1-19). In Jerusalem the church was made up purely of Jews, but the church in Rome was made up of Jews and Gentiles; two different cultures. Paul gives us two exhortations for promoting unity (Romans 15:5-7).

I. HOW TO PROMOTE UNITY:
A. "Be like-minded" (Romans 15:5; 1 Corinthians 1:10; Philippians 2:3-8). Peace is not the result of total agreement. The Lord's church is so huge and diverse, we will never have unity if it means we must line up on every matter of opinion. Unity is the result of deciding the interests of others are more important than our own.

B. "Accept one another" (Romans 15:7; John 13:35). The Christ that unites us is bigger than the opinions that divide us. The convicting testimony of Christian unity is not that we are alike, but that we are all one, even though we are not alike. What made the Lord's church in the First Century so incredible and convicting, was that the Jews stayed Jews and the Gentiles stayed Gentiles and for the first time in history, they treated each other like family.

II. HOW TO MAINTAIN UNITY:
A. By God's standard (Acts 2:37-47; John 8:31-32). We have a brother when anyone enters Christ church on God's terms. And we must continue in His word.

B. By the right to forgo our right (Romans 15:1). We must be able to give up any opinion, practice, or conviction, not bound by God, for the sake of harmony in the Body.

C. By selfless discipleship (Romans 15:5). When our focus is on Christ there is beautiful harmony.

Today, I will... Let God's word direct my life and seek peace and unity even at the sake of my own opinion.

ADMONISHING ONE ANOTHER

TODAY'S SCRIPTURE: 1 Thessalonians 5:12-14

The task of "admonishing one another" is very difficult. The New Testament word "admonish" means to instruct, counsel, warn or correct. The word implies re-direction. There is a place in the Lord's church for positive instruction and correction. Admonishment is not judgmental-ism nor is it something we use to label or criticize someone. Admonishment is for our Christian family and it springs from a sense of concern. When God instructs parents to train up their children in the "admonition of the Lord" (Ephesians 6:4), we know He means out of tremendous love, and not out of a spirit of criticism.

I. WHO HAS THE RESPONSIBILITY OF ADMONISHMENT?
A. Elders (1 Thessalonians 5:12-13). Elders cannot lead the Lord's church if they turn their heads to sin.

B. Christians (1 Thessalonians 5:14). Christians help share in this responsibility because they are members of one another.

II. WHAT IS AN ADMONISHER LIKE?
A. Full of goodness (Romans 15:14). Those who are admonished must perceive that their admonisher is coming to them because they care about them like family.

B. Filled with knowledge (Romans 15:14). Admonishers must be able to take scripture in life situations and apply it to where they are living (2 Timothy 3:16-17). Those whose spiritual walk lacks credibility should not be admonishers.

III. WHEN SHOULD WE ADMONISH?
A. Only when God's truth has been violated, and not in matters of opinion or personal convictions. Biblical admonitions bring someone face to face with the teaching of God's word (Romans 14; Romans 10:17).

B. Only if we are sure we have examined our own lives (Matthew 7:3). The chief difference between admonishers and judgers is that those who judge give no credibility to what they say.

C. Only if we admonish them personally (Matthew 18:15-17). Public admonition should always be the last resort and not the first response.

The Lord's church must embrace sinners, but it must also confront sinning. If we do not care enough to admonish one another, we do not care enough.

Today, I will...make sure I walk in God's truth; I care for everyone; I admonish lovingly.

Be Humble Toward One Another

RUSS CROSSWHITE

SUBMIT TO ONE ANOTHER

TODAY'S SCRIPTURE: Ephesians 5:15-21

In verses 15-21 we are exhorted to look carefully with a focus on God and others. We are to "be filled with the Spirit" (verse 18) and Paul gives three participles showing the results of this Spirit filled life. For our study in this lesson we will look at the third participle found in verse 21. Here Paul says we should be "submitting to one another out of reverence for Christ." So how can we be "humble toward one another?" Verse 21 gives us insight on how we can do it.

First, we must "submit" to one another. To "submit" conveys the concept of "mutual honor and respect" (William Barclay). A good commentary on this is found in Romans 12:10 where Paul says, "Love one another with brotherly affection. Outdo one another in showing honor."

Second, because of our "reverence" for Christ we show respect for all those who are of Christ. Therefore, we treat one another with love and grace just like Jesus does. Because Christ is the object of our faith and the affection of our love, all our relationships with fellow Christians find their meaning under the authority of Christ and our relationship with Him.

"They saw each other not in the light of their profession or social standing but in the light of Christ; and therefore they saw the dignity of every man" (William Barclay). Christ sees the value of every soul and humbled Himself to the Father's will by dying on the cross for everyone. Likewise, out of respect for the Lord, shouldn't we be willing to humble ourselves toward one another?

Today, I will...humble myself to my brethren by treating them on the basis of the dignity Christ gives to all His disciples and not upon personal, social, or economic standing.

BEARING WITH ONE ANOTHER

TODAY'S SCRIPTURE: Ephesians 4:1-3

The context of this section is a "worthy walk." A part of that walk is to "bear with one another." How can we do that? Two observations from verse two will help us answer that question.

First, there must be the right attitude toward oneself. Instead of "humility", the Amplified Bible translates it as "lowliness of mind." It means to have a humble opinion of one's self; a deep sense of one's need for God's grace at all times. Sometimes we can learn what a word means by looking at it's opposite meaning. And the opposite of "humility" is pride. Peter gives us a good commentary on this by saying "...Clothe yourselves, all of you, with humility toward one another, for God opposes the proud but gives grace to the humble" (1 Peter 5:5). Pride is an enemy of unity among brethren. Pride keeps one from "bearing with one another." When we remember what Christ has done for us and what we have in Christ (Ephesians chapters 1-3), we realize we have nothing of ourselves to boast about but instead are humble and grateful before God. No one has the right to have the "big head."

Second, there must be the proper attitudes toward our brothers and sisters in Christ. We are to be gentle, patient, and loving towards those who have been redeemed by the blood of Christ just like we have been redeemed. Gentleness means that we act unselfishly and exercise courtesy and considerateness toward brethren. We don't have to have our own way all the time. Patience means that we are "longsuffering" (NKJV) toward one another regarding differences of opinion and the weaknesses of others. Being loving is to love the brethren like Jesus loves us (cf. John 13:34-35).

Today, I will...exercise humility toward others by having the right attitude towards myself and demonstrating the right attitudes toward my brethren: gentleness, patience (longsuffering), and love.

CHARACTERISTICS OF HUMILITY

TODAY'S SCRIPTURE: Philippians 2:1-4

In verses three and four the apostle Paul gives at least two characteristics of humility. It is a challenge for every Christian. But we must meet the test if we want true unity with fellow Christians and to be genuine disciples of Jesus.

First, "do nothing from rivalry or conceit." The spirit of rivalry ("selfish ambition" NKJV) is contrary the spirit of Christ (Philippians 2:5-11). William Barclay rightly said, "There is always the danger that people should work not to advance the work but to advance themselves." In Mark 10 Jesus was confronted with this attitude from James and John and indirectly the other disciples because they probably wanted the same thing. This should not be characteristic of Jesus' followers.

Second, instead of selfish ambition or conceit (pride), Paul said, "in humility count others more significant than yourselves." I read somewhere that humility is not thinking less of yourself (that is self-depreciation), it is thinking of yourself less. When my father died, my mother was just forty-nine years old. But instead of feeling sorry for herself, she spent a lot of time cooking and taking food to people. She didn't think less of herself, she was just thinking about others more.

Humility will "look not only to his own interests, but also to the interests of others." Several years ago, the wife of a close friend of mine left him. During one of my visits with him he said, "One day I'm going to help someone that's going through what I'm going through." I believe that's a good illustration of what Paul is saying in this passage. My friend was not minimizing what had happened to him, but he was determined to use this bad situation as an opportunity to help others who are going through something similar.

Today, I will...make sure my motives are sincere and keep thoughts off myself by constantly looking for opportunities to help others.

SUBMIT TO LEADERS

TODAY'S SCRIPTURE: Hebrews 13:17

Humility toward others includes submitting to the eldership of the church. Leadership is important in the Lord's church but so is the follower-ship of the members. The writer of Hebrews had already mentioned those who had led them in the past (Hebrews 13:7). Now according to today's Bible reading, they were to follow the direction of their current leadership. How can we do that?

First, we "obey" and "submit" to the authority of the leaders of God's church. These men have met God's qualifications and therefore we trust their leadership. They are called "elders" (Acts 20:17) because they are to be mature in age and in faith (1 Timothy 3:5-6; Hebrews 13:7). We trust the decisions they have to make. They are called "overseers" (Acts 20:28; 1 Peter 5:1-4) because they monitor the spiritual welfare of the church. We cooperate with them in their oversight. They are called "shepherds" because they are responsible for the overall welfare of God's flock (Acts 20:28; 1 Peter 5:1-4). We know our leaders want us to be fed the proper spiritual diet and be protected from the wolves. Therefore, we "obey" the leaders of God's church.

Second, we are considerate of the leaders because we want their work to be productive. Humility involves thinking about the welfare of others. We know the elders have a tremendous responsibility and therefore, we want their work be as pleasant as possible. Our text says, "Let them do this with joy and not with groaning, for that would be of no advantage to you." Therefore, we must "obey and submit" to the leaders, we must "respect those who labor among you and are over you in the Lord and admonish you, and to esteem them very highly in love because of their work" (1 Thessalonians 5:12-13).

Today, I will...pray for the eldership of the church and that I will help them fulfill their responsibilities with joy.

LESSONS FROM A SELF-RIGHTEOUS MAN

TODAY'S SCRIPTURE: Luke 18:9-14

Our devotional thoughts this week have been about "being humble to one another." This last devotional lesson might be the most challenging of all. We learn from a man who was not humble and how that affected his attitude toward others. Therefore by doing the opposite of what this man did, we can treat others, even those in sin, with the right attitude.

First, when we are not humble and do not recognized our own spiritual need, we treat others with "contempt" (*despised* NKJV). According to Lenski's Commentary the result of the Pharisees not being humble "was that they were considering others as nothing; in their estimation they alone amounted to something – and that just about everything – before God." McCord's translation renders verse nine "while looking down on everyone else." A lack of humility will cause one to treat others in an ungodly way.

Second, when we are truly humble in spirit, we will treat all people right. Didn't Jesus "eat with publicans and sinners?" He talked with (not talk down to) the Samaritan woman in John 4. The humble person recognizes he is completely dependent upon the grace of God, unlike the Pharisee in our text who "trusted in Himself that he was righteous." When we realize that our spiritual need is found only in the atoning death of Jesus, we are humbled as we rely upon Christ. This will cause us to look at others in a different light. In John 13 Jesus shows us how our relations should be toward one another. Jesus taught them humility by serving them (washing their feet) and that our humility toward one another will show by our actions. *Humble people pay attention to others, look for opportunities to serve, and are modest when it comes to their accomplishments.*

Today, I will...thank Jesus for His death for my sins (for which I am totally dependent for salvation) and instead of looking at others with contempt, look for opportunities to serve them.

Pray for One Another

GARRETT BOOKOUT

PRAY FOR ONE ANOTHER

TODAY'S SCRIPTURE: Ephesians 3:14-19

This week I want you to think about your prayer life. How often do you pray for the church? When you pray for the church what do you pray about? We often pray for each other's physical health. Usually our prayer requests are filled with those who are sick, injured, or scheduled for surgery. I don't want to suggest that we should stop praying for each other in this way but maybe add some things to that prayer list. As you read through scripture you will notice that when biblical writers prayed for the church, they emphasized spiritual health. A great example of this is found in Ephesians 3:14-19. This week we will look at the different reasons Paul prayed for the church. But for today let's just appreciate that he prayed for them.

Paul wrote: "For this reason I bow my knees before the Father, from whom every family in heaven and on earth is named, that according to the riches of his glory he may grant you to be strengthened with power through his Spirit in your inner being, so that Christ may dwell in your hearts through faith—that you, being rooted and grounded in love, may have strength to comprehend with all the saints what is the breadth and length and height and depth, and to know the love of Christ that surpasses knowledge, that you may be filled with all the fullness of God" (Ephesians 3:14-19).

As you read that passage you should have noticed that Paul said he bowed his knees before the Father on their behalf for four basic reasons: 1) their strength; 2) that Christ would dwell in their hearts through faith; 3) that they would be rooted and grounded in love; 4) and that they would be filled with all the fullness of God. This week we will examine each of these more closely. Today appreciate that Paul prayed for the church and make sure you do the same.

Today, I will...pray for the spiritual health of my church family.

PRAY FOR STRENGTH

TODAY'S SCRIPTURE: Ephesians 3:16

When I was in high school, I participated in the sport of power lifting. I will not tell you how good (or bad) I was, but I'll tell you about someone I competed against. He squatted 700 lbs. If you're unfamiliar with the strength exercise known as "squatting" I'll just let you know "that's a lot." I'm comfortable telling you that it was (and is) way more than I could do. He was very strong. Physically speaking we understand strength. A strong person can lift more weight than a weaker person. The stronger you are the more weight you can hold. However, this is not only true physically but also spiritually and emotionally. I think we all know that this world can be hard. Unfortunately, we often act as if it's not. It's quite common to "put our heads in the sand" and pretend that everyone is doing great. I can assure you they are not. So many in your church family are carrying weight that they aren't strong enough to carry. They are burdened down with trials and temptation. They are trying to live for God but are struggling to do so. So, what can I do to help? Maybe several things; but, not the least among them is to pray that God would strengthen them. That's what Paul did for the church.

Paul wrote: "For this reason I bow my knees before the Father, from whom every family in heaven and on earth is named, that according to the riches of his glory he may grant you to be strengthened with power through his Spirit in your inner being" (Ephesians 3:14-16).

Yesterday we noticed that Paul prayed for the church. Now we know that when he prayed for them, he prayed that God would strengthen them. People are carrying heavy loads. They might need your help and they certainly need Gods.

Today, I will...pray that God would strengthen my church family.

PRAY FOR CHRIST TO DWELL IN HEARTS

TODAY'S SCRIPTURE: Ephesians 3:17a

Have you ever had someone outstay their welcome? Most of us like to have company, but rarely will we invite that company to stay forever. We typically like friends and family to visit and then leave. We are extremely uncomfortable with someone moving into our homes permanently. Living with someone requires change. They might have a different routine or want to organize the house differently. Most of us like to do things our way and we don't want to consider what someone else wants. Kids typically grow to a point when they're ready to move out of their parent's homes and get a place of their own. Believe it or not, parents usually reach a point with their kids when they're ready for them to move out. That is one of the unique things about marriage. Two people agree to live with each other until death. Obviously, that takes a lot of patience and sacrifice if it's going to work. However, when Paul prayed for the church, he prayed that they would not just invite Jesus into their homes but that He would dwell in their hearts.

Paul wrote: "For this reason I bow my knees before the Father" … "so that Christ may dwell in your hearts through faith" (Ephesians 3:14-17a).

When Paul prayed, he was aware that most don't invite Jesus to dwell in their hearts. Most want Jesus to stay the weekend. They want a short visit, but they don't really want Jesus to come and stay forever. Once Jesus starts moving around furniture, they want him to leave. Most don't want Him changing anything about who they are. Paul's prayer was that the church would have enough faith to invite Jesus into their hearts forever so that Jesus would change the things that He wanted to change and organize their lives the way He saw fit.

Today, I will...pray that Jesus will dwell in the hearts of my church family.

PRAY FOR A FOUNDATION OF LOVE

TODAY'S SCRIPTURE: Ephesians 3:17b-19

I'm not much of a gardener but I took it upon myself to plant some trees in my backyard this year. Time will tell if I did a good job and if those trees will live and grow. Probably most of us know that a tree is only as strong as its root system. If the roots are strong, then the tree will be strong. Obviously, the reverse of this is also true. Weak roots will cause the whole tree to be weak. If the roots die, then the visible parts of the tree will also soon die.

I planted the trees in my backyard soon after my house was built. When they were building the house, they laid a solid foundation. Of course, we know why the builders did this. If a house does not have a strong foundation, it will easily fall in harsh conditions. Jesus gave a very well-known illustration about this very thing (Matthew 7:24-27). So, like the root system to a tree, the foundation of a house determines the strength of that house.

I say all of this because when Paul prayed for the church he prayed for their "root system" and "foundation".

Paul wrote: "For this reason I bow my knees before the Father" ... "that you, being rooted and grounded in love, may have strength to comprehend with all the saints what is the breadth and length and height and depth, and to know the love of Christ that surpasses knowledge" (Ephesians 3:14).

Unfortunately, many will never have the strength to comprehend the blessing of Christ's love. So, many live in fear and uncertainty because they don't comprehend how much Christ loves them. This causes many to be weak and sick. Paul's prayer is that the church would be strong because of the love of Christ; however, this is only possible when they are rooted and grounded in love.

Today, I will...pray that my church family be rooted and grounded in love so they can comprehend the love of Christ.

PRAY FOR FULLNESS

TODAY'S SCRIPTURE: Ephesians 3:19b-21

How much of God do you want in your life? Most want some, but few want a lot. Like water in a house. We enjoy having running water. Life would be more difficult without it. We want water in the tub, sink, refrigerator, and water heater. But we don't want water all over the place. We happily invite water into our homes so long as it stays where we want it and doesn't take over. That's good with water, but detrimental when we treat God that way. We often want God to have a small part of our lives but Paul prayed that God will overflow in the lives of the church.

Paul wrote: "For this reason I bow my knees before the Father" ... "that you may be filled with all the fullness of God" (Ephesians 3:14-19).

It's not enough to have a little God here and there. We should be FILLED with ALL His FULLNESS. Paul wanted God to completely take over the lives of the church. We should pray the same.

We have been looking at Paul's prayer all week, but I want you to see what he wrote next.

Paul wrote: "Now to him who is able to do far more abundantly than all that we ask or think, according to the power at work within us, to him be glory in the church and in Christ Jesus throughout all generations, forever and ever. Amen" (Ephesians 3:20-21).

When Paul prayed for their strength, their hearts, their love, or their fullness he prayed knowing that God could do, not only what he asked, but so much more. And he glorified God because of it. Let us make sure that we pray for one another and that we pray with confidence in our God who deserves all glory.

Today, I will...pray with confidence that God will overflow in the lives of my church family.

Recreation

DON'T WAIT FOR A PANDEMIC
TODAY'S SCRIPTURE: Mark 6:30-31

The impact of COVID-19 has been different for different people. Some have lost homes and businesses. Others have been terribly sick or have had loved ones and friends who are terribly sick. Some have been so overwhelmed with depression because of being cut off from others, that they have contemplated taking their lives. Others have actually taken their lives. For many people, the Coronavirus has been devastating. It is important that we acknowledge that this pandemic has broken many hearts and lives and we need to pray for and minister to them.

Yet, for some it has actually been a blessing. It forced them to slow down and spend time with family and close loved ones. In a matter of days, I went from making plans for a six-week span in which I would only be home for six days to having all my travel plans cancelled. One blessing that came out of COVID-19 for me is that I had some time with my family that I would not have had.

Life can be tough. Mark 6 gives a glimpse into the ministry of Jesus. He trained and sent out the apostles. They had dealt with the loss of John the immerser. Jesus and the apostles not only dealt with the normal stress and fatigue of ministry, but people thronged to them so much that they struggled to have time even to eat. Jesus felt that they needed a break. This devotional and several that follow, will focus on potential lessons we can learn from Mark 6. We need to begin by noting that Jesus called the apostles to come away "by yourselves" (6:31). They were the only ones on the planet who truly understood what life was like for them. They had just returned from the two-man mission trips on which Jesus had sent them. Now, they all needed some time together. Who are the people that refresh you? Who are the people who understand you, that care about you, that will have your back? Don't become so busy, that you cut yourself off from those who enliven your spirit.

Today, I will... treasure the time I have with my loved ones and I will seek opportunities to be with them.

DETERMINE YOUR DESOLATE PLACE

TODAY'S SCRIPTURE: Mark 6:30-31

What is your desolate place? At one congregation where I worked, it was an attic behind the balcony in the church building. I kept a songbook and a Bible there. I thank God for smartphones...and I hate them! The beauty is that they allow us to minister and connect to people anytime and anywhere. I can connect my phone to Apple Play in my vehicle and get all kinds of hands-free work done while driving across the country to make visits for Heritage Christian. It is amazing! The ugly side is that that these same phones allow us access anytime and anywhere. We become addicted. We start to twitch if we go too long without checking Instagram or our email. People can access us around the clock and around the world. It is awful!

Jesus had to deal with people overload. He was a miracle worker and an amazing teacher. People came from miles around to see him. He and the apostles struggled to have private time. Mark 6 says, "For many were coming and going, and they had no leisure even to eat" (Mark 6:31). A similar statement is found in Mark 3:20. The situation was so bad in Mark 3 that the text says, "When His own people heard this, they went out to take custody of Him; for they were saying, 'He has lost his senses'" (Mark 3:21). Returning to Mark 6, we find that to deal with fatigue and people overload, Jesus encouraged the apostles to come away "to a desolate place" (6:31). Jesus knew they needed to "unplug" for a while.

We need to unplug as well (literally, unplug from our phones). The area around my beehives has become my desolate place. I have a couple of benches in front of the hives where I just sit and relax. I sing, I pray, I read, I think, I listen to the symphony of the birds, and I watch the flights of the bees as they take turns landing on the front porches of their hives while ladened down with pouches full of sweet nectar or nutritious pollen. As I sit there, I never cease to be amazed at our Awesome God. Where do you unplug?

Today, I will... unplug and spend time away from distractions and alone with God.

DETERMINE YOUR DIVERSION

TODAY'S SCRIPTURE: Mark 6:30-31

Webster's dictionary says that "recreation" means "refreshment of strength and spirits after work" and also "a means of refreshment or diversion" (merriam-webster.com). In other words, recreation "re-creates" us and brings us back to full strength when work and life have worn us down. In Mark 6, Jesus encouraged the disciples to "Come away...and rest a while." Sometimes we need rest. Sometimes we need a diversion (to use Merriam-Webster language).

Servant leadership in the kingdom of God, and the physical and emotional fatigue that accompanies it, can drain our energies. Sometimes we just need to do something that is totally different. We need a healthy and wholesome diversion. Some use exercise as a diversion. Paul used several illustrations from the ancient Olympic games in his letters. In 1 Timothy 4, He said that bodily exercise had some value, though we must admit that he also said that it was of little value compared to practicing godliness. When my knees still worked, I ran a lot, not only to get in shape, but to clear my mind and feel better. There was time I worked out at a boxing gym to de-stress.

John 21 tells us that in the aftermath of the cross and the resurrection, seven of Jesus' disciples went fishing. It was something they were used to. It would have felt comfortable and familiar. It would have taken their minds off of the emotional roller coaster ride they had been on. Fishing does that for me as well. Also, over the last couple of years, beekeeping has become an escape for me. It is work, but it is work unlike any other work I do. It relaxes me; it takes my mind off of other concerns; it reminds me that God has made an amazing world and some incredible creatures. What does that for you?

Today, I will... find something wholesome that "recreates" me and allows me to be more effective and less aggressive (i.e., grumpy).

DON'T LET RECREATION REPLACE COMPASSION

TODAY'S SCRIPTURE: Mark 6:34

Flavil Nichols preached for several years in my hometown of Elizabethtown, KY. He and sister Mary were great encouragers to me. After Sunday morning worship and before lunch, brother Nichols used to say, "I've got to go wash the brethren off my hands." That comment is even more interesting to me now as I write this devotional during a pandemic in which the CDC encourages us to wash our hands more frequently. Brother Flavil knew that sometimes, to be healthy, he needed to wash off the germs that come with contact with people. Yet, he loved being with God's people. He loved shaking their hands and hugging their necks and would go right back to doing it on every Sunday night.

Sometimes we need to "de-people." We have already noted in our previous devotionals that we can sometimes have people overload. Jesus and the apostles had so many people thronging around them that they could not even eat (Mark 6:31). That is why Jesus encouraged them to come away to a desolate place (Mark 6:30). Yet, it turned out that the desolate place was not so desolate. Imagine going to a cabin in the Smokey Mountains for a little rest and relaxation and when you arrive, you find the church bus full of church members is there waiting for you. That is basically what happened to Jesus and the apostles in Mark 6:34. Jesus needed a break from people. Just like brother Nichols needed to wash off the germs that come from interacting with people, Jesus needed to "wash off" the stress that comes from interacting with people. He needed a few moments away. In spite of that, He still loved people. When He saw the crowd, he had compassion (Mark 9:34).

There is a word of caution here for us. We can go too far in our efforts to find recreation. We can go from too much work to too much focus on play. We can become self-absorbed and start thinking of ourselves and forget thinking about the hurts and needs of others.

Today, I will... ask for God's forgiveness for being selfish and look for ways to put compassion into action.

DON'T LET DIVERSION BECOME A DISTRACTION

TODAY'S SCRIPTURE: John 21:6

The apostles had been in the eye of the storm. They had experienced the mountains and valleys of traveling with Jesus. They had dealt with the heartache of watching Jesus die, the guilt of their own denials, the doubt of their initial reaction to the resurrection, and the uncertainty of what would happen next. It was one adrenaline rush after another, and they likely felt drained and unsure. What did they do? They went fishing. They had been fisherman before Jesus called them to be fishers of men (cf. Luke 5:10). It would have been both comforting, because it was natural and easy for them, and it would have also served as a diversion because it was different from what they had been doing while traveling with Jesus.

When Jesus met them on the seashore, he asked them how their fishing was going. Asking a fisherman who has worked all night and caught nothing about his catch is like rubbing salt in an open wound. When they said, "No," He said, "Cast the net on the right side of the boat" (John 21:6). The end result was a large catch of fish. Does this sound familiar? It should. Jesus performed the same miracle when he first called them (Luke 5:4-6).

Why the repeat? Maybe He was trying to get them to refocus on their mission. The repetition was a reminder. They were not longer fishermen; they were fishers of men. He did not want their diversion to become a distraction from their mission. Can we be guilty of the same thing? Paul said, "Rather train yourself for godliness; for while bodily training is of some value, godliness is of value in every way, as it holds promise for the present life and also for the life to come" (1 Timothy 4:7b-8). Have we lost perspective? Do we have mixed up priorities? Have we allowed recreation to reign in our lives and families? Are we worshiping at the ballpark temple on Sunday mornings instead of with God's people? Are we spending more time lifting weights than lifting God's word to study? Have our diversions become a distractions?

Today, I will... remember that my mission is to serve Jesus and to be a fisher of people.

Sacrifice

THE BATTLE FOR THE HEART

TODAY'S SCRIPTURE: 2 Samuel 11, 12

We're at war! No! The battleground is not on some foreign soil. It is not being fought upon our shores. It is not even being engaged in the cyber world. The struggles of this war are being carried out upon the battlefield of the heart.

King David was a warrior. He was the master of guerilla warfare, hand to hand combat, and was unequaled on the front-line of mass engagement. The Philistines were afraid of him. His mighty men feared him. Israel lauded him. But David was utterly defeated in the arena of his heart.

His eyes wandered at the wrong place, the wrong time, and with the wrong person. He wanted Bathsheba, and he had her. Then, he covered it up, even to the point of murdering her husband. It sounds like a Hollywood production. But no, this is real. He almost got away with it, but one thing he forgot. While he thought, "Nobody knows!" He forgot about the all-seeing God. He got caught! Oh, yes! He got caught! His "you are the man" moment has rung in the ears of us all for thousands of years.

Later, David wrote these words, "For you will not delight in sacrifice, or I would give it; you will not be pleased with a burnt offering. The sacrifices of God are a broken spirit; a broken and contrite heart, O God, you will not despise" Psalm 51:16–17. After his "you are the man" moment, he would have offered 10,000 sacrifices if he thought God would be pleased with it. But he realized God didn't want the blood of bulls and goats. He wanted a contrite/penitent/broken heart. That is what God has always wanted from His people. You can "do church" 10,000 times, but if your heart is not broken at your sin, what good is your worship?

Today, I will... find ways to be broken-hearted because of what Jesus endured so that I could be forgiven. I will talk about it in at least one conversation with a trusted friend.

LIVES ON THE LINE

TODAY'S SCRIPTURE: Romans 12

What would cause a person to run into a burning building to save a stranger? Ask a fireman! Who would put on a badge knowing that their lives are in harm's way? Ask a policeman! Who in their right mind would allow themselves to endure great affliction, even the threat of death, for the faith they have in Jesus? Ask a Christian!

Christians do not mind turning the other cheek when slapped or going the second mile when asked to go one, Matthew 5:38-42. Christians love their wives like Christ loved the church, are submissive to their husbands as to the Lord, raise their children in the admonition of the Lord, and are obedient to their parents, Ephesians 5-6. Christians love God with all their heart, soul, mind, and strength. And, they love their neighbors as they love themselves, Matthew 22:37,39. Christians are even happy to love their enemies, Matthew 5:44. Christians worship together on the Lord's Day because they want to worship God and provoke others to love and good works, Hebrews 10:24-25. All these things, and so many more, Christians do because they have learned the instructions of the Lord and desire to follow them.

But why? Why are we willing to go to such lengths? Why are we motivated to do what God says? Simple! Look what He has done for me. He has made this world for me. He has made me. He has given me blessing after blessing. He has given me Jesus. He has given me salvation. He has given me faith, hope, and love. He has given me the promise of eternal life. He sacrificed so much for me! He has given me a reason to sacrifice my whole life for him, Romans 12:1-2.

Today, I will... give up myself to show Christ to the world around me.

SPIRITUAL DISTANCING

TODAY'S SCRIPTURES: Hebrews 12:1-2; Colossians 3

Over the last year, we have been introduced to what became an everyday concern. Potential exposure to harmful viruses meant taking protective precautions. Washing hands for at least twenty seconds, wearing masks, and socially distancing ourselves became an across the board, worldwide, way of life.

Early on in the struggle, a most illuminating parallel emerged when comparing what the authorities said about things to do for protection from the virus and what the Bible teaches about protecting oneself from sin's effects. While a virus can kill the body, sin can kill the soul. While social distancing can protect you from contracting a virus, spiritual distancing can protect you from evil.

The Bible is clear when it comes to dealing with sin. Stay away from it! "Flee from sexual immorality" 1 Corinthians 6:18. "Flee from idolatry" 1 Corinthians 10:14. "Flee youthful passions!" 2 Timothy 2:22. "Submit yourselves therefore to God. Resist the devil, and he will flee from you," James 4:7,17.

When I was thirteen, my Granny decided it was time for us to have a heart to heart talk about temptation. When she spoke of getting away from sin, she threw her hands in the air and shaking them back and forth as fast ask she could, saying, "Run away from sin! You've got to RUN away!" She was dramatic and emphatic, almost funny to see, but she was dead serious.

Spiritual separation is not an easy task. Sometimes it's not something from which you can jump up and run physically. Sin has a way of taking over your thoughts as well. So, how do you run from your thoughts? Change your focus. Replace evil thoughts with good ones. Read Philippians 4:8. Empower your faith with Bible study, prayer, and surround yourself with God's people to protect you from the devil's attacks.

Today, I will... put some distance between me and the sin which clings so near to me with an action that fills my time.

TAKE TIME TO PRAY

TODAY'S SCRIPTURES: Matthew 6; 1 Thess. 1:2; 3:10; 5:17, 25

When is the last time you got down on your knees beside your bed, closed your eyes, brought your hands together under your chin, and just poured your heart out to God?

When I was a kid, I remember Gus Nichols (1892-1975) preaching a gospel meeting. He was an older man, but I recall being intrigued by the way he carried himself. He seemed to be bigger than life. At one worship service, while the church was being led in prayer, I did the unthinkable. I opened my eyes! And, when I did, my eyes locked on brother Nichols. His eyes were closed. His head was bowed, and his hands were raised and pressed together under his chin. The psalmist wrote, "Let my prayer be counted as incense before you, and the lifting up of my hands as the evening sacrifice" Psalm 141:2.

What is to be said about the folding or pressing together of one's hands in prayer? It is humbling. It is focused, submissive, and even child-like. The very idea of prayer is sacrificial. It is the humbling of one's self before the Lord. Solomon said, "The sacrifice of the wicked is an abomination to the Lord, but the prayer of the upright is acceptable to Him," Proverbs 15:8.

Our greatest temptation is to be self-reliant, like the old adage, "Look out for Number 1!" Praying to God is giving Him a win over self. Requesting God's provision in our lives is an admission of our powerlessness.

Commands as to posture in prayer are not outlined in the Scriptures. You can read of people bowing the knees before the Lord, Ephesians 3:14; Philippians 2:10. Perhaps our traditions have forced us to think that praying must be done in a particular way. You can pray on your knees, or standing, in your car with eyes wide open, or the closet with them closed, with hands folded or at 10 and 2 on the steering wheel. But pray!

Today, I will... schedule times to pray to God.

FRIDAY

WHAT DOES IT COST?

TODAY'S SCRIPTURE: Philippians 2:5-11

Do you like deals? We live in the day when nobody pays MSRP. Why? Because money has to go along way. We work hard to make ends meet. We have to get the most bang for our bucks. So, how much will this set me back? What will it cost me?

Cost is about giving up some things. The Bible says Jesus gave up some things when he left heaven, Philippians 2:5-8. Buying something—anything really—means potentially not being able to buy something else. Whether losing weight, buying a car, or giving up a bad habit, part of the cost means doing without something. Somebody rightly said, "I can afford anything, but I can't afford everything."

Twelve men were trained by Jesus to preach the gospel to the whole world, Matthew 28:19. One failed, but what was to become of the eleven? Peter needed Jesus with him. So did Simon and Thomas. So, do you! All had to give up something. All of us had to give up his physical presence. Thanks be to God, that's not the end of the story. Jesus told his men, "I will not leave you as orphans, I will come to you," John 14:18. But how? His last words on earth were, "And behold, I am with you always, to the end of the age" Matthew 28:20. But how?

His Comforter came! His Holy Spirit came the day the church began, Acts 2. Three thousand people gave up everything and were immersed for the forgiveness of their sins to follow Jesus that day. What did they get out of it? At least four big things: 1. Salvation; 2. The Church; 3. The hope of heaven; 4. His presence in their/our lives. In this way, Jesus could then, and can now, be with you, me, and all who love Him.

Today, I will... remember that whatever I face, I will not face alone. Jesus is with me, and I can overcome it. And, seeing the face of Jesus someday is worth giving up whatever it takes.

My Social Life

CRAIG EVANS

BACK TO BASICS

TODAY'S SCRIPTURE: 2 Timothy 3:14-17; 1 Timothy 4:12

Several years ago, when I was teaching school, I heard a disturbance at the end of the hallway. I could hear a mother scolding her middle school son, the middle school son protesting saying "but mama" and the mother escalating the discipline of her son. I cautiously approached and asked the mother what she needed, and she said she needed a place to appropriately discipline her son. I took them to the principal's office where she told her son she was embarrassed on how he was acting toward his teacher and other students and how he knows better. She emphasized how she and her husband have taught him principles that require a higher standard than the world. She continued to explain to her son how his actions were not in concert with their teaching and she expected better. His actions at school were different than parents teaching and expectations and reflected poorly on his parents and his mom emphasized that behavior would not be tolerated.

Are you actions a reflection of Jesus and what scripture teaches? Each of us has a standard we must base our actions on the standard of God's word. Paul told Timothy to be an example in speech, conduct, love, faith, and purity in 1 Timothy 4, but in 1 Timothy 3 Paul reminded Timothy of his training in scripture given to him by his grandmother and mother and the authority, power, and relevance of God's breathed-out word. Paul gives a challenging charge to Timothy reminding him that life and conduct make an impact for Jesus on this world, and the basis of his actions must be God's word.

Today, I will... examine by speech, conduct, love, faith and purity do determine if they are shaped by scripture or my feelings and I will act in accordance with scripture to make the biggest impact for Jesus.

MAKING A DIFFERENCE

TODAY'S SCRIPTURE: Acts 10:38

I have heard it said that death is a part of life. After someone dies, there is usually an obituary published in the local paper and on the website of the funeral home. An obituary is a brief article written about the person who died. Their birth date and death date, their family who has already passed and their family who is still living, and funeral arrangements are all part of the obituary. The biggest part of most obituaries is the description of how the deceased spent his or her life, listing their relationships, accomplishments, hobbies, work, and likes.

It is interesting to look at what is said about Jesus after he passed away. Luke writes "He went about doing good and healing all who were oppressed by the devil, for God was with him (Acts 10:38)." Jesus life summed up in the phrase "He went about doing good."

Jesus' life was spent making a difference in the lives of others, and he accomplished this by doing good. Jesus not only loved his Father, but he loved people and spent his ministry serving them. Jesus's fed, healed, raised from the dead, and cast out demons, changing the lives of those who he came in contact with. Ultimately his good was dying on a cross and changing eternity. It is sobering to think of his challenge in John 13:34 to love others and He loved them.

We can make a difference in the lives of others by going around doing good. I know we cannot heal the sick or raise the dead, but we can feed, comfort, encourage, support, and provide for those in need. We cannot take away their sins, but we can show others the one who did so they might come to love and follow Jesus. Life is to be spent making a difference in the lives of others in the name of Jesus.

Today, I will... do good for someone knowing I am following the example of Jesus and loving others as He loved them.

SOCIAL MEDIA

TODAY'S SCRIPTURE: Matthew 5-7

There have been many inventions that have changed the world: gunpowder, microscopes, refrigeration, automobiles, airplanes, and television just to name a few. The internet and other inventions that use internet (smartphones) have done more to shape the world in the past 30 years than anything else. One of the tools and one of those ways is through social media. Facebook, Instagram, and Twitter allow for sharing of news, building of relationships. These were built with thought of connecting with others, hence the name "social media."

Does God care how we use social media? There are many opportunities for good with social media: encouragement, prayer, connection, and sharing our lives with one another. It seems social media has devolved into a place of division, hate, bragging, envy, immodesty, political hatred, echo chambers, fake news, affairs, arguments, strife, immorality, and much more. I feel like I just listed the works of the flesh Paul mentioned in Galatians. A place designed for connection and positivity has become for many a place of loneliness, depression, and sin.

In the Sermon on the Mount in Matthew 5-7 Jesus shows the life citizens of His kingdom should and must live to impact the world around them, and the picture he uses is Salt and Light. Salt and light impact everything they contact. Social media allows for connection between people and allows us to have influence. Being salt and light shows people Jesus and can draw people to Jesus. We not only have the opportunity, we have the responsibility to be salt and light in this world.

Imagine spreading joy instead sorrow, peace instead of division, truth instead of lies, gentleness instead of aggression, kindness instead of meanness, love instead of hate, humility instead of arrogance, self-control instead of self-indulgence, or encouragement instead of criticism. Wow!!! we would be salt and light for Jesus, and He would make a difference in the world.

Today, (and everyday) I will... use social media for Jesus as a reflection of Him.

THE PROBLEM OF PEOPLE

TODAY'S SCRIPTURE: Matthew 9:39

I just want to be a hermit! Have you ever said those words? There are times being around people is frustrating and exhausting. After so much frustration it might be easy to determine you would be better off living in a mountain cabin away from everyone, but is that what God wants for you?

For 3 years, Jesus was the greatest show on earth. Jesus turned water into wine, made the deaf hear, made the blind to see, healed lepers, opened the mouths of the mute, fixed the legs of the lame, freed people for demon possession, fed the hungry, gave paralytics back feeling and movement, and raised people from the dead. Multitudes of people gathered to follow Him wherever he would go. Jesus was constantly hounded by those who wanted something from him. Jesus saw crowds and had compassion on them. There are times he would go out by himself to find a place to rest and pray only to be told that everyone is looking for him.

Jesus was criticized, worshiped, loved, followed, abandoned, hated, beaten, slapped, insulted, flogged, and murdered. What all of these actions had in common, is all of these actions were done by people.

Jesus knew his purpose, and His purpose was to proclaim the good news of the kingdom, and that meant spending time with people. Jesus knew the world needed Him, so He gave Himself fully to making a difference in the lives of people.

The world needs you!! People need you to make a difference in their lives by being Jesus to them. Your husband, wife, children, friend, enemy, neighbor, co-worker, boss, teammate, server, cashier, all need you to show them Jesus, and Jesus will be seen and heard in how you live and interact with them. As much as people can hurt and frustrate you, they still need Jesus.

Today, I will... bless others by showing them Jesus through all my interactions with them.

DO YOU KNOW YOUR A-B-C's?

TODAY'S SCRIPTURE: John 13:34

I am often amazed by my nineteen-month-old little boy. Like most we end our prayers with the word Amen, and if I say "A" and hold it out he will say "MEN" to finish the amen. The other day I finished the prayer and said "A" and he said B, C, D. We laughed. I am thankful he is also learning his alphabet. Do you know your alphabet?

Jesus created his church to be a community of believers, where there is not only a spiritual component but a social component. Actually, those two things are interconnected and must not be separated. If we look through the New Testament there are fifty-nine one another verses that show our inter-relation and responsibility to one another.

Each person is created in the image of God and is worthy of our love and respect, and we, as God's people, must champion this by showing everyone they are significant and loved. How do we do accomplish this task? By practicing the ABC's.

The A is Attention. We make a difference in the lives of others by showing them Attention. Talking to them, learning their name, and reaching out to them show them there are Significant and Loved.

The B is Belonging. We make a difference in the lives of others when we are inclusive of them. We all have a desire for acceptance and need for belonging, and we must help people feel as though they belong. I find it interesting Jesus chose twelve apostles and soon they went from being named individually to being know as "the twelve" or "the disciples." They belonged to a group that was greater than they were as individuals. We must not only show attention, but help others to see we are a part of the same family.

The C is Caring. We need to show care and support. When we offer acts of care through encouragement and prayer, we continue to reinforce each person as significant and loved.

The ABC's take what Jesus has done for each of us, and allow us to share his love with those in our world.

Today, I will... intentionally show Attention, Belonging, and Care so someone knows they are loved.

My Life and Peer Pressure

JACOB HAWK

DEFINING PEER PRESSURE

TODAY'S SCRIPTURE: Psalm 1

The great author and theologian, C.S. Lewis, defended the justification for his faith with this timeless quote, memorialized through history—"I believe in Christianity as I believe that the sun has risen: not only because I see it, but because by it I see everything else." These powerfully penned words remind us that the prettiest sights and brightest lights define not only how we see the moment at hand, but many moments that follow.

In this regard, peer pressure follows suit. We know it exists. We have seen it first-hand. We have felt the power of its "heat" on the back of our neck. It can give life or destroy. Yet peer pressure does not just affect us now, but for years to come. Delusion makes undoing decisions.

Peer pressure is real. It has challenged and conquered for centuries. It creates insecurity and instability. The psalmist of old began the holy volume of Psalms with these words—"Blessed is the man who walks not in the counsel of the wicked, nor stands in the way of sinners, nor sits in the seat of scoffers" (Psalm 1:1, ESV). Said in another way, the man who sees the quicksand of peer pressure in his midst—and chooses a different, safer path—is a happy, successful man. He makes the right decision not just for that moment, but many moments that follow. He survives today and thrives tomorrow.

Life's greatest dangers tend to be the ones we refuse to define. Peer pressure is as real as the sun that rises. Not only because we see it, but because by it we see everything else. Every moment is a chance to rise or fall by its rays. Refusing this acknowledgement is guaranteed destruction.

Today, I will...admit that peer pressure is a real poison that seeks to destroy my life. I will, to the best of my ability, refuse its poison at all costs.

ENCOUNTERING PEER PRESSURE

TODAY'S SCRIPTURE: Galatians 5:16-17

Yesterday we acknowledged the unfortunate reality that peer pressure exists. Like money to banks, medicine to sick patients, is peer pressure to Christians. We meet its power daily, but how do we recognize it? When do we know we are walking into its trapping snare?

Guilt. Longing for acceptance. Curiosity. Adrenalin rush. Regret. Highs followed by lows. These, and others, are all effects of peer pressure's controlling cause. Some are positive. Some are negative. None are neutral. Words like "I wish I would not have..." most often fall victim to peer pressure's sword.

How do you know when peer pressure is knocking on your door? When the flesh and the spirit conflict. When the voice in your head says you should while the megaphone in your heart screams you should not. Scripture cuts the tension with its spiritual knife. The apostle Paul becomes the everyman with these prophetic, inspired words of humanity.

"For the desires of the flesh are against the Spirit, and the desires of the Spirit are against the flesh, for these are opposed to each other, to keep you from doing the things you want to do" (Galatians 5:17, ESV).

"For I do not understand my own actions. For I do not do what I want, but I do the very thing I hate" (Romans 7:15, ESV).

Within the inner being of every disciple is a God-ordained, God-directed moral compass that speaks sufficiently when things go array. We encounter peer pressure when peace exits. If something does not feel right, it probably is not. You can thank God for the grace and blame Satan for the guilt.

Today, I will...trust my God-given instincts. I will know that when my spirit and flesh conflict, I have not only encountered, but entered peer pressure's arena. I will turn to Scripture for direction and trust God's way more than others.

MINIMIZING PEER PRESSURE

TODAY'S SCRIPTURE: 1 Corinthians 15:33

We have defined that peer pressure exists. We have discussed when we encounter it. How do we keep it at bay? Or at the very least, minimize its hold on our life?

There is a common pill many refuse to swallow. The dosage is simple in theory, complicated in practice, but powerfully prescribed in the New Testament. The apostle Paul spoke on behalf of Jesus, the Great Physician. Lucky for us the instructions are not composed or inscribed with a doctor's secret handwriting.

"I wrote to you in my letter not to associate with sexually immoral people—not at all meaning the sexually immoral of this world, or the greedy and swindlers, or idolaters, since then you would need to go out of the world. But now I am writing to you not to associate with anyone who bears the name of brother if he is guilty of sexual immorality or greed, or is an idolater, reviler, drunkard or swindler —not even to eat with such a one" (1 Corinthians 5: 11-12, ESV).

We begin with the strongest words, hardest to go down. The context was disfellowshipping a brother in the church who was causing others to sin. His lifestyle was diluting God's design. Paul knew this brother needed to exit the Corinthian church stage right before the entire body was compromised. He asked a few verses earlier— "Do you not know that a little leaven leavens the whole lump" (1 Corinthians 5:6, ESV)?

Now easier words to swallow. Even our brave military, champion sports teams, and profitable businesses understand that choosing the wrong soldiers, teammates, or employees ruins organizations. Christians choosing the wrong friends ruins faith journeys. Paul also warned the church at Corinth "Do not be deceived: 'Bad company ruins good morals'" (1 Corinthians 15:33, ESV). Do you want to minimize peer pressure? Minimize your peers.

Today, I will...make a promise to evaluate my roster of relationships. I will remove those who are toxic, re-engage with those who are a blessing, and renew my commitment to choosing my friends with careful precision.

OVERCOMING PEER PRESSURE

TODAY'S SCRIPTURE: 1 Thessalonians 5:22

The soul wants to be victorious. The heart longs for success. Barriers often stand in the way of the soul and heart's satisfaction, but overcoming obstacles produces beautiful stories. Zeroes become heroes through the struggle. Even in its challenges and unmistakable presence, peer pressure can be won. It can provide what the soul and heart desire.

Life's best advice is often packaged in the simplest of wrapping. The apostle Paul untied the bow and peeled off the paper when he wrote, "Abstain for every form of evil" (1 Thessalonians 5:22, ESV). That small soundbite is all encompassing. Abstain from every form of evil. Every form. Every fashion. From a bottle to a basement. From a casino to a courthouse, we are urged as God's people to run from potential trouble. Paul does not say be careful. Paul does not even say to use moderation. Paul says to abstain. To avoid. To refuse to participate. Each day we must decide how seriously and passionately we will observe this command. That decision, without fail, defines the direction of our lives. Ask any prisoner behind bars or addict in rehab for confirmation.

Peer pressure can shake the unshakeable and sink the unsinkable, but peer pressure loses its power when saying "yes" is not an option. Overcoming its sting is possible, but only probable through discipline and determination. Its bark is less than its bite. When left to our own vices, peer pressure forms a tight grip on our lives. When surrendered to God's way, peer pressure's grasp loosens as heaven's grace takes the wheel. Do you want to overcome peer pressure? Abstain from every form of evil.

Today, I will... I will...listen to Scripture's advice. I will make a promise to abstain from every from evil, and I will make a commitment to abound in every form of righteousness. I will realize that overcoming or underperforming is completely up to me.

BENEFITING FROM PEER PRESSURE

TODAY'S SCRIPTURE: Philippians 3:17

Each article in this series has highlighted the damaging and destructive characteristics of peer pressure. This seems reasonable and fair. Without a doubt, there are too many to count. Peer pressure can digress the most promising leaders into broken dreams. We close today with a different approach. Peer pressure can be used for a different purpose.

With any negative, a positive can still be found. With any storm, the sun can still shine. Promising good can still rise from peer pressure's perpetual grave.

A few biblical scenes and passages illustrate this truth.

On the Day of Pentecost, one committed voice led to 3,000 converted Christians. Peter's single sermon encouraged thousands of salvations. Can you imagine the morning of critical curiosity transforming into an evening of positive affirmation? One for the history books.

In a Roman prison, Paul mentioned the power of his influence to the Philippians in two profound, unforgettable ways. Listen to what he said peer pressure could, and did, do.

"And most of the brothers, having become confident in the Lord by my imprisonment, are much more bold to speak the word without fear" (Philippians 1:14, ESV).

"Brothers, join in imitating me, and keep your eyes on those who walk according to the example you have in us" (Philippians 3:17, ESV).

There is power in numbers. Numbers build up or tear down. Strengthen or weaken. When anchored in evil, peer pressure becomes a nightmare. When harnessed for good, peer pressure becomes a dream. We can help others see the God of Peace through our guidance, or the Father of Lies through our deceit. What about you? Does your peer pressure produce glory or shame?

Today, I will...see that I can lead others down the broad road of eternal destruction or the narrow path of eternal life. In the same way others can influence me for the world, they can influence me for Jesus. I will let peer pressure's positive traits, not negative features, write the script.

Temptation

VAN VANSANDT

MONDAY

THE FIRST TEMPTATION
TODAY'S SCRIPTURE: Genesis 3:6

The prospect for each of us to sin is very real. All who are in Christ have sinned and are still battling with sin daily, All who are outside of Christ have sinned and are presently living in that sinful state. Many have moved temptation as described in scripture to a place even "greater," than sin itself. Some portray the temptation as being as ungodly as giving in to the temptation and sinning. This cannot be the case.

For our purpose in this series, we will visit several examples in scripture which will help us separate temptation from the sin itself. Thus, we will better understand temptation and how to combat it. Let's begin with the first recorded temptation in scripture and the subsequent sin.

Genesis 3:6 describes for us the work of temptation and the first sin by man. The Bible says: "When the woman saw that the tree was good for food, and. that it was a delight to the eyes, and that the tree was desired to make one wise, .. " THIS IS TEMPTATION! If Eve had stopped before taking of the fruit and eating it, she would have still been free from sin. We know from reading further she did not stop, "She took of the fruit and ate, and she gave some to her husband who was with her, and he ate."

Temptation comes to everyone. We seek to overcome temptation in order to overcoming sin.

Today, I will...try to overcome temptation first. I will ask God to help me not to give in. God bless you all.

LURED AND ENTICED

TODAY'S SCRIPTURE: James 1:14

To reset our minds for today's thoughts we must be grounded in the truth concerning sin. Romans 3:23, "For all have sinned and fall short of the glory of God." The best defense against sin is to overcome temptation.

James dissects the work and will of temptation in the first chapter of his epistle, in James 1:14. "But each person is tempted when he is lured and enticed by his own desire." To this point I refer to the historical record of Commodore Oliver Hazard Perry stated to William Henry Harrison, after the Battle of Lake Erie: "We have met the enemy and they are ours." In 1970, cartoonist Walt Kelly turned the quote around to say, "We have met the enemy and he is us." Scripture taught this long before it was coined by men.

James says that one's temptations are based in the seat of one's own desires. Therefore, our struggles and temptations are brought about from within ourselves. We know the devil is the father of lies. We also know the devil was present in the first recorded account of sin. Oh, he had his place, but it was still the desire of Eve that moved her from being tempted to being sinful.

Paul describes it this way in Romans 7:23, "But I see in my members another law waging war against the law of my mind and making me captive to the law of sin that dwells in my members." If one wants to win the war over temptation, they must battle within themselves.

Today, I will...try to overcome myself first. I will ask God to help me keep my eyes on Him and not turn towards myself. God bless you all.

THE PROOF IS IN THE PUDDING

TODAY'S SCRIPTURE: Genesis 4:1-17

We now know the foundation of temptation comes from within each one according to their own desires. This is not to say there are no things, times, places, or even people who serve as triggers or encourage the intensity of one's desires. That old devil said to Eve, "You will not surely die."

Still, looking at the book of beginnings in chapter four we find Cain kills Abel. We know the sin. What was the encourager to send Cain's desire to such an evil place? Where do we find triggers? "The Lord said to Cain, 'Why are you angry. And why has your face fallen? If you do well. Will you not be accepted? And if you do not do well, sin is crouching at the door. Its desire is contrary to you, but you must rule over it" (Genesis 4:7).

In today's way of thinking, some would venture to say that God pushed Cain over the edge and therefore it was God's fault that Abel died. THIS IS NEVER THE ANSWER! Remember the words of James: "Let no one say when he is tempted, 'I am tempted of God.' For God cannot be tempted with evil; and he himself tempts no one."

Knowing these truths, man—because of all God has done and given—must be able to know, not only where the temptation may lead, but the triggers as well. For Eve, it was the beauty of the fruit, but also that she might be wise like God. For Cain the trigger was his own jealousy of his brother's sacrifice being accepted by God, and not his own. Triggers to temptation can be just as powerful as the temptation itself.

Today, I will...be more aware of what opens the door to temptation, which leads me to ungodly desires. I will ask God to help me not be moved by seemingly trivial things which may carry me closer to being enticed. God bless you all.

JESUS WAS TEMPTED

TODAY'S SCRIPTURE: Matthew 4:1-11

The reason I firmly know, and am sure, temptation itself is not sin, is because Jesus was tempted. The Bible teaches that Jesus was tempted, just like us, but never sinned. One of the best known accounts of Jesus being tempted is found in Matthew 4. There we find out the devil was the instigator of the temptation. We also find out that Jesus' present circumstances were the trigger. Jesus fasted forty days and nights and was hungry. The devil used that hunger to tempt Jesus.

In Jesus we see the same thing that we have seen in our other examples leading up to today's study. There is a trigger that leads to the temptation. There is a battle going on in Jesus. Yet, he does not falter. In Jesus, we see the difference between Eve's ending and that of the Lord's. In Jesus, we see the difference between him and the apostle Paul. We especially see a difference in Jesus and Cain.

What is the difference? Jesus did not give in to the trigger, nor to the instigator, or even the temptations themselves. Jesus never let the desire conceive, much less be planted. Remember what James said: "The one lured and enticed." When we are not lured in, or pulled away, then no sin will be conceived.

Today, I will...strive to know how not to be lured and enticed by my own desire. I will ask God for strength, convictions and understanding. God bless you all.

JESUS IS THE ANSWER

TODAY'S SCRIPTURE: John 1:14

The devil was serious about wanting Jesus to fail. Satan's own arrogance gave him the idea he could overcome the savior. Jesus was different. Jesus was man alright—living, breathing, feeling, flesh and blood. Yet, he was different.

Jesus knew the Father face-to-face. John tells us that Jesus was God in the flesh (John 1:14). Jesus overcame the devil's temptations, not because of his great physical strength, or his knowledge of his opponent's weakness, but because Jesus had a two-pronged spiritual approach to temptation.

Jesus was one who knew the will and word of the Father. Jesus used this knowledge as his strength. With each temptation Jesus would answer with the word of God. Secondly Jesus also was one who trusted God without wavering. Jesus was not afraid to tell God his woes, sorrows, or even his own desires. When push came to shove, Jesus always chose God. Jesus would choose God's plan because of his own trust in the father.

We are all "mere" men and women,· but we can learn from the Master teacher. We can follow in his steps and be able to overcome temptation.

Today, I will...seek to draw closer to God through his word. I want to know him face to face. I Will ask God to help me be more trusting of him and his word, like his Son, Jesus. For Jesus shows us all how to overcome temptation, and in so doing has given me better weapons against sin. God bless you.

As a Teenager

REED SWINDLE

STOP TRYING TO BE AN EXAMPLE

TODAY'S SCRIPTURE: Matthew 5:13-16

"Trying" to be an example can accidentally make Christianity about what others think about me. If I please God, I am the example.

One of the quickest answers to my Bible class teacher growing up was "to be an example." Why shouldn't a Christian smoke? "Because they are supposed to be an example." Why shouldn't a Christian cuss? "Because they are supposed to be an example." Why should Christians go to church? "Because they are supposed to be examples."

A 15-year-old young man was at a gathering where irresponsible adults offered the underaged teenagers beer with the promise of secrecy. One of the young men quickly, because of his moral convictions, excused himself. As he pulled the door closed, he felt resistance on the other side of the door handle. He let go of the door and turned to find a line of his friends following out the door. Later, one of those young men explained he wanted to leave, but didn't have the courage, and he was very glad the first young man made the first move. He didn't leave because he was trying to be an example. He left because of his convictions. That made him the example.

There are dangers for a Christian when they begin to be motivated by who is watching. First, it becomes easy for a Christian to turn their Christianity on and off depending on who is watching. Second, our motivation to prove to those watching how faithful we are, can quickly replace our desire to please God. Third, Matthew 5:13-16 does not encourage us to "try" to be an example. It tells us we "are" examples. One chapter later, Jesus warns the same audience of "practicing righteousness in order to be seen by" others (Matthew 6:1-4).

Today, I will... focus on doing what is right to be seen by God.

IT'S WORTH IT

TODAY'S SCRIPTURE: Hebrews 11

God will bless you later for decisions you make now.

When kids are little we want them to love the Bible so we teach them the "fairy tale" type stories in hopes of making them love the Word of God. We rightfully teach them stories about creation, Noah and his ark, and spend a lot of time teaching about Jesus and His miracles.

Once these kids reach middle school, we have a tendency to worry about them. We want them to be faithful and love God and His word. We are worried and do not want them to make mistakes. In our attempt, it becomes easy to make the Bible look like a book of rules and guidelines.

As teenagers mature and begin to question, it is sometimes difficult for them to see that following God is anything more than a lifestyle of commands and prohibitions. Teenagers find themselves with a faith in God but no real motivation for following Him. If they have grown up going to church, the have full intentions of coming back when they find themselves drifting off.

Hebrews 11:6 says we must "believe that he exists and that he rewards those who seek Him". Hebrews 11:23-29 shows a progression of Moses and his decisions. He refused to enjoy the pleasures of sin but rather be mistreated with the people of God. He left Egypt because he knew it was better to follow God than be rich in Egypt. Hebrews 11:27 interestingly says Moses was more concerned with pleasing "him who was invisible" referring to God than the king of Egypt. As the Red Sea divided and Moses led the people across on dry land, I have no doubt he understood "It's worth it!"

Today, I will... decide to keep myself pure for marriage. It's worth it! I won't drink alcohol. It's worth it! I won't use bad language or hang around the wrong people. It's worth it! I will commit myself to God, attend worship, and find ways to serve Him. It's worth it!

NO PAIN, NO GAIN

TODAY'S SCRIPTURE: Hebrews 12:1-17

God might not make things easy on purpose.

A phrase commonly used to motivate athletes is, "No pain, no gain." It used to inspire hard work and motivate successful habits. You have to go to practice when you don't want to go. You have to run faster, focus more intensely, push yourself harder or go for one more set! Maybe it's too cold. Maybe it's too hot. Maybe you are sleepy or you have something else you could be doing. "No pain, no gain" reminds us that we become better because of the hard things we decide to handle correctly.

Hebrews 12:7 explains that God might make us go through some hard things to make us stronger. He continues in verse 11 that some things we go through are not easy but they are for our good. The previous chapter includes an extensive list of people like named and unnamed believers who successfully navigated tough situations and were better because of it.

In Acts 4, Jesus' followers were strongly threatened by the Jewish rulers because they were teaching about their Lord. Once released, their prayer was a bit surprising. Under strong intimidation and promise of punishment, it would be easy to ask God to take away the problems. Acts 4:29 says the Christians prayed for boldness to continue teaching under the harsh circumstances. They refused to ask for the mountain to be taken away. Rather, they asked for strength to cross over it.

Sometimes, God could take away the problem, but He might want you to have to deal with it. He asked Abraham to offer a son, Noah to build an ark, and Moses to lead a restless nation. God might make you cross a mountain you do not want to cross. He might want you to deal with a situation you might would rather overlook. God is trying to make us stronger and prepare us for greater things.

Today, I will... recognize that my problems might be God giving me the opportunity to become more useful in His kingdom.

JUST KEEP SWIMMING

TODAY'S SCRIPTURE: Genesis 39

Sometimes NOT messing up IS success!

Many Bible class lessons, youth rally keynotes, and sermons from the pulpit remind us of characters who did great things in their lives. David and Goliath, for example, reminds us that when we give God the glory and have confidence in Him, we can slay giants. We are also encouraged to evangelize and take every opportunity, like the apostle Paul, to teach people the Bible.

BUT, some days aren't giant slaying, bible teaching days. Some days do not provide these glaring opportunities to stand up for God or go to bed feeling like conquerors. Some days, the very best thing you can do is NOT MESS UP!

Joseph in Genesis 39 did not convert anyone. He didn't slay a giant, conquer a fear or begin a Bible study. He just simply did not mess up. Potipher's wife invited him to be a part of something that could potentially be a secret sin. She offered him an option of messing up with few or no consequences. His response is as strong today as it was then. "How then can I do this great wickedness and sin against God?" In essence Joseph said "I will not mess up today!"

Another quote that can get caught in your mind is of a great Pixar blue tang fish named Dory. "Just keep swimming, Just keep swimming." Dory encouraged her friend Nemo to continue swimming through the difficult times.

Joseph had to go through "just keep swimming" days in order to be available for God's plan. David had to keep the sheep from wandering off in order to get to the battle with Goliath. There are days where the absolute most successful thing you can do is NOT mess up. Some days are a complete victory if you can go to bed and still be clean. God can use that!

Today, I will... not feel guilty if I did not slay a giant. Instead, I will allow my victories to also be measured by what I did not do.

CONFIDENCE IN YOUR OBEDIENCE

TODAY'S SCRIPTURE: Philemon

One of the biggest compliments a Christian can be given is for God to have confidence in their obedience.

There is a railroad track near my house. As you approach the crossing it becomes apparent that you cannot see what is coming down the tracks from either direction. The trees are grown up and visibility is low. At the crossing are signals with large arms that come down when a train is approaching. Even though I always slow down to check both directions, there are many who simply drive straight through when the arms are up. They have driven this road their whole lives and have become very confident in the consistency of the signaling arms.

The book of Philemon is a short letter from Paul to his friend, Philemon. This letter is a plea to this landowner to take back his runaway slave, Onesimus, without punishment. The slavery system of the time was more like a legal agreement to fulfill a predetermined timeframe of service to repay debt or earn wages. Onesimus had broken the agreement by running away. Along his way, he met Paul and was converted. Paul must have explained that repentance would include returning to fulfill his obligation even though Philemon might be upset enough to sell his debt to another landowner or even have him thrown in prison.

Paul had the authority of an apostle and had the right to tell Philemon exactly what he had to do. But Paul decided to appeal to him. He asked him to voluntarily do the right thing. It was obvious that Philemon and Paul had a strong history of trust and respect. As he concludes his letter, he says "having confidence in your obedience, I write to you, knowing you will do even more than I say" (1:22). Paul knew because of Philemon's moral consistency, that he could trust a correct response.

Today, I will... begin getting the important things right consistently, so God can have confidence in my obedience.

Suffering

DON & RON
WILLIAMS

WHERE IS GOD IN TIMES OF TROUBLE?

TODAY'S SCRIPTURE: Hebrews 13:6

In times of heartache, or when trials are many, as in the COVID-19 pandemic, it is familiar to wonder where God is in the midst of these trials and tribulations.

His Word tells us that for his people who love and follow Him, He is there for them.

1. God is before us. In Exodus 13:21, it says, "And the Lord went before them by day in a pillar of cloud to lead the way, and by night in a pillar of fire to give them, so as to go by day and night". We often sing the song,"Where He leads me, I will follow."

2. God is behind us. In Genesis 17:1, He appeared unto an aged Abram and said to him," I am Almighty God;walk before me and be blameless." He promises his people, "I will never leave you, nor forsake you, so that we may boldly say, The Lord is my helper-what can man do to me?" (Hebrews 13:6)

3. God is over us. In 1 Peter 3:12, it reads, "For the eyes of the Lord are over the righteous, and His ears are open to their prayers; but the face of the Lord is against them that do evil." God watches over his people and helps them in the midst of their struggles.

4. God is underneath us. Deuteronomy 33:27 tells us, "The eternal God is your refuge and underneath are the everlasting arms". In a pandemic world where social distancing is necessary, and hugs and touching others are against CDC regulations, we do not have a stay at home God! We can sing the song, "Precious Jesus, hold my hand-yes I need thee every hour!" One of my favorites has as its chorus "Hold my hand all the way, every hour, every hour, everyday, from here to the great unknown, Take my hand, let me stand, where no one stands alone!"

Today, I will... remember, that as a child of God, I have a Father who is before me, behind me, over me and underneath me. How blessed I am!

HIS SUFFERING WAS VERY GREAT

TODAY'S SCRIPTURE: Job 2:13

No one should ever have to suffer alone. We need others to care.

Job likely wished he could wake up and discover his losses were just a bad dream. Every valuable item of wealth had been destroyed or taken away from him. His servants had been killed and his livestock either killed or captured by others. His ten children were killed when a wind destroyed the house they were in. Although he did not know it, permission had been granted for Satan to afflict him bodily since he received sores from the top of his head to the soles of his feet. His wife, perhaps out of pity for him, told him to curse God and die.

Job had three friends that decided to come join Job in his circle of suffering. No doubt, Eliphaz, Bildad, and Zophar, did not know what they were going to see when they came to Job on the ash pile. The text says, "And they sat with him on the ground seven days and seven nights, and no one spoke a word to him, for they saw that his suffering was very great" (Job 2:13).

Suffering is universal but unfortunately having friends while we suffer is not. Too many people are oblivious to the pain of others. Too many people are too self-centered to see others that are hurting. Too many people are wrapped up in their world that they do not see others that are hurting terribly and desperately need someone to care for them.

Suffering hurts but compassion helps ease the pain. These three friends came where Job was to their own inconvenience. They felt Job's pain and wept and put ashes on their heads like that of Job. They sat "where he sat" and did not enumerate worn out words of cheer and comfort that would have made Job feel worse. They stayed with him in his pain. They cared. It showed in what they did.

Today, I will...feel what others are feeling. I will hurt with them. I will show care

WHERE IS GOD IN TIME OF LOSS?

TODAY'S SCRIPTURE: Hebrews 13:5, 6

If I had a favorite verse in the Bible, it would be Hebrews 13:5,6. "Let your conduct be without covetousness; be content with such things as you have. For He himself has said, "I will never leave you nor forsake you." So we may boldly say: "The Lord is my help; I will not fear. What can man do to me?"

It is my understanding that in the original Greek language, the phrase " I will never leave you nor forsake you" is a double negative. In other words, God is saying, "I will not leave, I will not leave you" and "I will not forsake, I will not forsake you." Isn't it wonderful to know that in the midst of adversity or loss, we are not alone. God tells us that He is there with us, in the midst of our trials.

This message is reaffirmed in a beautiful statement made by Dorothy Mercer. She writes, "Help! I can't stand this anymore! Get me out of here, God! The mud of my distress has sapped my strength, disrupted my belief, drowned my faith. Where are you, God? Why won't you rescue me from this mire?"

"Move over. I didn't promise to remove you from the pain of living. But I do ask you to give me room to sit in the mud beside you. Remember my promise to never leave you? Trust me. Move over!"

Today, I will... be thankful that as God's child, I do not have to walk through trials and sadness alone. God is with me!

SUFFERING: A BADGE OF HONOR?

TODAY'S SCRIPTURE: Hebrews 11:13-15

Human suffering in life reminds us of the better eternity ahead of us

I live in a town that has a sizable military base in our community. Many military personnel go through training here and veterans retire here after their service is completed. On Veterans Day, our town has a very large celebration parade and many soldiers come from our local area to march for this procession.

As I watch our men and women of the military march on Veteran's Day, the retired military often wear their uniforms of honor. On their uniforms those men and women may wear service medals which were awarded for good conduct, achievement, and participation in a conflict. Other soldiers may wear decoration medals honoring the recipient because of acts of gallantry, valor, and meritorious service. These soldiers earned the right to receive these medals through the faithful service they gave to our country.

I cannot know all the struggles of life that a person may face as a Christian. I cannot know why some Christians seem to have less challenges of life than others do. I cannot fully understand why some Christians seem to deal with their challenges of life more effectively than other Christians (as if we are experts in being judges of such matters).

I know this. Suffering in this world happens. It happens from the choices we make, from the choices of others that affect us, or by directional misfortune (we are at the right place at the wrong time). Read Luke 13:1-5 for two historical occurrences of this misfortune.

When suffering for Christ occurs (and it will) I know that God sees me as I suffer. I know He cares that I suffer for Him. I would like to think that heaven will be filled with medals of honor for Christians who gained the victory in Jesus Christ.

Today, I will... look at suffering from the vantage point of God. I will accept whatever my suffering may be because heaven will be worth it all.

HEALING SCRIPTURES TO COMFORT ONE'S HEART

TODAY'S SCRIPTURE: Psalm 147:3

One of the greatest fears is of being alone. In times of agony and suffering, we fear the pain, but we also fear that we will have to suffer without others being there with us. This has been one of the great travesties caused by COVID-19. Many who are sick cannot have family or friends around them, especially in the hospital or ICU.

Isn't it wonderful to know that our Heavenly Father is not a "stay-at-home" Father? He is there for us and with us, even in the midst of our suffering. Consider these following scriptures of Comfort:

Psalm 147:3-"He heals the brokenhearted and binds up their wounds."

Psalm 56:8-"You number my wanderings; put my tears into your bottle; are they not in your book?"

Psalm 41:1-3-"Blessed is he who considers the poor; The Lord will deliver him in time of trouble. The Lord will preserve him and keep him alive. And he will be blessed on the earth; You will not deliver him to the will of his enemies. The Lord will strengthen him on his bed of illness. You will sustain him on his sickbed."

Jeremiah 17:14-"Heal me O Lord, and I shall be healed; Save me, and I shall be saved, for You are my praise".

2 Corinthians 12:7-9 "And lest I should be exalted above measure, by the abundance of the revelations, a thorn in the flesh was given to me, a messenger of Satan to buffet me, lest I be exalted above measure. Concerning this thing I pleaded with the Lord three times, that it might depart from me. And He said to me, 'My grace is sufficient for you, for My strength is made perfect in weakness'. Therefore, most gladly I will rather boast in my infirmities, that the power of Christ may rest upon me."

Today, I will... be grateful for the comforting messages of God that will sustain me, even when I suffer.

In View of Eternity

LARRY ACUFF

THE FACT OF ETERNITY

TODAY'S SCRIPTURE: John 5:24

The Holy scriptures say, "Truly, truly, I say to you, whoever hears my word and believes him who sent me has eternal life. He does not come into judgment, but has passed from death to life" (John 5:24).

Atheist do not believe there is an eternity for man. Note the following quote, "I have always felt that when I die, I am dead and gone, my conscious life will end, my interactions with others will end, and I will be simply GONE."**

We know eternity means "infinite or unending time," but understanding what that means to those who believe in The Christ is underscored by the Holy Bible. Viewing such passages as, "For the wages of sin is death, but the free gift of God is eternal life in Christ Jesus our Lord" (Romans 6:23). Notice, "the free gift of God is eternal life." Another great passage reminds us of this fact, "And this is the promise that he made to us—eternal life" (1 John 2:25). Contrast this with the idea that when this life is over there is nothing. Zilch! Zero! Nata! I read one time that an atheist described death as we simply go back to the dust and that is it. It is like seeing the wind blow dust and we say, "Well, there goes grandpa."

The Christian has great comfort in the fact of eternity. Death is a transition when we move out of this old body into a "place prepared for you from the foundation of the world" (Matthew 25:34). We have a new body, one that is incorruptible (1 Corinthians 15).

If the Bible is right, and I believe that it is, – there will be an eternity! The old song expresses it like this:
>*"To Canaan's land, I'm on my way*
>*Where the soul of man never dies*
>*My darkest night will turn to day*
>*Where the soul of man never dies."*

Today, I will... determine to live in such a way as to be in that place called heaven for eternity.

**https://www.theatlantic.com/daily-dish/archive/2010/05/what-do-atheists-think-of-death/187003/

THE CHOICE OF A LIFETIME
TODAY'S SCRIPTURE: Revelation 22:1-4

The Holy Scriptures say, "Then I saw a new heaven and a new earth, for the first heaven and the first earth had passed away, and the sea was no more. And I saw the holy city, new Jerusalem, coming down out of heaven from God, prepared as a bride adorned for her husband. And I heard a loud voice from the throne saying, "Behold, the dwelling place of God is with man. He will dwell with them, and they will be his people, and God himself will be with them as their God. He will wipe away every tear from their eyes, and death shall be no more, neither shall there be mourning, nor crying, nor pain anymore, for the former things have passed away" (Revelation 21:1-4). The Christian has this as his goal.

When a person chooses to become a Christian through faith, repentance, confession, and baptism that is not just a choice for today but for a lifetime. A life that never ends. Oh, we leave this old body behind (1 Corinthians 15) but we take on a new incorruptible body, one that will live forever.

There is a song in which these words are said,
> *"This life is filled with sorrow and troubles here below.*
> *We oft are made to wonder just why it should be so.*
> *In every tribulation this life must bring to view.*
> *Oh Lord we need a friend like You."*

When we make the choice of a lifetime we leave this world that is filled with trouble, pain, and sorrow for a place where, "death shall be no more, neither shall there be mourning, nor crying, nor pain anymore, for the former things have passed away." Wow! All because we made that choice.

Joshua made the choice of a lifetime when he said "...But as for me and my house, we will serve the LORD" (Joshua 24:15).

Today, I will...make the right choices so that I may live eternally with God.

I WANT TO GO HOME

TODAY'S SCRIPTURE: Philippians 3:20-21

Have you traveled away from home for a period of time staying in motels and eating in restaurants, and then it hits you – I want to go home. Having traveled in foreign countries on missionary journeys, I would find myself counting the days until leaving for home. I remember one mission trip WHEN my wife, and I and another couple could not wait to land because we were dreaming of and talking about going to Wendy's. It reminded me of a story that I had read where the writer wrote, as the wheels of the plane hit the runway, "He said all through the plane you could hear the unfastening of seatbelts. As the voice came over the intercom saying, 'Please remain seated with your seatbelt fastened until the plane comes to a complete stop,' he said, no one was paying attention. People were already out of their seats, opening the overhead compartments, getting their stuff out. Why? Because they were home. Their final destination was not that plane. They wanted to get off of that plane, and get out, and get home with those they love. He said he didn't see any of the stewardesses having to struggle to pull people out of their seats, with people going, 'Wait a minute. I want to stay on the plane for a few more hours. The food is really good. These seats are so comfy, I want to stay.' No. They were home. They wanted to get off of that plane."

Todays scripture reminds us that our citizenship is in heaven. The song says, "This world is not my home I'm just a passing through my treasures are laid up somewhere beyond the blue...." Don't you love Paul's description, "For we know that if the tent that is our earthly home is destroyed, we have a building from God, a house not made with hands, eternal in the heavens" (2 Corinthians 5:1).

Today, I will... pray that my life will be lived in such a way as to reflect the citizenship I have in heaven.

DECISIONS THAT AFFECT MY LIFE

TODAY'S SCRIPTURE: Luke 15:18

The Holy scriptures say, "I will arise and go to my father, and I will say to him, "Father, I have sinned against heaven and before you" (Luke 15:18). The Prodigal Son made a decision, "I will arise and go to my father...." Decisions affect our lives which in turn affects our eternities. Here are some decisions that will make a difference.

The decision to obey the gospel affects my life in view of eternity. We are saved by the blood of Jesus Christ (Ephesians 1:7). Jesus said, "Whoever believes and is baptized will be saved, but whoever does not believe will be condemned" (Mark 16:16). That choice affects my view of eternity.

The decision to worship affects my life in view of eternity. "God is spirit, and those who worship him must worship in spirit and truth" (John 4:24). The decision to meet on the first day of the week to worship God is vital to spiritual strength. When I sing, pray, take communion, give and study, it keeps my view directed toward God. Worship on the Lord's Day keeps my focus on seeking first the kingdom of God (Matthew 6:33). In addition, a Christian is encouraged by being with other Christians. The Hebrew writer declared, "And let us consider how to stir up one another to love and good works" (Hebrews 10:24).

The decision to pray affects my life in view of eternity. Jesus said, "Ask, and it will be given to you; seek, and you will find; knock, and it will be opened to you" (Matthew 7:7). Jeremiah says it like this, "Then you will call upon me and come and pray to me, and I will hear you" (Jeremiah 29:12). What a great comforting passage.

Today, I will...make the decisions that will help me stay focused on eternity.

GETTING ALL YOKED UP
TODAY'S SCRIPTURE: Matthew 11:28-30

Jesus said, "Come to me, all who labor and are heavy laden, and I will give you rest. Take my yoke upon you, and learn from me, for I am gentle and lowly in heart, and you will find rest for your souls. For my yoke is easy, and my burden is light" (Matthew 11:28-30). This passage is one of the great invitations of our Lord. He says, "Take my yoke upon you..." When we are yoked to Jesus, it altars our eternal view. To be "yoked " means: "to become joined or linked" (Merriam-Webster Dictionary). How does being yoked to Christ altar our eternal view? Here are several ways:

Being yoked to Christ means we are closer to God. Jesus Christ is the Son of God, therefore when we are yoked to Christ, we will be closer to God. "Draw near to God, and he will draw near to you. Cleanse your hands, you sinners, and purify your hearts, you double-minded" (James 4:8).

Being yoked to Christ means separation from the world. "No one can serve two masters, for either he will hate the one and love the other, or he will be devoted to the one and despise the other. You cannot serve God and money" (Matthew 6:24). Being yoked to Christ means you can not turn aside to the right hand or to the left.

Being yoked to Christ also draws you closer to the word of God. Jesus said it like this, "The one who rejects me and does not receive my words has a judge; the word that I have spoken will judge him on the last day" (John 12:48). To be yoked to Christ means your yoked to the word of God also.

Today, I will...yoke myself to Christ so that I may take advantage of the opportunities that are presented to me.

Dealing with Anger

TERRY TOWNSEND

FACIAL FURY

TODAY'S SCRIPTURE: Daniel 3:19

Have you ever seen someone get so angry that their facial features change almost instantaneously? You know what I am talking about: their face turns blood red, they grind their teeth, the veins in their forehead begin to appear, and their eyes look like they are ready to pop out of their head. I call it "facial fury!" I suppose all of us have experienced this transformation, whether directly or indirectly. It can be a rather intense situation, and one we'd all just as soon forget.

When I think of "facial fury," I immediately think back to the account of Daniel's three Hebrew cohorts, Shadrach, Meshach, and Abednego and their refusal to bow down to the image that had been erected to honor King Nebuchadnezzar (cf. Daniel 3:1ff). Nebuchadnezzar, when learning of their refusal to bow, became very angry. The Bible gives us a vivid picture of just how angry he was: "Then Nebuchadnezzar in furious rage commanded that Shadrach, Meshach, and Abednego be brought" (Daniel 3:13), and again, after they refused to bow a second time, the Bible states, "Then Nebuchadnezzar was filled with fury, and the expression of his face was changed against Shadrach, Meshach, and Abednego" (Daniel 3:19). How dare these men defy me, the king! Thus, he ordered the fiery furnace to be heated seven times hotter (an indication of just how HOT he had become), and then commanded that the three men be cast therein (Daniel 3:20ff). Thankfully, because of their remarkable faith, God saved these three men, prompting Nebuchadnezzar to acknowledge the One true and living God (Daniel 3:26ff).

Make no mistake about it, when God's people stand up for truth in the face of opposition, the adversary will become fiery mad, even to the point of responding with violence. When those situations arise, may we have the fortitude to stand strong in the faith and at the same time the inner control to avoid any retaliatory response.

Today, I will... know how to properly respond to those who are angry with me, knowing that God is watching over me.

BE ANGRY AND DO NOT SIN

TODAY'S SCRIPTURE: Ephesians 4:26-27

Have you ever uttered some angry words and soon thereafter felt bad about it? I suppose most of us have said things in haste that we later regretted. I recall a time when I was working in the kitchen trying to repair a cabinet door that was broken. When things didn't go back together the way I had anticipated (they seemingly never do), I slammed the doors out of anger and pinched my thumb, and then proceeded to spew a laundry list of angry words from my mouth (not bad words, just angry words toward the cabinet doors). Little did I know standing behind me watching and hearing everything I was saying was my young daughter. As I grasped my throbbing thumb and turned around and saw her standing there, I heard her say, "Dad, why are you yelling at the cabinet door? You should be yelling at yourself for your own stupidity!" Ouch! At that very moment, my heart hurt more than did my thumb. She was right. I had no business speaking harshly to anybody or anything. After the pain and swelling had subsided, I sat down with my daughter and apologized to her for my actions.

Being angry is not a sin, but one's attitude and actions to situations that spawn anger can be. Paul writes, "Be angry and do not sin; do not let the sun go down on your anger, and give no opportunity to the devil" (Ephesians 4:26-27). There are things that should anger all of God's people (doctrinal error, injustice, racism, etc.), but we must maintain the proper attitudes and actions in response to such things. My reaction to a repair of a cabinet door not going as planned was wrong. My response should have been to take a deep breath, maybe even walk away momentarily, and then patiently try again. Had I done so, I would not have gone through the agony of a pinched thumb, and I certainly would have been a better example to my daughter.

Today, I will... watch what I say and respond to adverse situations with patience.

ANGER = ACTION

TODAY'S SCRIPTURE: John 2:13-22

Several years ago, a gentleman called the church office seeking financial assistance. After discussing the need with the elders, it was decided that help be granted, which resulted in a Bible study and conversion. Within a few months, additional needs for this man and his family were brought to our attention, and again, the church helped. This became a pattern, and eventually the elders told this man that they couldn't continue to assist him because there were others in the congregation who also needed help. Soon thereafter, the man quit coming to services and began a social-media attack on the church, her members, and her leadership. It was later brought to our attention that this man had, for years, preyed upon the good hearts of Christian people to support he and his family. I was angry because I had gone to bat for this man and thought he was sincere. Church discipline was eventually implemented, not out of hate, but out of love in hopes that this man would repent.

I do believe the anger I, along with my elders, had about this situation was justified and that the actions taken were Scriptural. A similar situation is recorded in the Sacred Scripture (cf. John 2:13-22). Jesus was justly angered that worldly commercial activities had corrupted the sanctity of the temple, and the actions He took were appropriate. As He drove them all out of the temple He said, "Take these things away; do not make my Father's house a house of trade" (John 2:16).

It should anger God's people when folks corrupt the holiness of the church, blaspheme God and His Holy Word, sow discord, speak falsehoods, and make merchandise of her. The action that the church should take (like the Lord's actions at the temple) should be to drive out the wrong in hopes of maintaining spiritual purity.

Today, I will... take the appropriate action for any just anger I might have (of myself and or for others) for purity sake.

AN ANGRY MOB

TODAY'S SCRIPTURE: Luke 23:13-25

The year 2020 will forever be remembered as the year of the "virus" (Covid-19) and civil unrest. It is a year I suppose most of us would just soon forget. Never, in my fifty-plus years of life, have I seen as much chaos, fear, division, anger and hate. The images of the angry and rebellious mobs reaping havoc within our inner cities is disheartening. I understand the hurt and pain associated with racial injustice. But as we've seen, peaceful protests can quickly escalate into an angry and violent mob. The loud and angry voices of a few can lead the masses into doing things they wouldn't otherwise do.

What we saw playing out in 2020 wasn't a new phenomenon. In fact, a little over 2,000 years ago on the streets of Jerusalem an angry and rebellious mob was formed. The anger and hate of a few Jewish elite toward Christ spawned a violent mob bent on stamping out any-and-all associated with Him. Once Christ was taken into custody, Pilate quickly surmised His innocence (cf. Luke 23:13-16). In hopes of appeasing and disbanding the angry mob, Pilate had Jesus scourged, but to no avail. The mob refused to listen to any voice of reason. So focused on destroying Jesus, they demanded Barabbas, a known felon, be released. They vehemently cried out, "Crucify Him, crucify Him!" Pilate ultimately relented and granted their demand. "He released the man who had been thrown into prison for insurrection and murder, for whom they asked, but he delivered Jesus over to their will" (Luke 23:25). An angry mob may have crucified an innocent man on that occasion, but ultimately the Truth would prevail!

I wonder how many assembled on the day of Pentecost to hear the Gospel preached were part of that mob that some 50 days earlier had angerly cried out for Jesus' crucifixion? My guess is most, if not all, who were "cut to the heart, and said to Peter and the rest of the apostles, 'Brothers, what shall we do?'" (Acts 2:37) were present on the day the Lord was delivered over to be crucified. What started out as an angry mob bent on the destruction of Truth ended with a penitent people resolved to obey that Truth!

Today, I will... seek to uncover for myself all the facts (truth) before giving in to the media mob and political activists.

A JAVELIN IN THE HAND OF AN ANGRY MAN

TODAY'S SCRIPTURE: 1 Samuel 18:1-30

Mark Twain once wrote, "Anger is an acid that can do more harm to the vessel in which it is stored than to anything on which it is poured." What a profound, and might I add, Biblically based statement! In many ways, king Saul (his attitude and actions toward David) is the epitome of what Mr. Twain was describing. Saul, God's anointed servant and first king of Israel, allowed his jealousy of a young shepherd soldier servant to consume him, which in turn gave way to anger and rage that would ultimately lead to his demise.

Soon after David's victory over Goliath (1 Samuel 17:41-54), king Saul brought David to live within the palace, setting him over the men of war. David quickly gained the favor of the people, and Saul, when learning of David's appeal, became filled with jealousy, anger and hate. The Bible says, "And Saul was very angry" (1 Samuel 18:8). How angry was Saul? I think a javelin in the hand of this man and then hurled not once, but twice at David answers that question conclusively (cf. 1 Samuel 18:11). Imagine being so angry with someone that you grab a spear and throw it at them in hopes of ending their life! But who does anger harm more? A careful examination of the context under consideration will answer that question for us. Saul's anger led him to violence, fear and distrust, while catapulting David into the national spotlight (cf. 1 Samuel 18:12-30).

Saul's anger at David was unwarranted, and he allowed that rage to contaminate his inner self to the point of destroying everything good around him. May we learn from Saul's mistake, and rid our hearts of any unjust anger we might have toward a fellow human being.

Today, I will...lay down the proverbial javelin of anger and hate and extend a hand of love and support to everyone around me

Dealing with Depression

DOUG TOOLEY

A MATTER OF PERSPECTIVE

TODAY'S SCRIPTURE: 2 Corinthians 12:10

One of the first things we must do is realize that even the Christian life is not going to be a bed of roses. The Bible tells us over and over that we are going to face trials. Peter warned his readers not to be surprised by fiery trials they were about to face (1 Peter 4:12). Paul preached that it was through many tribulations one must enter the kingdom of God (Acts 14:22). Jesus faced persecutions. Surely, we do not think we are greater than our master (John 15:20).

The Bible even gives us examples of people that fell into bouts with depression. Elijah went from defeating the prophets of Baal to asking God to take his life (1 Kings 18:20-40; 19:4). He was losing his trust in God, and he believed he was the only faithful person left (1 Kings 19:10, 14). Elijah's perspective was incorrect. God was still with him. He was not the last of the faithful (1 Kings 19:15-18).

Perspective can have a profound effect on our success and happiness. I once read a book called Running with Kenyans. The author set out to find out why Kenyans were so successful at running. While he found various contributing factors, there was one that stuck out, their perspective. When the author was with the Kenyan runners and they came to a hill, he approached it with dread and slowed down. The Kenyans saw a hill as an opportunity to train harder. They attacked the hills. They had a similar perspective in every aspect of running.

In the Bible, Moses lost favor with Pharaoh and had to tend sheep for forty years (Exodus 2:11-21; Acts 7:25-31). How would that help Moses tend a flock of grumbling Israelites? When David overcame Goliath, he rose to prominence (1 Samuel 17:1-18:6). Paul found strength in his time of weakness (2 Corinthians 12:10). Who could see anything positive in facing trials like these? Yet, each case had a positive outcome.

Today, I will... pray for God to help me keep a positive outlook even when I am faced with mountains.

AVOIDING ANXIETY

TODAY'S SCRIPTURE: Proverbs 12:25

For the next four days, we are going to look at a few ways we can build a life that helps us to avoid depression. Today we are considering anxiety. In Proverbs 12:25, we read, "Anxiety in a man's heart weighs him down, but a good word makes him glad (ESV)." The New King James Version translates "weighs him down" as "causes depression." Most of us have dealt with some kind of anxiety and know it will weigh you down.

Jesus instructed us that we should not be anxious about our lives, what we will eat, drink, or about our body, what we will put on (Matthew 6:25). When I think about His teaching on this matter, I realize that we must find balance in our lives. Otherwise, someone could read Matthew 6, and decide to just quit their jobs, become homeless, and wait for the judgment.

From other Bible passages, I can deduce that was not what God had in mind. Paul instructed the saints at Ephesus that a person should labor, working with their hands, that they might have something to give to the person that has need (Ephesians 4:28). He also wrote on a similar matter to Thessalonica. Apparently, some there had actually quit working because of their misunderstanding and anticipation of the time of second coming. He told them that if anyone will not work, neither shall he eat (2 Thessalonians 3:10). That is about as straightforward as it gets.

When I combine these teachings, I realize we must find balance. God expects us to have enough concern to be able to move through life and make a decent contribution. He also expects us to have enough trust in Him to let Him handle the things we cannot change or control. If we allow Him, He can give us peace that surpasses understanding (Philippians 4:6-8). We must be able to turn the things we cannot control over to Him because He cares for us (1 Peter 5:6-7).

Today, I will... pray for the faith to fall into God's caring hands.

BEING CONTENT

TODAY'S SCRIPTURE: Hebrews 13:5,6

Chasing things of the world brings sorrow.
Chasing heaven brings contentment.

When you try to find contentment in possessions you are only going to find sorrow. Paul wrote, "For the love of money is a root of all kinds of evils. It is through this craving that some have wandered away from the faith and pierced themselves with many pangs (1 Timothy 6:10)." Did you ever see a documentary about "happy" lottery winners?

Jesus taught, "Do not lay up for yourselves treasures on earth, where moth and rust destroy and where thieves break in and steal, but lay up for yourselves treasures in heaven, where neither moth nor rust destroys and where thieves do not break in and steal (Matthew 6:19-20)."

This advice will help us to be right with God, but it will also help us to be happier in this life. If we truly followed this advice, we would not be found overextending ourselves financially, because we would always be putting God first.

I will be the first to admit, I like "things." I love to see the Amazon van pull up in front of my house, but where does it end? I struggle with this and need work myself. The pleasure I get from that new package from Amazon is very short-lived, and if we are not careful, we can find ourselves in a place where we are overextended financially. Unexpected things happen. People get sick. People lose their jobs. Pandemics arise.

If we find ourselves getting constant calls and letters from creditors, it is going to be hard to avoid depression. Financial problems can also lead to marital problems. The Hebrews advised us to keep our lives free from the love of money and be content with the things we have (Hebrews 13:5-6). The devil wants us to think God is trying to keep us from happiness, but God is trying to help us.

Today, I will... pray to find contentment in the blessings I already have and move my focus toward heaven.

PHYSICAL PROBLEMS

TODAY'S SCRIPTURE: Revelation 21:4

When it comes to physical problems, I can hardly think of anything that will more quickly lead to depression. I am placing diseases, cancer, injury, or anything else that causes physical ailment, in the category of physical problems. I would also include the physical sickness of a loved one or the death of a loved one.

All of these things can be very difficult. Thus far in my life, I have been fortunate that my medical conditions have been short-lived. It is hard for me to imagine being in a situation of constant pain, or just physically unable to do the things that I have been able to do in the past. I have lost loved ones, but I have not yet lost my wife, a parent, or a child. Those things are hard for me to imagine.

Many of the same principles apply here that we talked about in dealing with anxiety. The things we cannot change must be given to God (Philippians 4:6-8; 1 Peter 5:6-7). I am not a fan of rehearsed prayers. However, the serenity prayer has some great thoughts. The short version says, "God grant me the serenity to accept the things I cannot change, the courage to change the things I can, and the wisdom to know the difference (Reinhold Niebuhr).

One day Christian parents will be united with children they have lost (2 Samuel 12:22-23). One day every Christian's crippled, disease-ridden body will be replaced with a glorious body (1 Corinthians 15:42-45; Philippians 3:20-21). One day Christians will live in a place where God will wipe their tears away, there will be no more death, nor sorrow, nor crying, nor pain (Revelation 21:24). What a day that will be!

Today, I will... pray to accept the things I cannot change in this life and focus on preparing for the life come.

SIN

TODAY'S SCRIPTURE: Matthew 11:28-30

We are continuing to try to be proactive in avoiding depression. Today, I want us to consider how we can slip into the depths of sin.

Sin is much like weight gain. Several years ago, I woke up one day and found myself very overweight. Do not get me wrong, I knew before this point that I needed to lose some weight. However, it was on this day that I had one of those "aha" moments where I realized how bad it was. When you get to this point you know you need to change, but it is hard to get back to where you need to be. Sin is very similar.

Sin is a hard master. It will take control of your life a little at a time. The process starts with choosing the thing you want right now over the thing you should want most. For instance, Adam and Eve chose the right now pleasure of the forbidden fruit over eternal life in a garden paradise (Genesis 3). However, Moses chose to be mistreated with the people of God rather than to enjoy the fleeting pleasures of sin. Moses knew the reward in Christ would be greater than all the riches of Egypt (Hebrews 11:24-26).

The old saying is "sin will take you farther than you want to go, cost you more than you want to pay, and keep you longer than you want to stay." Satan is a hard master and his devices will lead you to the depths of depression. Jesus on the other hand is calling for all those who labor and are heavy laden. He will give you rest. His yoke is easy, and His burden is light (Matthew 11:28-30).

The depths of sin can be hard to escape, but God is like the father of the prodigal, looking down the road and waiting for you to come home. He will receive you with open arms.

Today, I will... pray for the strength to turn down what I desire right now and hold fast to what I want most.

Dealing with Anxiety

BRYAN McALISTER

THE PROBLEM

TODAY'S SCRIPTURE: 1 Peter 5:7

Take time to make even a cursory search through a biased and skewed search engines (I'm looking at you Google), and it will reveal the ever-present and metastasizing reality of anxiety among hearts of all ages and demographics.

When Christians talk about the problem of anxiety, part of our challenge is to not view the problem as novel, or that it somehow exists outside the realm of God's Sovereign power to help. Likewise, a dismissive intervention of "Just pray more; have more faith" does not a remedy make. Both in the Old and New Testaments, words translated "anxiety" come from word derivatives which point to a divided mind.

Anxiety, in its most pervasive and debilitating forms, touches our lives because of the layered divisions of our thoughts and minds. The anxious mind looks at, focuses on, and obsesses over unknown events or outcomes, unknown conclusions of thoughts of people, and unknown consequences of un-lived circumstances.

Given the dramatic increase in the scope of anxiety, people have reinvented ways to divide our thoughts. From our news binging, to our social media consumption and comparisons, to our relying on emotive thinking and not reasoned thinking, our minds are divided and we are riddled with anxiety. We are the only created being that can produce an emotional and physiological response to a threat that is imagined, perceived, and non-existent. It brings a new understanding to Solomon's wisdom that declares a man's inward calculations reveal him (Proverbs 23:7).

Like any other problem, our perception must not cast any problem in a greater role of power or potency than what our God possesses. To begin addressing this problem, Christian hearts are given the simple yet sufficient beginning step, "casting all your anxieties on him, because he cares for you" (1 Peter 5:7).

Today, I will... Make a list of my anxieties, being honest with myself about the number of things I have allowed to divide my mind, and trust that God is greater than my divided mind.

THE PURPOSE

TODAY'S SCRIPTURE: Psalm 139:24-25

If anxiety is viewed as something that should not be a part of our lives, then our response to the presence of anxiety (in any of its inevitable forms) will only be to resist its presence and, in so doing, fail to see its purpose. We were not created, simply to fall and remain fallen, but to find redemption by grace through Jesus Christ (Romans 3:23-24).

Anxiety, as a function, serves to warn and alert the individual as to potential threats or dangers. Without some measure of anxiety (fear), we would likely find ourselves dealing with greater difficulties from injury or other harm, were it not for the anxieties which can prompt us to be alert and aware of needs for self and others. There is a functional purpose to our anxiety. However, the purpose becomes problematic when the alert mechanism is always "running" or responding to everything around us or worse, responding to everything that is not around us as though it were.

Once David describes God as being everywhere (omnipresent) and knowing everything (omniscient). He turns the attention to God being ever capable (omnipotent) to lead the follower in the "way everlasting" (Psalm 139:24-25). David calls for God to "search" his heart and to "try" his life to reveal his "thoughts" or "anxieties" as translated in the NKJV. This inviting prayer looks not to live without anxiety, but to listen to it in order to see what it reveals.

When anxiety is present, it communicates a presence of a problem, or the perceived presence of a problem. In other words, a feared threat may can be real or can be created and imagined. But what is this anxiety telling me? What does it communicate to me? What does it tell me about the way I am thinking? Could it be that my revealed anxieties point to a pattern of thinking and feeling that does not profit me?

Today, I will... Pray the prayer of Psalm 139:24-25 and trust God to lead me to grow in my faith even through my anxieties.

WEDNESDAY

THE PAIN

TODAY'S SCRIPTURE: Proverbs 12:25

"Anxiety in a man's heart weighs him down, but a good word makes him glad" (Proverbs 12:25).

"Anxiety" or "Heaviness" as the KJV translation reads, indicates the depth of pain in the anxiety-riddled heart. The description of the condition of the heart indicates that it is "weighed" down, giving a picture of one surrendering, or paying attention to, even worshiping the occupant of the heart. This is not an indictment as though the pain of anxiety is wanted, but rather it is an indicator that the pain/weight of anxiety is so heavy, so great, it cannot be denied the attention it demands. The pain takes on many shapes and shades.

Americans have witnessed an alarming rise in the suicide rate over the last 15 years. This is especially evident in the lives of our youth. We've seen an exponential rise in reported loneliness among people, young and old. Furthermore, when you think of the weight of anxiety, you see symptoms ranging from high heart rate, shortness of breath, feeling nervous or powerless, sweating, and an impending sense of danger or doom. People hurt with this pain of their heart. It does weigh them down in their lives.

There is no insinuation that a heart wants to struggle in the ways already listed. Yet, the truth is that our anxiety demands our attention, it demands the peace and calm of our lives be surrendered to the never-satisfied altar of anxiety.

Words matter. Their meaning matters. "[B]ut a good word makes him glad" are words that matter too (Proverbs 12:25). If the anxiety in my heart is a weight, then "good words" are a counterbalance to the unjust weights of anxiety. Created and perpetuated fears of the heart are not worthy of your attention and energy. Words of affirmation, truth, value, worth, purpose, and power, are "good" words for the heart to consume, and offering surrender to those words can transform the weight of the heart.

Today, I will... Meditate on the passage of Philippians 4:8-9, creating lists of all things that are mentioned in this passage, filling my heart with these good words.

THE PERSON

TODAY'S SCRIPTURE: Luke 12:22-34

Honestly, how did He do it? In three words He spoke a message that would be incumbent on every heart that has ever been or will ever be burdened. His words in summary do not tell the whole story, but they tell us the whole theme of the story, "do not worry" (Luke 12:22). Worry is a malignant cancer of the mind, keeping us in a constant state of anxiety and panic; uneasiness and pain. God frequently reveals the pains of worry in muscle aches, body aches, racing thoughts, sleeplessness, loss of appetite, and inexplicable body aches.

Lest you think I'm reading the symptoms relegated to merely our time or our state, give your attention to the Psalmist's dilemma. "My days are consumed like smoke, and my bones are burned like a hearth. My heart is stricken and withered like grass, so that I forget to eat my bread. Because of the sound of my groaning my bones cling to my skin" (Psalm 102:3-5). Worry drills deep into the soul, and buried burdens, ignored ills, and unnerving unknowns, will find a way out of the person. Worry is toxic to the body, leading to deadly behaviors attempting to ignore it, and can even distract us with chronic illnesses, unresolved with mere medicines.

Yet to hearts beset by anxiety and worry, just hearing the words, "do not worry" are not enough, in fact they become almost insulting and demeaning. It stands to reason, our Lord did not stop there with His instruction at those words and neither should we.

Jesus offered words of proactive response to the reality of worry and anxiety. He spoke of guarding the heart against the burden of temporary or exaggerated needs (Luke 12:-24). Jesus offered an alternative to obsessing over felt needs or emotional thinking. The alternative was a focus upon the kingdom and the God of the kingdom, whose care is constant and whose desire is to preserve (Luke 12:29-34).

Today, I will... List the ways my God has delivered and preserved me in the past, as a reminder of how He can and will do it in the present. (If you're reading this today, you woke up. Start there if you're having trouble writing your list.)

THE PLAN

TODAY'S SCRIPTURE: 2 Corinthians 10:5

Dr. Ronald Dworkin, conveyed a story some years ago of a patient's distress over her husband's handling of the family finances. Wanting to keep the books, but fearing confronting her husband might hurt his feelings, she sought medical intervention to ease her troubled mind. She began to feel better, but consequently, the woman's husband led the family into financial ruin.

Jesus said, "do not worry" (Luke 12:22). When He said these words, His audience heard, "do not have a divided mind...do not be anxious, troubled with cares, take thought beforehand, be drawn in different directions." The Anglicized word means, "to choke or strangle." Jesus said the Word in men's hearts can be choked out by cares (Luke 8:14). Literally we are not to cut our minds into pieces; but we do when we worry. We choke our hearts, we strangle our self. Jesus offered the alternative with the word, "Consider." The audience heard, "attentively fix one's eyes or mind upon." The reason Jesus said, "do not worry" is because of the temptation and possibility to worry or be anxious. Thus Jesus instructs a better way for us. When worry has been brought into subjection, and every thought captive for Christ, a plan is put in place (2 Corinthians 10:5).

This is the power of the mind—not that it is divided or susceptible to anxiety or burden, but that each thought can be brought captive, literally imprisoning the thoughts which are imprisoning our hearts, and presenting them as captive to Jesus Christ. While our feelings may be real in every way, the thoughts driving those feelings may be distorted or exaggerated. Bringing our thoughts into captivity is intentionally measuring, weighing, and examining the truth, and value of our thoughts toward self, circumstances, and others through the lens of scripture.

In all our ways of life and living, thinking and feeling, the Lord's truth in the face of all untruths, even the ones we tell our selves, must be remembered, "he who is in you is greater than he who is in the world" (1 John 4:4).

Today, I will... Create a list of things I for which I feel anxiety. I'll use this list to compare what is in my control and what is out of my control. For those things out of my control, I will acknowledge what's out of my control, and fix my mind's eye upon what I can control.

Dealing with Busy-ness

DOUG BURLESON

BUSY ISN'T ALWAYS BEST

TODAY'S SCRIPTURE: Ecclesiastes 2:11; Romans 12:2

It is not a sin to be busy, but busyness has destroyed the faith of many Christians. Workaholism can become an idol that distracts Christians from doing the first things first. Busyness can become a means of being, "putting me before He." One of Satan's lies is that the busier a person becomes the important they are, yet a life that is too full can be a warning that a person has built an idol to themselves, their possessions, or their career. Things that we are busy doing may not be the best things.

King Solomon had been busy in Jerusalem. Because of his lack of faith, he turned away from God and busied himself with treaties, military strength, and romantic/political interests. The Lord became angry with Solomon because of his poor choices (1 Kings 11:1-9). In Ecclesiastes 2:11 a reflective Solomon was taking inventory of the things that brought purpose to his life under the sun when he wrote, "Then I considered all that my hands had done and the toil that I had expended in doing it, and behold, all was vanity and a striving after wind, and there was nothing to be gained under the sun." While Solomon was speaking of what happens when a person seeks to find worth in life without God, the reality is that being busy can leave a person empty and zapped of any spiritual storage.

Perhaps this is part of the reason the apostle Paul challenged his readers to avoid conformity with the world instead seeking transformation so that they could discern the will of God (Romans 12:2). By not being conformed to the world, Christians can truly know "what is good and acceptable and perfect." Everyone is busy, but as we sing "We'll Work 'til Jesus Comes" let us ask if we are investing ourselves in the best work? Let us sit with Mary at the feet of Jesus when many Christians act like Martha (Luke 10:39-40). What is the most important work? Are we doing the first things first?

Today, I will... survey my priorities for the purpose of making sure I have not built an idol, falling into using the excuse of busyness to avoid doing the work God really desires.

RETREATING TO REST

TODAY'S SCRIPTURE: Exodus 20:8-11; Mark 6:31

Even in the seven days of creation God was already setting an example for His people (Genesis 2:1-3). Why did God rest on the seventh day of creation? He did not take a nap or make time to relax. The omnipotent God of creation does not need to rest. God rested as an example for His people. Holy people should take notice of the inaction of the Holy God on that day of rest.

Later when Moses stood before the assembly of Israel and described the laws of God as summarized in ten commands, he said, "Remember the Sabbath day, to keep it holy. Six days you shall labor, and do all your work, but the seventh day is a Sabbath to the Lord your God [...] For in six days the Lord made heaven and earth, the sea, and all that is in them, and rested on the seventh day" (Exodus 20:8-11). Later Moses repeated these sentiments adding that the purpose of this day of rest was for the people to "remember that you were a slave in the land of Egypt, and that the Lord your God brought you out from there with a mighty hand and an outstretched arm" (Deuteronomy 5:12-16).

Sadly in Jesus' world many Jews forgot the Sabbath principle out of a concern to keep Sabbath tradition. As Jesus challenged these traditions He reminded His hearers that the Sabbath was made for man and not man for the Sabbath (Mark 2:27-28). While some might argue over the specifics of what the Sabbath principle ought to look like for Christians, the point Jesus was making was that God's people need to take time to not only rest, but to reflect on and remember God's blessings. Jesus protected His disciples knowing that it wasn't good to be so busy that they did not have time to eat or think (Mark 6:31). Jesus invited His disciples to "come away by yourselves to a desolate place and rest for a while" in one of the busiest stretches of His public ministry. While many may strive to wear themselves out in service to the Lord, there is also something to be said for being good stewards of our time and health. Be intentional about living out the Sabbath principle. Take time to be holy, which means that we will first take the time.

Today, I will... take a deep breath and remember God's goodness in the stillness of thirty minutes. I will write, reflect, and pray focusing exclusively on what God has done for me.

MAKE THE TIME TO HELP

TODAY'S SCRIPTURE: Psalm 1:1-2; Luke 10:38-42

Robert Frost was not the first to write about two roads diverging from one another. In Psalm 1, readers are confronted by the reality that we have a choice to make between the road of righteousness and the wicked way. The righteous path involves meditating on the law of God day and night, while yielding fruit in its appropriate season (Psalm 1:2-3).

We see an example of such God-centered fruit coming to fruition in the Parable of the Good Samaritan. In answering the lawyer's question, "Who is my neighbor?" (Luke 10:29), Jesus spoke of the choices three men made on the road from Jerusalem to Jericho. A traveller who had been stripped, beaten, and left for dead by robbers provided an opportunity for someone to take the time to show the love of God. We are not told why the priest and the Levi "passed by on the other side" (vv. 31-32), but I suspect at least one of the reasons is that they thought they were too busy. After all there are only 86,400 seconds in a day and there was important work to be done! One of the most endearing qualities of the Samaritan, who did stop to help, was the time he took in the situation. Luke describes how he bound up the traveler's wounds, poured oil and wine on him, set him on his own animal, spent the night caring for him, and asked the innkeeper the next day to provide further care (vv. 33-34). The one who proved to be a neighbor was the one who took the time to do the right thing.

Sometimes good seed falls among thorns. Jesus warns that thorns cause worries, riches, and pleasures of this life to choke out good growth in the heart of a disciple (Luke 8:14). Renouncing materialism and focusing on the things of God can help God's people to shape our thinking to reflect God's priorities.

Today, I will... consider ways to use my time to invest myself in a kind of ministry that I typically do not participate in for the purpose of seeing how God's work can be done in spaces and times that I sometimes overlook.

LET GO AND LET GOD

TODAY'S SCRIPTURE: Exodus 18; Philippians 4:6-7

Jethro was certainly proud of how the Lord had blessed Moses and the people of Israel when he accompanied Zipporah, Ephraim, and Manasseh as they journeyed towards a sweet reunion at the mountain of God (Exodus 18:1-9). It did not take long for Moses' father-in-law to realize Moses was overworked and to ask two important questions, "What is this that you are doing for the people? Why do you sit alone, and all the people stand around you from morning to evening?" (v. 14) He then added a warning that many Christians need to hear, "What you are doing is not good [...] the thing is too heavy for you. You are not able to do it alone" (vv. 17-18). Jethro's reproof and the plan he proposed helped to rescue Moses from real difficulty. Even the wise prophet and judge would certainly have been burned out and used up if he had continued down that path. Jethro reminded him that he needed to share the work, delegate jobs to responsible men, and to trust in God for strength.

Years later a persecuted apostle sent some jail mail to his Macedonian brethren in Philippi. As he expressed gratitude for their generosity, Paul wrote, "Do not be anxious about anything, but in everything by prayer and supplication with thanksgiving let your requests be made known to God. And the peace of God which surpasses all understanding, will guard your hearts and your minds in Christ Jesus" (Philippians 4:6-7). How could a man who had been wrongly accused, imprisoned, and now sat in Rome awaiting trial speak with such assurance about God's peace? He knew that while there is a season for everything (Ecclesiastes 3:1-8), God's peaceful presence is greater than any season. God is greater than any work or burden. If we trust God like Moses or Paul surely we can feel relief even today by trusting in God enough to let go of some of the burden.

Today, I will... trust that my brothers and sisters will labor beside me in the kingdom, while relying on the Savior who is the only One capable of bearing the burdens that I sometimes erroneously seek to bear.

FRIDAY

SCRIPTURE SAYS BEING SLOW IS A GOOD THING

TODAY'S SCRIPTURE: Psalm 46:10; James 1:19-20

We generally do not like the word slow. When we are on the road, in the kitchen, waiting on something to download, or watching our favorite athletes play, the word SLOW is a considered a bad word.

Yet, to my knowledge, the word slow is only used twice with a negative connotation in Scripture. In Exodus 4:10 Moses made excuses before God saying that he was "slow of speech and of tongue." In Luke 24:25 Jesus rebuked the two men walking with Him on the road to Emmaus for being "slow of heart to believe" (Luke 24:25).

In contrast to these two negative examples consider the majority view of slowness as a good thing in Scripture. Nine times in the Old Testament God is described as being "slow to anger" (Exodus 34:6; Numbers 14:18; Nehemiah 9:17; Psalms 86:15; 103:8; 145:8; Joel 2:13; Jonah 4:2; Nahum 1:3). As those who deserve God's wrath aren't we thankful that God takes it slow in this regard? Furthermore God is not slow concerning His promises (2 Peter 3:9). God's people are also commended when being slow to anger or slow in their reactions (Proverbs 14:29; 15:18; 16:32; 19:11). It is in this same line of thinking that James challenges us, "Let every person be quick to hear, slow to speak, slow to anger; for the anger of man does not produce the righteousness of God" (James 1:19-20).

Scripture invites us to slow down. Christians must be still long enough to contemplate God's goodness. God can be honored when we take it slow. Let us accept His challenge to take the time to meditate on Him and respond with love by taking the time to be still and know that He is God (Psalm 46:10).

Today, I will... give a little time and space, not speaking rashly, lashing out in the heat of the moment, or returning fire. I will take the slow path to making peace (Matthew 5:9).

Dealing with Loneliness

JON PODEIN

MY GOD, MY GOD!

TODAY'S SCRIPTURE: Matthew 26:26-44

In the story by Hans Christian Anderson, "The Ugly Duckling," one of the birds perceived that he was different from the other birds and farm animals and suffered tremendous abuse because of this. He ventures away from place to place looking for creatures with whom he belongs. Along the way, he decides to end it all until he eventually finds where he belonged and who he truly was. The "ugly duckling's" struggle was more than self-esteem challenges or even social acceptance...it was loneliness!

We all long for happiness. But to be happy, we need intimate bonds to connect with and a common obstacle along that path is loneliness. Yet here's the interesting thing ... none of us are immune to its reach. A recent Gallop poll showed that over 1/3 of Americans suffer from loneliness and it is a determining factor in many mental health challenges. And yet, though many will admit when they suffer with different addictions, often many people struggle admitting they are sometimes lonely.

Even Jesus had to face loneliness in his life. As He approached the end, Jesus took His closest friends with Him to watch while He went to pray. Each time He returned to find them sleeping and even expressed His frustration when He asked, "Could you not watch with me one hour?" (Matthew 26:40). This was more than a question of frustration; it was an expression of loneliness that would be fully realized when He cried out, "My God, My God, why have you forsaken me?" (Matthew 27:46).

If you are in a season of loneliness, take heart, you are not different, you are not strange, and you are not alone. As part of God's family, we have a network of brothers and sisters that are more than faces we see within a church building. So, if you are one that is not in a season of loneliness, look for those that are and "love one another with brotherly affection. Outdo one another in showing honor" (Romans 12:10).

Today, I will... look for those that are experiencing loneliness and strive to show them that they are not alone, but part of a family that rejoices with those that rejoice and weeps with those that weep!

BUT IT'S NOT MY FAULT!

TODAY'S SCRIPTURE: Psalm 142

Psychologist tell us that there are two types of loneliness. One is the loneliness of spirit where even in a crowded room, one can feel alone. The other is loneliness of isolation. This comes when there is a separation from the ones we love, whether because of a loss from death, a dissolving of a marriage, an empty nest when a child goes to college, or even a move to a new location. Whatever we think of loneliness, there are times when it affects us, not as a result of something we have done, but because of outside influences that can cut us deep emotionally.

When David began to pen Psalm 142, he had come to pretty low point in his life. He had come to the cave of Adullam in 1 Samuel 22 as he was fleeing for his life. King Saul had determined that he was the number one enemy. Then Jonathan, David's best friend and son to King Saul was now separated from David because of Saul's hatred for David, and eventually David ran into enemy territory out of desperation. It was under these conditions that David cried out, "... there is none who takes notice of me" (Psalm 142:4). David, the man after God's own heart, was in a season of loneliness, not by his doing, but because of others.

Are you in a cave? Have things happened to you that brought upon a season of loneliness in your life? Do you feel helpless and overwhelmed because of grief or anxiety because of this time of loneliness? Good news... God is the one who hears every cry and every whisper. As David realized, "The righteous will surround me, for You will deal bountifully with me" (Psalm 142:7).

Today, I will... look beyond my circumstances and cry out to the One that gives everything that is sufficient for you.

DON'T LET YOUR MIND PLAY TRICKS!

TODAY'S SCRIPTURE: 1 Kings 18:1-19:18

When I was a kid, my parents and I would sometimes go and visit my aunt and uncle in Valdosta, Georgia. I always enjoyed going there for a visit because they had a huge yard. To a 7-year-old, it felt like miles of land to play and explore. As I got older, and a little more daring, I decided to take a bike around their neighborhood and explore the "greater territory." On one occasion, I found myself lost. Fear started to set in as I was alone and in a strange, unfamiliar place. As the minutes, which felt like hours, passed, I began to think that I would be forever lost and never see my family again. Even though I was a couple of streets over and had houses all around, I was losing all hope of being found again.

After Elijah faced the prophets of Baal on Mount Carmel in 1 Kings 18, he finds himself on the run for his life from Jezebel and her order to hunt him down. The fear for his life, with the encompassing dread of loneliness, caused Elijah to fall into a deep depression and even to plead for God to take his life. All Elijah could see in his mind was that he was alone, fighting a battle by himself. It wasn't until God cleared his thoughts and explained that there were "seven thousand in Israel, all the knees that have not bowed to Baal" (1 Kings 19:18) that Elijah was able to get over his loneliness.

Research has shown that loneliness is purely subjective and depends on how much a person feels connected socially and emotionally to those around them. Psychologist have also found that people in a state of loneliness struggle to get out of that stage because their minds and thoughts don't allow them to break the cycle of loneliness. This is one reason Paul encourages us to think on the things that are honorable, just, pure, lovely, commendable, excellent, and worthy of praise (Philippians 4:8).

Today, I will... not allow my mind to play tricks on me and keep me enslaved to a stage of loneliness, but rather I will focus on the things that are positive and worthy of praise.

IT'S EVIL, BUT GOD MEANT IT FOR GOOD

TODAY'S SCRIPTURE: Genesis 50:15-21

I can't imagine what it must have felt like to be 17 years old and have your family turn against you. Feeling like an orphan in a strange land must be the epitome of loneliness and yet, that is where Joseph finds himself in Genesis 37. For the next 33 or so years, Joseph works for Potiphar only later to be jailed for a false accusation, indentured into service for Pharaoh, and eventually works his way up to second in command of all of Egypt as they prepared for the coming famine.

I have often wondered, did Joseph, during this time of loneliness and rejection, ever question God as to the "why" he was going through this for such a long time? Once he was reconciled to his family during the famine, he came to an understanding that though they meant evil against Joseph, "God meant it for good, to bring it about that many people should be kept alive" (Genesis 50:20).

Can loneliness be a good thing? Loneliness isn't something that many people want to experience. It can make everything in your world feel small and fragile. Loneliness can cause your food to taste bland, your nights to be sleepless, pondering why you are in this lonely phase, and make every day feel longer and longer. But loneliness doesn't always have to be a bad thing if you are comfortable with yourself and focus on positive things that can sometimes be overlooked because of our busy lives. We can:

· Remind ourselves of how blessed we are.
· Open our creative side.
· Force ourselves to open up and meet new people.
· Inspire ourselves to become more active for the Lord and His Kingdom
· Spend time in quiet meditation and prayer with the Lord.

The possibilities are abundant. How can you use loneliness for good?

Today, I will...not allow my circumstances to control my happiness. Even in times of loneliness, I will use them for God and to His glory.

WHAT CAN I DO TO HELP?

TODAY'S SCRIPTURE: 1 Thessalonians 3

Loneliness is an affliction that can often hide itself. We can incorrectly assume that loneliness must deal with being physically alone. However, being surrounded by friends, coworkers, and even church members can leave one feeling the pangs of loneliness deep inside. There are often subtle hints that a friend or loved one is going through these moments, and it is in these situations, that Christians rise to the challenge and encourage those around us experiencing loneliness.

But what can I really do to help someone struggling with loneliness? Becoming aware that someone is lonely is one thing, figuring out how to encourage someone... that can become confusing. When Paul faced great affliction and had to leave Thessalonica because of the Jews, he reached out to the church there, not for money or even people to journey with him. Instead he reached out to learn about their faith (1 Thessalonians 3:5). It was the good news that they had stayed faithful in the presence of trouble that encouraged Paul to continue his journey despite the loneliness he was facing.

Jesus understood that His disciples would need this same encouragement as his death approached. He encouraged them to not let their "hearts be troubled" (John 14:1). He knew that the loneliness they were about to encounter was going to challenge them emotionally and challenge their faith in God. "I will come again and will take you to myself" (John 14:3) must have been the most calming promise they could have received that night.

Look for ways to encourage someone today. It could be something small... often it is the small things that mean more than the biggest gift in the world. Perhaps it's just an ear to listen that would show interest in what they are saying. Or it could just be an optimistic gesture that shows them that you support them and that they are not alone in this world.

Today, I will... look for someone that is dealing with loneliness and get to know them better and to pray for them each day.

Dealing with Fear

ROBERT DODSON

YOU CAN HAVE CONFIDENCE IN GOD

TODAY'S SCRIPTURE: Philippians 1:19-20

How many times have you become frightened because of circumstances in your life? Have they caused you to doubt God? Have you wondered if God could really help you out?

The apostle Paul teaches us to have confidence in God no matter what our situation. He wrote,

"for I know that through your prayers and the help of the Spirit of Jesus Christ this will turn out for my deliverance, as it is my eager expectation and hope that I will not be at all ashamed, but that with full courage now as always Christ will be honored in my body, whether by life or by death" (Philippians 1:19-20).

Though he was under guard in Rome and did not know whether he would live or die, still Paul was confident that God would deliver him from shame and use him to magnify Christ.

What was it that gave Paul such confidence in God?

Paul was confident because he knew the Philippians were praying for him and he knew that God listens to prayer.

He knew that he had received from God the gift of the Holy Spirit when he became a Christian and that He would provide all that he would ever need to accomplish God's purposes in his life.

He had an "eager expectation and hope". This "eager expectation" was a compound word that means to stretch the neck. Like a chick stretching its neck eagerly awaiting nourishment from its mother, Paul was confident in God's ability to deliver him.

These three things gave Paul "all boldness." It gave him the power, strength and courage to endure. The same God who sustained him when he was flogged five times by the Jews and the same God who helped him survive three shipwrecks would continue to embolden him in the present situation.

Today, I will...show my confidence in God to deal with every circumstance of life and death so that all can know that He will not fail us.

WHERE WAS GOD?

TODAY'S SCRIPTURE: Acts 17:27

Hurricane winds hit the Gulf Coast. People died. Many were injured. Homes and businesses were destroyed.

We ask, "Where was God?"

Some say that He doesn't exist, but what happened in the Gulf does not change the fact that there is a God. God is the only logical, reasonable explanation for the existence of our universe.

Some wonder how He could let these things happen, but this does not change the fact that God is in control of all things. Children do not always understand what happens under the control of their parents, but it doesn't mean their parents are not in control. Just because we don't understand what happens under God's control does not mean that He is not in control.

Some doubt His love for us, but no matter what, we can know that He loves us. He proved that once and for all in the giving of His Son, Jesus Christ. We have no reason to ever doubt how much He loves us.

So, where was God? He was in the same place that He has always been, the same place He was when He made this world for us, the same place He was every other time we asked, "Why?" The same place He was when Jesus died for our sins upon the cruel cross of Calvary, the same place He will always be.

God promises, "'I will never leave you nor forsake you.' So we can confidently say, 'The Lord is my helper; I will not fear; what can man do to me?'" (Hebrews 13:5-6).

You are never alone. You are not on your own. He is always with you. Even for those who don't know the Lord, He is right there for them "that they should seek God, and perhaps feel their way toward him and find him. Yet he is actually not far from each one of us" (Acts 17:27).

Today, I will...not let the situation and circumstances of my life dictate my faith in God but trust that He is always there for me.

DON'T BE SCARED!

TODAY'S SCRIPTURE: Isaiah 41:10

We all get scared. Maybe it's a terrible weather event. Or, it could be you have lost your job and don't know what to do. Perhaps, you just found out you have cancer. The many violent acts of terrorism around the world and here in America are very scary, too.

When Isaiah prophesied, it was a scary time for Israel. Many had forsaken God's law. There was much injustice in the land. They suffered famine, pestilence, and war. Their future was dark. It is then that Isaiah gave these very encouraging words from the Lord: "fear not, for I am with you; be not dismayed, for I am your God; I will strengthen you, I will help you, I will uphold you with my righteous right hand" (Isaiah 41:10).

Here's why we don't have to be scared!

God is with us. We are not alone.

God is our God. He is on our side. He will fight for us. He will protect us. He loves us. He cares for us.

God will strengthen us. We are scared because the fears we face look very powerful, but God is stronger. He is greater. He will strengthen us in our weakness so that we are able to overcome our fears.

God will help us. Unable to deal with our fears alone, He stands by us to share the burden and help carry the load that would destroy our confidence. So, with God's help we are able to face our fears with courage.

God will uphold us. Even when we are ready to give up and lay down in defeat, He is there for us to support us. When we are falling, He is powerful to stand us back up again.

Yes, our fears are real, but so is God. So, don't be scared.

Today, I will...thank God for being there for me and look to Him for the courage to overcome all my fears.

HE HOLDS THE FUTURE IN HIS HANDS

TODAY'S SCRIPTURE: Revelation 5:1-5

When Christians were being severely persecuted for their faith, Jesus gave them a message of comfort and hope.

"Then I saw in the right hand of him who was seated on the throne a scroll written within and on the back, sealed with seven seals. 2 And I saw a mighty angel proclaiming with a loud voice, 'Who is worthy to open the scroll and break its seals?' And no one in heaven or on earth or under the earth was able to open the scroll or to look into it, and I began to weep loudly because no one was found worthy to open the scroll or to look into it. And one of the elders said to me, 'Weep no more; behold, the Lion of the tribe of Judah, the Root of David, has conquered, so that he can open the scroll and its seven seals'" (Revelation 5:1-5).

The One sitting on the throne is God. The right hand speaks of strength. The scroll written on both sides represents all that is to happen in the future. God holds the future in His strong hand.

The seals kept the scroll hidden so no one could see into the future. The Lion who prevailed to open the scroll is Jesus Christ. He can make known what the future holds. Through His death for our sins and the power of His resurrection He has overcome Satan, sin and death so that the faithful have assurance of a victorious future.

Knowing who holds the future in His hands, and its glorious outcome, we have no need to fear. We may be at peace and rest no matter what may come our way because we have hope of eternal life.

Such faith will courageously live for God. It will show and tell others that there is a powerful, loving Savior who is the only way for us all to be delivered from this world of sin and death.

Today, I will...boldly praise the Lord before all people.

IT WILL ALL WORK OUT

TODAY'S SCRIPTURE: Romans 8:28

In March 2020, the world was attacked by one of the worse pandemics in history. Many died of the coronavirus and even more were hospitalized. Workers lost their jobs and owners their businesses. Schools and churches closed their doors. People were scared.

I'll tell you like I used to tell my kids, "It will all work out." We don't have to fear because God will work it all out for our good.

"And we know that for those who love God all things work together for good, for those who are called according to his purpose" (Romans 8:28).

Paul says, "we know". We don't have to wonder or doubt, there is no uncertainty in those words. Those are words of faith and hope.

Paul says, "all things work together." It doesn't matter what happens, even the coronavirus, even a broken economy, even sickness and death.

Paul says it all works together "for good." It is often in the scariest times that people will come to Christ, draw closer to God, reach out to help one another, spend time together as a family, and be reminded of the important things that really matter. Amidst all the bad news out there, there are good stories of real love, kindness, and unselfish service.

Paul says, "for those who love God...for those who are called according to his purpose." That's us, Christians. It's our promise and it's His purpose. Instead of recoiling in fear, be encouraged by the good that God has done, is doing and will do for us.

Jeremiah 29:11 "For I know the plans I have for you, declares the Lord, plans for welfare and not for evil, to give you a future and a hope."

Without God there is no future and there is no hope, but because of Him we can rest assured even in the worst of times. With God in your corner you don't have to fear anyone or anything.

Today, I will...trust the Lord with everyone and everything knowing that the future is in His hands.

Dealing with Worry

J.J. HENDRIX

ALWAYS GET BACK UP

TODAY'S SCRIPTURE: 2 Timothy 4:7

Boxer Mike Tyson once said, "Everyone has a plan until you get punched in the mouth." Sometimes worry can be the same way. We want to be committed to casting our burdens on the Lord (Psalm 55:22). We want to show the world that worry doesn't bother us, yet it can hit you like a punch to the face. The question becomes, will you get up?

Guglielmo Papaleo, better known to boxing fans as Willie Pep, was a world champion pugilist who went on a 5-year winning streak. Remarkably, during that stretch, he was involved in a plane crash and continued to fight and win. That streak stopped on October 29, 1948 when Willie Pep met a grisly defeat at the hands of Sandy Saddler. This wasn't just any defeat. This was a humiliation. Pep came into the fight with a record of 134-1-1 as the Featherweight Champion. The world believed that Willie Pep would make short work of Sandy Saddle, and the world was wrong. Saddler knocked the champion down four times in route to a fourth-round victory, the first knock out loss in Pep's career.

What did Willie Pep do? Give up? No. Less than six months later, Willie Pep recaptured the world championship from Sandy Saddler by judges' decision.

Sometimes we can be Willie Pep, can't we? Sometimes we cast our burdens where they belong and serve God to the best of our ability then, out of nowhere, worry hits. The ultimate underdog, worry, knocks us to the mat. What we do next is important.

Paul stated in 2 Timothy 4:7, "I have fought the good fight, I have finished the race, I have kept the faith." What had Paul endured? We need to look at 2 Corinthians 11. He faced beatings, stonings, hunger, and many dangers. He endured. Paul, when hit hard, got back to his feet.

Get back up. Always get back up.

Today, I will...understand that sometimes worry overtakes me. I cannot give up. I can never give up. When knocked down, I will get back to my spiritual feet and living for Jesus.

IMAGINE YOU ARE NEHEMIAH

TODAY'S SCRIPTURE: Nehemiah 1:4

Imagine you are Nehemiah.

Imagine you are Nehemiah and serving a ruler. Nehemiah was the cupbearer for the king. This position was held by an official that the king trusted. The cupbearer would test the drink to ensure that the drink was not poisoned. While this job was dangerous, the job also was beneficial, not only financially, but because of the proximity to the king.

In the first few verses of his book, Nehemiah hears news about the walls of Jerusalem being ruined and how the gates were destroyed by fire. The news hit Nehemiah hard. He wrote, "As soon as I heard these words I sat down and wept and mourned for days, and I continued fasting and praying before the God of heaven" (Nehemiah 1:4).

When faced with disastrous news, sometimes we do not respond in the way we ought. Worry causes people, Christians included, to sometimes do things they would not do. Worry will cause some to seek advice from places advice shouldn't be sought. Worry can cause some to blame God. Many times worry leads to anger, which is taken out on someone else. Still others internalize their worry causing other health problems. No matter the news, the first place we should go is to God in prayer.

We should strive to be like Nehemiah when we hear news that worries us. Seek God in prayer.

After Nehemiah prayed, something wonderful happened. The king saw something was wrong and asked what could be done. He then allowed Nehemiah to return to Jerusalem and rebuild the walls he was so concerned about.

Again, imagine you are Nehemiah.

Imagine you are Nehemiah after he heard the negative news and after he prayed to God. He found himself on a journey to give God glory. What an incredible example to follow!

Today, I will...make sure my first action when faced with worry is to seek God in prayer.

LEAVING SOMETHING VALUABLE

TODAY'S SCRIPTURE: James 1:2-4

Many people are concerned about the legacy they will leave behind. Some view that importance in the form of money while others hold accolades in high regard. No matter the motive, people are concerned about what people will think of them after they are gone. They are concerned about what they will leave for those they love after taking their final breath, be it money or acclaim. This worry drives people to work longer hours, take jobs they do not like, or shoot for objectives that will make no difference in eternity.

What if, instead of worrying about those things, we considered the spiritual legacy we are leaving behind. Let us devote our lives to leaving a legacy of a Christian who faced adversity and stayed faithful to God. Everyone faces trials; what makes a Christian different is how we persevere through them while staying committed to the Lord.

The Holy Spirit inspired James to write, "Count it all joy, my brothers, when you meet trials of various kinds, for you know that the testing of your faith produces steadfastness. And let steadfastness have its full effect, that you may be perfect and complete, lacking in nothing" (James 1:2-4).

When we read "count it all joy", that doesn't mean that during sad times we have to click our heels and go, "Yippeee!" Christians are allowed to mourn just as Christians are allowed to be happy! Even in the difficult times, we can take joy in God our Father, that no matter what trial we endure, that He is faithful to us.

Let's keep our focus on what truly matters, keeping God first even in the face of adversity. Our friends, family, coworkers, and fellow Christians will see our resolve and remember it for many years after we have gone on to our eternal reward.

Today, I will...pray that when I face a trial of any kind, that I will keep God first and foremost in my life and actions. This will not only give me peace but will leave a lasting legacy for those around me.

LEARNING TO SUCCEED THROUGH DIFFICULT SITUATIONS

TODAY'S SCRIPTURE: Lamentations 3:27

Taking up a hobby can be a lot of fun, but also a great source of frustration. As we learn something new, we make many mistakes trying to master our new craft. Persevering through all those mistakes can lead to proficiency and enjoyment. Sometimes, when met with an obstacle that we do not know how to overcome, we reach out to someone who is learned in the field. Often they will say they made the same mistakes and walk you through the process, or even give you advice to avoid future mishaps. Your perseverance and the advice from their previous difficulties can help bring success.

There comes a time when the frustration of a new hobby can lead to pondering if quitting and finding something new would be easier. If it is something we really want to learn, we ditch the negativity and continue striving for success.

What if we did this in our spiritual walk, too?

When you consider your life, think about the hard times and how you stayed faithful to God. Those challenges have made you more valuable to the Kingdom as you are able to give the advice that you needed to others dealing with similar trials.

The prophet writes in Lamentations 3:25-27, "The Lord is good to those who wait for him, to those who seek him. It is good that the one should wait quietly for the salvation of the Lord. It is good for a man that he bear the yoke in his youth."

The writer of Lamentations talks about the benefit of dedication to God early in life. In the face of adversity, when we put on the yoke of God and continue to live, we learn humility, dedication, and perseverance.

Today, I will...pray for strength in the face of worry. I will take the yoke of God upon myself and bear it proudly into the future.

A SMOOTH SEA NEVER MADE A SKILLED SAILOR

TODAY'S SCRIPTURE: Galatians 6:2

When we deal with worry, we can feel like a ship in the midst of a massive storm. US President Franklin D. Roosevelt once said, "A smooth sea never made a skilled sailor." A simple, but profound, saying. Sometimes we think we cannot handle what is going on around us. In times of trial, seek those who have weathered life's storms. Seek those who have been through spiritual battles and stayed faithful to God. We seek the counsel of those who experienced the trials we are enduring or have years of dedicated Bible study who can share with us God's Word in continuing to be faithful.

Paul wrote, "Bear one another's burdens, and so fulfill the law of Christ" (Galatians 6:2).

Although each of us will stand before God individually on the day of judgment, Christianity is very much a team effort. When you are worried, those emotions can make you feel isolated. Rest assured that there are people you can lean on who can help you with your burden. The first step is letting the Christians around you know you are struggling. While some may view that as scary, it is better to face the storm with people helping you and cheering you on to spiritual success.

As you mature in your Christian faith, you will find that people will begin to seek you out for advice because of the storms you have endured. You will be able to help people because of the difficulties you have faced. Instead of worrying, think about how these things will make you stronger for Him. The choppy waters of life will help you be a skilled sailor, equipped to help others dealing with spiritual storms.

Today, I will...to not be bitter about the trials I have endured but look for opportunities to help others dealing with the storms that I have weathered.

Dealing with Envy

KEITH HARRIS

MAKING BONES ROT

TODAY'S SCRIPTURE: Proverbs 14:30

It is common knowledge that fishermen know that one never needs a top for crab baskets. If one of the crabs starts to climb up the side of the basket, the other crabs will reach up and pull it back down. As strange as this sounds, I am afraid we can relate more than we care to admit. Envy and jealousy seem to be part of our human nature, or more accurately, our fallen human nature.

Merriam-Webster defines envy as "painful or resentful awareness of an advantage enjoyed by another joined with a desire to possess the same advantage." The Oxford Dictionary explains that envy is "a feeling of discontented or resentful longing aroused by someone else's possessions, qualities, or luck." Certainly, we can all relate to the feeling of envy or jealousy. The truth is we have all faced the challenge of seeing the fortunes of others and desiring them for ourselves.

J. I. Packer, in his book, Knowing God, pointed out that "Envy is one of the most cancerous and soul-destroying vices there is...It is terribly potent, for it feeds and is fed by, the taproot of our fallen nature." Envy and jealousy are not new to humanity. As a matter of fact, early in the book of Genesis we see envy and its destructive end.

Envy often destroys relationships and hinders our spiritual growth. The destructive reality of envy and jealousy are made clear in Proverbs 14:30, "A tranquil heart gives life to the flesh, but envy makes the bones rot." Envy makes bones rot. This is an interesting statement that speaks to the negative power of envy. It is the skeleton that lasts for many, many years. Think of the bones that have been discovered through the work of archaeologists. Some bone discoveries have dated back thousands of years, with minimal decay. Yet, the wisdom of Proverbs says "envy makes the bones rot." We must recognize the true nature of envy, guarding against this destructive sin.

Today, I will...ask God to remind me of the destructiveness of envy.

CAIN & ABEL

TODAY'S SCRIPTURE: Genesis 4:1-16

Early in the history of humanity, envy reared its ugly head. Interestingly enough, the first instance of envy did not involve material possessions, but rather spiritual sacrifices made to God. Adam and Eve were blessed with their first son, Cain, followed by their second son, Abel. As they grew, Cain became a worker of the ground, while Abel was a shepherd. The Bible says, "In the course of time Cain brought to the LORD an offering of the fruit of the ground, and Abel also brought of the firstborn of his flock and of their fat portions" (Genesis 4:3-4a).

The offering itself caused no issues between these brothers. Both brothers made a conscious decision to present their offering to God. The problem arose when God regarded one over the other. The Bible goes on to explain, "the LORD had regard for Abel and his offering, but for Cain and his offering he had no regard. So Cain was very angry, and his face fell" (Genesis 4:4b-5). God questioned Cain concerning his anger and warned Cain that he must work to control the subtle pull of sin that was "crouching at the door" (Genesis 4:7). Cain, failing to do what God instructed, rose up against his brother and murdered him. As a result, Cain would be a fugitive and wanderer. The ground that once produced so plentifully would no longer yield to Cain its strength.

Envy in the spiritual sense is being jealous of the blessings God has given to someone else. Certainly, envy is seen in the story of Cain and Abel. God had regard for Abel and his offering but not for Cain. This angered Cain. The Hebrew word used in Genesis 4:5 for anger means to blaze up with anger, zeal, or jealousy. Cain was jealous and burned with envy because his brother's sacrifice was accepted and his was not. Do we ever feel the same? Are we ever jealous of the blessings God gives to others?

Today, I will...ask God to rid my heart of spiritual envy and jealousy.

JOSEPH & HIS BROTHERS

TODAY'S SCRIPTURE: Genesis 37:12-36

Perhaps one of the most well-known stories in the Bible is the story of Joseph and his coat of many colors. Granted, many know it better by its stage name, "Joseph and the Amazing Technicolor Dreamcoat." While that portrayal doesn't quite fit the story revealed in the pages of Scripture, the feelings and sentiment on the part of the brothers is rather accurate.

Joseph, described as the son most loved by Jacob (Genesis 37:3), was given a robe of many colors by his father. No doubt the colorful robe attracted much attention. It is evident that Joseph's brothers were extremely jealous of Jacob's gift to their younger brother. To make matters worse, Joseph explained recent dreams he had to the whole family. These dreams seemed to suggest that Joseph would one day rule over his brothers. This added to their frustration and jealousy of Joseph.

While pasturing their flock in the fields of Dothan, Joseph's brothers saw him coming toward them while he was still far off, and they conspired against him. They stripped him of his colorful robe and threw him into a pit. As it happened, some Ishmaelites were traveling through from Gilead, and Joseph's brothers decided to sell Joseph to this caravan of traders for twenty shekels of silver. The brothers took Joseph's robe, dipped it in goat's blood, and presented it to their father saying that Joseph had been devoured by a fierce animal.

Envy and jealousy are powerful forces. They bring us to do and say things we would otherwise never do and say. Jealousy caused Joseph's brothers to want him dead. Jealousy caused them to ultimately sell Joseph and lie to their father concerning Joseph's whereabouts. Aristotle said, "Envy is pain at the good fortune of others." This is certainly evident in the actions of Joseph's brothers. They were hurt emotionally, envious and jealous of the good fortune of Joseph, both his colorful robe and his dreams.

Today, I will...ask God to help me overcome envious thoughts regarding God's blessings to others.

SAUL & DAVID

TODAY'S SCRIPTURE: 1 Samuel 18:6-16

It is no secret that, historically, kings desired to be praised and honored above all others. Many kings were ruthless in their treatment of any who dared regard others above the king. You can imagine how it must have made Saul feel when he and his army returned from defeating the Philistines. The Bible says, "As they were coming home, when David returned from striking down the Philistine, the women came out of all the cities of Israel, singing and dancing, to meet King Saul, with tambourines, with songs of joy, and with musical instruments. And the women sang to one another as they celebrated, 'Saul has struck down his thousands, and David his ten thousands'" (1 Samuel 18:6-7).

This is not the way it was supposed to be! These women should have been singing, "Saul has struck down his ten thousands, and David his thousands." It is not difficult to understand the feelings that Saul must have been experiencing. Why were they exalting David, this shepherd boy, over the king?

Saul was very angry, and this displeased him greatly. He feared the only thing remaining was for David to assume the throne. His anger, perhaps we should say his jealousy, drove Saul to seek to take David's life. As was noted above, this was the typical response of the king toward anyone by whom he felt threatened. So, this was not out of the norm. But we must acknowledge the catalysts for his actions. Anger. Pride. Envy. Jealousy.

Leslie Flynn once noted, "The envious man feels other's fortunes are his misfortunes; their profit, his loss; their blessing, his bane; their health, his illness; their promotion, his demotion; their success, his failure." Certainly, this is the way Saul felt about the situation. David's success, the praising of David by these women, created an envious spirit in Saul. Do we every feel a sense of jealousy and envy when we witness others being praised?

Today, I will...ask God to strengthen my resolve to push away envious, jealous feelings.

THE ULCER OF THE SOUL

TODAY'S SCRIPTURE: 2 Corinthians 10:12

Lloyd John Ogilvie said, "One of the major causes of stress is combative competition – more accurately, envy. Rooted in a lack of self-esteem, it grows in the soul-soil of comparisons and blossoms in noxious thorns of desire for what others have or achieve." We tend to look at those around us. The truth is we seldom ever just look. More times than not, we compare our life, our success, our possessions, with theirs. Sadly, it is not simply with material aspects of life that we compare but are guilty of comparing our spirituality as well. Paul wrote, "...when they measure themselves by one another and compare themselves with one another, they are without understanding" (2 Corinthians 10:12). Essentially, Paul is letting us know that it is not wise to compare. Comparison often leads to unhealthy thoughts and actions.

In his book, *The Winner Within*, the famous coach, Pat Riley, quoted John Dryden who described jealousy as being "the jaundice of the soul." Socrates said, "Envy is the ulcer of the soul." Envy and jealousy seem to take hold within us before we even realize it. Unfortunately, this can create a number of problems that can lead to damaged relationships and a weakened faith.

So, what can we do to help us overcome the destructiveness of envy and jealousy? First, we need to keep a watch on our feelings and own up to our envious thoughts. Second, we need to avoid making comparisons, and know that the success of others is not tied to our success or failure. Third, we need to look deeper than the surface level and remember how much God has blessed us. Finally, we need to be grateful for what God has given us.

An envious and jealous spirit is a dangerous thing. But with God's help, we can overcome its destructiveness. Thanks be to God who gives us strength through Jesus!

Today, I will...ask God to remind me of the blessings He has given me and will rejoice with others whom He has blessed.

Dealing with the Loss of a Child

LONNIE JONES

A PERSPECTIVE OF TIME

TODAY'S SCRIPTURE: Genesis 47:7-9; Romans 8:8

I always pictured Pharaoh as an old guy. I now see him as a contemporary to Joseph. After all who would have a much younger man as his chief advisor? It's just a thought and you don't have to agree with it. But when I picture Pharaoh as Joseph's age or younger then when he meets the old man that is Jacob his question is more poignant. Jacob enters the presence of Pharaoh and without apology lays a blessing on him. Senior citizens do whatever they want. The ruler of all Egypt asks, "How old are you?" To which Jacob replies, "The days of the years of my sojourn here (he acknowledges his status as a traveler or visitor to earth) are 130 years..." How shocked was Pharaoh to be in the presence of a man who had lived a century or more? Then he adds, "and they have not attained to the days of the years of the life of my fathers..." I'm a 130 but it's not near as long as my ancestors. I have a 130 years but it is short compared to...

That's the perspective of time. It is never enough time. When we lose a loved one it does not matter what the life span was: moments, hours, days, weeks, months, years, decades or a century our response to the death is usually, "This was too soon." Those thoughts are especially true when a child dies. This was too soon. This is not natural. Dying is as natural as being born. Everyone born on this planet is a temporary resident. That thought does not erase the pain, fear, and loss but it creates a perspective of time.

Compare the perspective of eternity with any pain, grief, loss, separation, or suffering and the idea that "this was too short" allows us to realize just how short any experience under the arch of time really is.

There is nothing right now that will ease the pain, heal the brokenness or fill the emptiness. The perspective of time is the assurance that when we compare the here with the hereafter, one will be very, very short indeed.

Today, I will...focus on the truth of eternity and set my hope in the everlasting rather than have my thoughts reside in the things that were never designed to be permanent. "For I consider that the sufferings of this present time are not worth comparing with the glory that is to be revealed to us (Romans 8:8).

THE RECIPE FOR HOPE

TODAY'S SCRIPTURE: Romans 5:1-5

Metal fatigue. Metal gets tired. Heat it and it will bend. Flex it often enough and it breaks. Rock climbing ropes are dynamic and catch falling climbers. Ropes are rated to catch only so many factor 1 falls. After that they fail. Steel cables rust and lose volume over time and have to be replaced.

Most everything in the known universe gets weaker under stress. Except you. Oh we get tired. Our bodies get sick. We die. All of us die. But our inner person, the real us is designed for eternity. We have this as a promised progression in scripture. Suffering produces endurance. Endurance produces character. Character produces hope. Hope is formed by the process of suffering, endurance, and character. Once we have suffered, endured, and been tempered, we then can rest in the hope that the process is repeatable. Hope formed in this way is based on what God has done in our lives up to the point of suffering. God's character in our past is indicative of His activity in the present and predictive for the future. We are reminded "hope does put us to shame, because God's love has been poured into our hearts through the Holy Spirit who has been given to us (Romans 5:5-6). The evidence of future hope is based in one single past act of God. "For while we were still weak, at the right time Christ died for the ungodly. For one will scarcely die for a righteous person-though perhaps for a good person one would dare to die-but God shows His love for us in that while we were still sinners, Christ died for us" (Romans 5:6-8).

So regardless of what suffering we have encountered or are enduring, the process is designed to build hope. God did not create the suffering, rather, He designed the process where suffering, any suffering, ultimately brings hope. The proof of hope is that He already declared how much He loves us by sending His Son.

Today, I will... Look for the character of God in what He has already done rather than what I am currently experiencing. I will not feel punished or rejected by what I am presently enduring but will seek hope that is rooted in the eternal love of God.

THE FOUR TASKS OF GRIEVING, Pt 1

TODAY'S SCRIPTURE: 2 Samuel 12:18-20

When life does not turn out like we expect, we suffer loss. Humans grieve all losses. There may be no greater loss than the bereavement-the robbing us- of an anticipated future of an entire life. It could be stated "The greater the disparity between the anticipated and the actual, the greater the grief." It is one thing to grieve a life that was and no longer is. That's what we experience when a lifelong friend or parent passes away. The loss of a child, especially a young child, is different. It is much different to grieve a life that could have been and was not. Grieving involves the four tasks outlined below.

Accepting the reality. Once we are faced with a loss we all have a sense of derealization. "This isn't happening." "I can't believe this has happened." There is time when one feels as if they are walking in a fog. After the funeral, after the crowds go away, after the cards stop coming, finality sets in. Often this is only after we experience all the "firsts." We go through the first birthday, Christmas, start of school, start of the season— that's when the reality is cemented. This is not what I expected but it is real.

The second task is to experience and express ALL the emotions. It is unfortunate that we can often be emotion dismissing, "Oh you don't really feel that way." Or emotion disapproving, "I can't believe you said that, feel that" or simply "Christians don't feel that way'. Emotions come from God and we are allowed to experience all of them. As long we express them rather than vent them, they are part of helping us return to balance and harmony. It is important to remember that emotions are more often information, rather than instruction.

Adjust to the "new norm." This is when our focus leaves the "what was" and we return to the "what is." This is when our focus leaves the "what could have been" and accepts the now. Especially in the premature death of a loved one, like loosing a child, we grieve a future that will never exist. They may or may not have played ball, gone to college, got married or liked hunting. The new norm is learning to live in the present and look at what you have in the here and the now, and not neglecting the people who are still living. I've seen spouses lose living spouses because of the focus on the missing child. I've actually heard children say, "They spent so much time hurting over the death of my sibling, that they ignored the living child in the other room."

Today, I will... Try and focus on the here and now. Even the here and now hurt. I will let my hurt tell me the truth of my love. We do not grieve the loss of things we do not love.

THE FOUR TASKS OF GRIEVING, Pt 2
TODAY'S SCRIPTURE: 2 Samuel 12:18-23; 2 Corinthians 5:4-5

Grieving "what might've been" is an effort in futility and guilt.

Being established in a future that is guaranteed is an exercise in recovery. The fourth task of grieving is to reinvest the grieving energy into something new or in a different aspect of the actual event. Experience is not what happens to you, but rather what you do with what happens to you.

An investment, after a time, into the grieving or healing of others is one of the by products of any experience. What did you do? What did others do that was helpful? What did others do or say that was not helpful? Sharing this information, even if unpleasant, might have a function in making any tragedy a way to help or bless others in a very dark time. People will say, "I just don't know what to say." My initial response is "Thank God. You aren't supposed to be talking you are supposed to be listening." But even then, those who have been through the suffering, perseverance, character, hope process have become uniquely qualified in the this area, and if they are willing, can share or even educate those of us who do not truly understand what they have gone through.

As a final look at this fourth task-Reinvest into the future or something new is the ultimate hope that all Christians have. This is the real function of Hope. We, like David, will go through the uncertainty, the refusal of taking care of ourselves, the lying on the floor in agony. Eventually the reality sets in and the finality fades. He got up off the ground, washed and anointed himself and changed his clothes. He then went into the house of the Lord and worshiped. His servants questioned him. You fasted and wept while the child was alive; but when the child died, you arose and carried on as normal. David's response is anchored in the ultimate hope. "But now he is dead. Why should I fast? Can I bring him back again? I shall go to him, but he will not return to me" (2 Samuel 12:23).

Grief and loss are not easy. This is not a sudden switch to "Oh I'm better." Rather this is a sustaining mindset that even when I am hurting, even while I am bitterly thinking that life has no purpose or meaning, I must look beyond the here and now and acknowledge the hope that all souls return to God. The innocent and saved return to God and remain in His presence forever.

Today, I will... Intentionally focus on the reunion I have been promised rather than the separation I have experienced. The separation is temporary the reunion is permanent.

WHAT SWALLOWS MORTALITY?

TODAY'S SCRIPTURE: 2 Corinthians 4:16-5:5

Read those verses and you will see that we have the choice to focus either on the external, the internal or the eternal. No one is minimizing pain, loss, or trauma. When our lives are properly understood, we understand that the external, the outward is designed to fade. The internal-which is eternal- is not designed to fade. When our spirits lose our bodies we are not naked, unclothed, or homeless. When our spirits are loosed from our bodies we get a building or a home made by God.

The body is a vehicle that houses the soul. When we die, we do not become spirits. We have always been spirits. That is true for people who are 88, 8 or 8 minutes. We are alive because the eternal nature of God is housed in our bodies. The life of the body only impacts the life of the soul in as much as we reach an age to be accountable for the actions we choose while in the body.

Why do we die? We die because we are mortal. Because we are mortal we die? Try this. Because we are mortal our bodies die. The death of our bodies usher us into life. "...not that we would be unclothed, but that we would be further clothed, so that what is mortal may be swallowed up by life. He who has prepared us for this very thing is God, who has given us the Spirit as a guarantee" (2 Corinthians 5:4-5). Did you get that? "What is mortal may be swallowed up by life." It is not that everything that lives dies; but rather that everything that dies lives. This process, this transformation is in our design. God made us from the beginning to live two lives; the temporary, transitional, sojourn of the external, physical world and the unending reunion with God and our loved ones in the spiritual world.

Today, I will...focus my energy away from the external and try to focus on the eternal. I will try to live in the here with a focus on the hereafter.

Dealing with the Loss of an Adult Child

STEVE BAGGETT

IN EVERYTHING GIVE THANKS

TODAY'S SCRIPTURE: 1 Thessalonians 5:18

The words still ring painfully in my inner being, "There's been an accident, and Matt did not survive." At that moment, a piece of my heart was taken away, never to return. The precious ladies in our office immediately surrounded me and held me together as best they could. One of our shepherds was on his way to the church office to drive me to Dickson County High School to be with Pam and tell her of our loss. While waiting, I called our youngest son Jason and informed him. The next few days were without a doubt the most difficult of our lives. Matt was our firstborn, a faithful husband, and a loving father to three children!

How do parents survive the death of a child? We see him everywhere and in everything. In our thoughts we immediately went to the last moment we were with him or spoke to him. We hardly had the strength to stand. Our minds were numb. We were greeted, loved, held, and prayed for by a houseful of our church family members. Yet, there was no template for this! Children are supposed to outlive their parents and care for them in their old age. Parents are not supposed to lose their children. We immediately knew we had to get to Cookeville to be with Matt's family, but how could we go to his home knowing he is not now and never will be there again.

As Pam and I prepared for Matt's funeral, the passage that came to our minds was Paul's statement, "In everything give thanks" 1 Thessalonians 5:18. Though our hearts were broken, we made the decision to be thankful rather than bitter. We wanted to rejoice in the blessings God had given us and not focus on our loss. We haven't always been successful, but that is our goal. In our devotionals this week, we will focus on things for which to be thankful while dealing with the loss of an adult child.

Today, I will... offer a prayer for parents everywhere who have lost a child.

I THANK GOD ON EVERY REMEMBRANCE OF YOU

TODAY'S SCRIPTURE: Philippians 1:3

When the apostle Paul wrote his love letter to the church in Philippi he was in prison. His imprisonment had nothing to do with crime. Instead, it had everything to do with jealousy and hatred. The religious leaders of his day vehemently opposed him, because the message which he preached was drawing people away from them and to Jesus! One of the blessings Paul enjoyed while in prison was his memory. He wrote to the Philippians, "I thank my God upon every remembrance of you" (Philippians 1:3). According to the subsequent verses, he: remembered them in every prayer, made his requests for them with joy, was thankful for their fellowship in the gospel, and was confident that God would continue to work through them (Philippians 1:4-7).

Matt was thirty-eight years old when the accident that took his life occurred. Though there is a void in our hearts that will never be filled, we are indeed thankful for the precious memories which flood our souls:
- Matt's 3-week-early arrival.
- His glistening smile.
- The time, as a toddler, he hid from us under the Christmas tree.
- The Christmas he was so excited about his "Talking Computron" that he asked his mom if she would open the rest of his gifts while he played with it.
- The Sunday we visited with the Jefferson Avenue church in Cookeville regarding working with them, and as an18-month-old, he smiled and shook every hand I shook.
- His brilliant mind which could remember almost anything.
- His vast vocabulary.
- His forgiving heart.
- His joy when playing with his children.
- His love for singing.

On and on I could go with precious memories! These wonderful memories have helped us deal with and live through the physical absence of our son.

Today, I will... offer a prayer of thanks for the precious memories of parents who have lost a child.

WITH THANKSGIVING LET YOUR REQUESTS BE MADE KNOWN TO GOD!

TODAY'S SCRIPTURE: Philippians 4:6

Perhaps like other parents who have lost an adult child, when Matt died, Pam and I were filled with questions: What happened? Why? How? What are Becca and the children going to do? How are we doing to survive? We were also filled with requests: God, will You please let Matt know how much we love him and how proud of him we are? Lord, will You please give us the strength to put one step in front of another? Father, will You help us to know how to grieve the loss of our son and still with thankful hearts serve You?

How do grieving parents make requests "with thanksgiving"? Paul wrote that it helps to be able to:
- "Rejoice in the Lord" in the midst of grief (4:4).
- Be "reasonable" or "gentle" with all people as we are grieving (4:5).
- Turn our "anxiousness" (grief, depression, and anxiety) over to God (4:6).

Above all, making requests with thanksgiving is possible because God promises that thankful requests are profitable. Paul followed the command to "with thanksgiving, let your requests be made known to God" (4:6) with the promise that "my God will supply every need of yours...in Christ Jesus" (4:19). He also promised "Likewise the Spirit helps us in our weakness. For we do not know what to pray for as we ought, but the Spirit himself intercedes for us with groanings too deep for words" (Romans 8:26). And James wrote, "...the prayer of a righteous person has great power as it is working" (James 5:16).

Choosing to express thanks to God for Matt, for the rest of our family, for who God is, for our church family, and for brethren the world over has helped us deal with the loss of our dear son.

Today, I will... offer a thankful request to God that grieving parents everywhere will be able to count their blessings and name them one by one.

THROUGH THEM, HE STILL SPEAKS

TODAY'S SCRIPTURE: Hebrews 11:4

When the writer of the book of Hebrews identified several great heroes of faith, he included Abel. Of Abel he said, "By faith Abel offered to God a more acceptable sacrifice than Cain, through which he was commended as righteous, God commending him by accepting his gifts. And through his faith, though he died, he still speaks" (Hebrews 11:4). It is a beautiful lesson for us that Abel still speaks today because of his faith!

One of the blessings our family has experienced which helps us deal with the loss of Matt, is that through his children, he also still speaks. These precious children all possess qualities which we see on a regular basis which remind us of their Dad. Lane, John Steven, and Anna Kathryn love hearing stories about their dad. Being able to share stories of "Daddy Matt" with them is not only good for them; it is also very helpful to us. We love reliving the memories of Matt and being able to talk about them.

Matt "still speaks" today through:
- Lane who has his love for and innate ability to easily work with technology. When Matt would answer a question for me about technology, he would usually begin by saying, "Dad, you probably won't understand this, but...." The reality is that most of the time he was correct!
- John Steven who is extremely talented in working with numbers, having a quick recall, and his love for climbing on just about anything. Matt was an excellent mathematician, was a member of his High School FBLA Parliamentary Procedure team which, by the way, won a national championship. And as a child, Matt climbed on anything he could find.
- Anna Kathryn who has a beautiful smile, a radiant personality, and a tenacious determination about life. I can still see Matt's smile, see him interacting with people, and remember his, "That's my stance, and I am sticking to it" approach to life.

Today, I will... offer a prayer for Matt's three precious children and all children who have lost a parent.

WE WILL GO TO HIM

TODAY'S SCRIPTURE: 2 Samuel 12:23

Following David's sin with Bathsheba, he was confronted by the prophet Nathan. David's response was, "I have sinned against the Lord.' And Nathan said to David, 'The Lord also has put away your sin; you shall not die'" (2 Samuel 12:13). However, one of the consequences of David's sin was the death of his child. Prior to his child's death, while he was very ill, David fervently prayed for his child and fasted for six days.

When finally, the child died the Bible says, "So David arose from the ground, washed and anointed himself, and changed his clothes; and he went into the house of the Lord and worshiped. Then he went to his own house; and when he requested, they set food before him, and he ate (2 Samuel 12:20). When David was asked what made the difference in his behavior he said, "While the child was alive, I fasted and wept; for I said, 'Who can tell whether the Lord will be gracious to me, that the child may live?' But now he is dead; why should I fast? Can I bring him back again? I shall go to him, but he shall not return to me" (2 Samuel 12:22-23).

Matt's death occurred without illness; he died suddenly in an automobile accident. Thus, Pam and I did not have the opportunity to fervently pray that he might be healed and live. However, like David, we know our son has left this life for good; and, like David, we have determined to go to him. We are so thankful to serve a God who promises eternal life to his children, and we are so thankful that one day we will be with Matt again!

Today, I will... offer a prayer of thanks for our son's faithfulness to God, the promise of eternal life with God, and our anticipation of joining him in the presence of God.

Dealing with the Loss of a Spouse

DON & RON WILLIAMS

A QUESTION NO ONE WANTS TO BE ASKED

TODAY'S SCRIPTURE: Ephesians 5:25

A Minister for over 50 years lost his wife, after a bout with cancer. As I stood in a long line of people who had come to pay their respect and love to the family, I finally reached the widowed husband. As I placed my hand upon his shoulder, he took me by the hand and looked at me and said, "Don, tell me-what does a man do without his wife?" Sometime later, I saw him visiting others at the hospital. He described himself as "making it, but dying on the inside."

In Ephesians 5:25, God commands husbands to "love your wives, just as Christ also loved the church, and gave Himself for her."

I do not know of a husband who would not be willing to give himself up for his wife. This particular godly Minister did just that, seeing after the daily needs of his good wife until the end. Often, the living mate feels empty because of the void left by the passing of his or her mate. It often takes a great deal of effort and time to fill the "emotional gap" that was previously held by his or her spouse.

Some widowers fill the gap with their work. Others fill the gap by investing themselves in various hobbies or interests. One's remaining family often becomes more important in daily living. Some, in time, may choose to re-invest their lives by dating or ultimately re-marrying.

A widow or widower who has given all they could, loving their mate as "Christ loved the church," should not feel guilty for reinvesting themselves in worthy manners. I knew of a wonderful man, who after losing his wife in a car accident, became even more involved in the work of the church. He was a great cook, and he had folks into his home regularly. He was a frequent companion with me when we went visiting. He reinvested his time by giving it to the church.

Today, I will... remember that God remembers the good that we do (Hebrews 6:10). I will use my life to honor my mate, and above all,God Almighty.

NO LOVE LIKE THAT LOVE IN LIFE

TODAY'S SCRIPTURE: Ephesians 5:31-33

The unique relationship of a husband and wife is so profound that it is compared to Jesus' love for His church

My brother, Don, and I were doing a grief workshop somewhere in Kentucky. I was meeting with a group of Christians who had lost their mates in death. I was emphasizing the marital relationship is special and unique in many kinds of way. I tried to validate the different feelings that several had previously mentioned. I then asked this question, "Why is the loss of a mate so devastating and difficult to bear?" A lady spoke up and said these words:

I lost my husband a few years ago in death. I have wonderful children and their mates that try to help me in my life. They are kind, giving, and I cannot thank them enough for what they have done for me these past few years. Having said that, when I leave this building and head home this evening, I know that there will not be that one special person that will meet me at the door whose one mission in life is to love me, care for me, and protect me as my husband did. My children will try but they have their own one person to love. That is why it is so hard for those of us as widows and widowers. No one is here to love us as our mate did.

God meant the marriage relationship to be special. He meant it to be a life fulfilling and life-changing experience. Marital love is so important as it is the only human relationship that the Holy Spirit used to compare the love of Jesus to His divine church. If you had that kind of love, know that you will grieve. Be grateful for that love like no other in your life.

Today, I will... be grateful to God for the marriage I have or had. If ended, I will cherish the memory and I will grieve that loss.

"DO NOT CALL ME PLEASANT—CALL ME BITTER!"

TODAY'S SCRIPTURE: Ruth 1:20, 21

Someone has equated the loss of a mate with a loss of an arm or a leg. In other words, your mate is an extension of yourself. They are vital, and they add stability and worth to your relationship.

Others have suggested that the loss of a child is like the loss of a lung. It is inward, because that child is a part of your makeup-he/she came from within you. Imagine someone losing both relationships in a period of time.

Such was the case of Naomi, whose name meant Pleasant. She and her husband left Bethlehem with their two sons and moved to Moab. The husband died, but she had her two sons to sustain her. In time, they married Moabite women, but then both of the sons died. Now, as she returns home, she makes the statement listed above to the women of Bethlehem. Her name needed to be changed because of the losses she had encountered!

I have known of mates who felt "cheated" because of the loss of their good mates. One lady in a grief class of mine lost her husband suddenly in an accident. She worked in a building where weddings were had, and marriages were dissolved. She talked about how sad ot was that some were "throwing away their marriages" and yet she had a wonderful marriage, only for it to end in such a sad manner.

It is important that we validate and allow grieving people to feel the pain and void because of the loss of their mate. Although some may, in time, choose to date and/or remarry, this does not take the place of the one whom they had given their life to in marriage.

The book of Ruth ends with Naomi being blessed through a faithful daughter-in-law and the ultimate marriage she had with Boaz. In time, they have a son named Obed, who becomes the grandfather of a young shepherd named David. He is included in the lineage of Jesus as found in Matthew 1. Thus, out of sadness a blessing came through this lineage that blesses mankind today.

Today, I will...remember that some good can come to me out of the ashes of my grief.

IN JUST A MOMENT OF TIME

TODAY'S SCRIPTURE: Genesis 19:15-26

Bad things happen when we least expect them.
A marriage partner can be gone in an instant and the mate is left empty and alone.

Today I write these words on 9/11/2020, the 19th anniversary of the attacks of terrorists on America soil in New York, Washington D.C, and on a plane in Pennsylvania. Several thousand of our citizens and others across the world woke up next to their mate, at home with their children or others they loved. Not any of those who died that day could imagine the horrible acts of death and destruction that would soon destroy their lives and inflict horrific pain on the surviving families for their rest of their lives.

Lot, his wife, and daughters were told by the angels to get out of Sodom as God was going to destroy that city for their gross disrespect to God and humanity. Lot pleaded with the angels for more time to get to some safe place that would preserve their lives. The angels agreed to Lot's bargaining to go to a city instead of the hills, but the angels reminded Lot and his family they were not to look back and to flee as fast as they could.

For some reason, Lot's wife disobeyed that command. "But Lot's wife, behind him, looked back, and she became a pillar of salt" (Genesis 19:26). I wonder, why was Lot's wife behind Lot and not in front of him as he hurriedly led his family to safety? Where were the daughters? Why didn't Lot, one more time, remind them what the angels said to them for them not to look back? We have questions but no answers to this terrible event of history. In just a moment of time, Lot's life (and that of his daughters' lives) changed forever. Lot's wife was gone.

Today, I will... love and cherish those most precious to me because in a moment of time those that I love can be gone forever.

AND SARAH DIED

TODAY'S SCRIPTURE: Genesis 23:1-2

The death of a spouse produces much pain and grief.

Abraham and Sarah had seen much change in their one hundred-plus years of life. They had traveled hundreds of miles from their birthplace to Canaan where God made a promise to Abram and his family (Genesis 12:1-3). They had encountered hardships, some from their own choices, and others, from the people around them where they lived. At age ninety-nine and Sarah ninety years old, they had a child together, Isaac, the child of promise, from which a nation eventually would come forth.

Sarah's death in Hebron was unique in several ways. First, it is the first notation in Scripture that a woman's death is recorded. Secondly, it is significant that a married woman is mentioned as to her death. The entirety of Genesis 23 deals with Abraham's dealings with the Hittites in obtaining a place to bury his wife. Prior to Sarah's death, no mentioning had been given as to burial arrangements being made to bury the body. Abraham wanted to honor his wife by taking care of her remains and solidifying a place of burial for his family for years to come.

A spouse's death produces feelings and emotions that one cannot imagine. It has been said that when a person loses a mate to death, it is like an appendage of their own body has been taken away. If a person loses an arm, a hand, or a leg, it will immediately and continually impact that person for the remainder of their life; so it is with the loss of a mate. It feels as if a person's past has ended, their present situation seems cloudy and unclear, and the future can look hopeless for time to come. Like Abraham, one grieves and mourns their great loss.

Today, I will...check on those acquaintances I know whose mate has died recently. I will be plan to be there for them and love them through their pain.

Dealing with the Loss of a Job or Income

ANDY CONNELLY

I'M SHOCKED, SCARED, AND ANGRY

TODAY'S SCRIPTURE: Matthew 6:25-34

One real problem that even Christians face is the potential loss of a job, and possibly ongoing loss of income in the family. When this happens, it is not unnatural for a Christian to feel what the world feels, too. He may feel shocked, scared, and even angry.

Does God condemn these emotions as inherently sinful? Certainly not. What we may do with them may become sinful, but not the emotions themselves. Jesus certainly addressed this moment and others in Matthew 6:25-34.

- Verse 25 - Jesus teaches the principle that God does not want me anxious. As "unnatural" as it may seem and even truly be, we are called to come out of that which is only natural. Part of being the "salt" and "light" of Matthew 5:13-16 involves contrast. I want to be different in this moment.

- Verse 27 - Jesus says my anxiety, which may be natural for man, is still not productive. He says it cannot "add a single hour to the span of life." Satan attempts to profit in disaster. I don't want to let him.

- Verses 26, 28-30, Jesus says my logic can rest in God's provisional intent and stated view of our worth. Our worth to God is clearly seen in Jesus' words, comparing his intentional blessings upon us to those of other parts of His creation, even saying that we are "much more valuable" than those things.

- Verses 31-32, I am reminded that God knows my need. This is referencing my real need, not just my perceived ones. I must ask, wouldn't the creator and sustainer of all things, including me, know my real need? Faith does not remove logic, it calls for it.

- Verses 33-34, Jesus says today has its own opportunities for righteousness, and in fact, maybe especially in such a time of natural anxiety. I don't want to miss today's opportunity for it.

Today, I will...provide a contrast to the world, relying on God's promise of provision, and thank him for it.

I'M QUESTIONING

TODAY'S SCRIPTURE: Daniel 3:16-25

Why Do The Unrighteous Profit While I Face Trouble?

An unexpected loss of a job and concern over ongoing income capability can create very real challenges. For the Christian, the cunning whispers from our adversary, Satan, may include tempting us to ask, "Why do the unrighteous prosper, while this happens to me?" While an understandable human tendency, we should have patience to search scripture to come to why this may be an allowance in our life. To this end, it may be there is something to learn from the attitudes seen from Daniel's friends when faced with a choice to deny faith or face certain death. Why would young men of such obvious faith be allowed to face such a day? Read Daniel chapter 3: 16-25, and note the following things as possible if facing faith questions due to fears over providing for others.

- **God might not immediately deliver me from it, but instead stand with me through it.** To see God's hand, the three young men had to go into the furnace. To see God's hand, David had to face the giant (I Samuel 17).

- **God may allow events to remind His children of things that are hard to learn in other ways.** Could it be a lesson of our chosen reliance? Even Job made the statement, "Though He slay me, I will hope in Him (Job 13:15) ." Does real faith have a chance to grow most when we take it to such an extent?

- **Someone in my world may need a clearer picture of God, His son, and our own faith.** People are watching and listening, and an evident faith response in contrast with the world's view of trouble gets noticed. Remember Peter's reminder to "always be prepared to make a defense to anyone who asks you for a reason for the hope that is within you (I Peter 3:15)."

Allow our great God to show Himself, to you, or to others through you.

Today, I will...pray to remember GOD, and only GOD, can supply every need (Philippians 4:19).

I'LL WAIT

TODAY'S SCRIPTURE: Psalm 37:7

The word "wait" or some form of it is a common term in scripture. Add to that word other similar ideas like that of patience and you begin to see it as an evident theme throughout scripture. While we have been blessed to live in a time and place of so many advancements compared to earlier generations, it hasn't necessarily helped us with that concept of patience. In fact, it may have conditioned us to have more trouble with it than ever. When I've been shocked, scared, and already questioning why I've lost my ability to provide for self and family, being patient is not easy. However, for spiritual well-being, it becomes of the utmost importance. Today, let's look at being able to say, "I'll wait for the Lord."

David uses such a term many times in his Psalms. In looking at how God dealt with His people in the Old Testament, just before victory or blessing, there is often a period of waiting and a calling for patience. The children of Israel had to go through a period of wandering before entering the promised land (the book of Exodus). God's people were allowed periods of oppression before God raised up judges to bring them to victory (the book of Judges). It is shown in the New Testament as well. All the world had waited, generation after generation, for the prophesied coming of the Messiah. Jesus chose to wait instead of immediately going to keep Lazarus from dying, so that they would see His power in raising him (John 11:6,14,40). The Lord's disciples had to wait three days before knowing that He had indeed conquered the grave as he said he would do. Then they had to wait to receive that power of the Holy Spirit our Lord had promised them (Acts 1:6-8; Acts 2:1-4).

In each of these situations, however, it always happened. It always came. He came.

"Be still before the Lord, and wait patiently for Him" (Psalm 37:7).

Today, I will...focus on the God who always came, who always kept His word.

I'LL DO

TODAY'S SCRIPTURE: Joshua 6:1-20

Have you ever heard the expression, "Trust in God, but lock your car."? That expression obviously means that protection from some things and opportunity for others involves a cooperative effort between both faith and common sense. Well, that idea runs throughout scripture, and it is not cheapening the love, power, or mercy of God. Throughout the Bible, both in the Old as well as the New Testament, there is evidence that God wants us to do right things while we are waiting upon Him.

As God was about to give Israel a great victory at Jericho. How would he do that? Well, first by His own power, a power that didn't need any help. However, as you may remember from a Sunday class from childhood, God told Joshua to tell the people to march around that city once a day for six days, then on the seventh day to march seven times (Joshua 6)! God could have done it without the march. When Naaman had leprosy, God's plan through the prophet Elisha was for him to wash in the Jordan River, which was not exactly a clean, understandable request. (2 Kings 5). In the book of Daniel, chapter three, the power of God was not limited and needing the help of a certain action by Daniel's three friends in order for them to be saved from the fiery furnace, but they took a right action anyway. In the New Testament, the great doctrines of grace, faith, and obedience are taught as flowing beautifully together to make man whole. Also, consider the fact that the Christians who wish to be approved are told "do your best to present yourself to God as one approved" (2 Timothy 2:15).

God wants us to do what we can to cooperate in His love and plans for us. With that in mind, while I am waiting in a hard time, I will study, work (John 9:4), recall (1 Peter 2:9), and believe (Luke 8:50).

Today, I will... exercise my faith into the goodness of God, and do something for Him.

I'LL BELIEVE, SO THAT I'LL SEE!
TODAY'S SCRIPTURE: John 11:1-44

Several years ago I preached a sermon from John 11, regarding Jesus' response to the sickness and death of Lazarus and suggesting that the same things we see from Him there are, by illustration, things we need to see Him doing for us during a tough challenge.

In John 11, verse 4, as Lazarus lay sick, the first thing I notice is that Jesus knows. That is important when I'm prone to wonder what the Lord is doing while I'm hurting. There are times when it seems Christians think they must explain their situation to God as they pray to Him. That is not the case.

In verse 6, we are told that even though He knew, the Lord decided to wait. What? Jesus waits? Why would He do that? Why, when He knows He could do it, would He not go immediately to save His friend from deeper sickness or death? Our society and even too many in the church seem to believe that love means making sure someone never has a time of challenge, that love would always swoop in and remove the possibility of pain. Scripture, however, shows that throughout history our God has, at times, allowed a period of difficulty so that His people will eventually see something more important and eventually even more protective than the avoidance of trouble. For a third point, however, later in the chapter it is clear that as Jesus waited, it was for a challenge (verse 25-26) and a purpose, as He later reminded Martha that had she only believed she would "see the glory of God" (verse 40).

Fourth, as seen in verse 15 and 17, Jesus comes to Lazarus, and to his family. That is what Jesus wants to do with us when we're hurting. He wants to come. Finally, when He comes, He acts with command (verses 39-44). Friend, this is what Jesus still does when we are in hurt or fear.

Today, I will...believe it, so that I may see the glory of God!

Fruit of the Spirit In My Life:
Love

JACOB RUTLEDGE

143 POUNDS OF LOVE

TODAY'S SCRIPTURE: *1 Corinthians 16:14*

Mr. Rogers was known throughout the country to be a loving and gentle man. Almost everyone that met him quickly learned to like him due to his innate kindness and generosity in his interactions. His program Mr. Rogers Neighborhood ran for an unprecedented 31 seasons. This accomplishment came despite a low budget, mundane props, and a lack of technological wizardry; the success of the show was due simply to Mr. Rogers commitment to loving others—a genuine concern that came through every episode. In fact, Mr. Rogers was so committed to his belief in love that it is said he always kept his weight at 143 pounds. This number, so significant to Rogers, was the numerical equivalent of his favorite phrase: I (1) Love (4) You (3).

Yet, as loving as this Mr. Rogers was, he can't compare the perfect embodiment of absolute love: Jesus. Jesus' entire life was spent loving and serving others. He remains the greatest example to humanity because the entirety of his being exuded love. God—both Father, Son, and Spirit—is love (1 John 4:8). Every definition and explanation of love must be measured by the standard or God's character as expressed in Jesus of Nazareth.

With this in view, as disciples of Jesus, shouldn't we strive every day to fully devote our lives to loving others? Paul wrote in 1 Corinthians 16:14: "Let all that you do be done in love." Everything? All 143 pounds of it. I imagine that the reason Paul used such an umbrella term ("All that you do") is due to our habit of excusing certain areas of our life from love. Maybe it is how we treat our spouse, our coworkers, our political enemies, or Christians we disagree with doctrinally. In our interactions with these groups we excuse our lack of love because we feel that such offers compromise and condones the sinful actions or beliefs of another. In reality, nothing could be farther from the truth. Love doesn't equate to accepting sin but refusing to fight sin on its terms. No matter the person or the situation, love always seeks to show itself in the life of the Christian.

Today, I will... Go out of my way to be loving to someone who has hurt me in the past or who I am at odds with in the present.

MORE LOVE PLEASE!

TODAY'S SCRIPTURE: 1 Thessalonians 4:9-10

I never cease to be amazed at the appetite of my two-year-old son, Lincoln. Recently we were eating spaghetti for dinner as a family, and it seemed as if he couldn't get enough. After his fourth bowl of spaghetti he finally tapped out but left me wondering if I would soon need a second job to keep our toddler content! Of course, I don't mind, and he can't help it: he keeps eating because his body tells him that he is hungry.

While the stomach might crave food, the heart hungers for love—and we just can't get enough of it. Just ask any husband who has been married for 20+ years. If he has a successful marriage it wasn't due to him depending on the love he offered his wife when they were dating. Marriages that depend on love expressed long ago, while failing to nurture love in the present moment, will soon fail. Marriages need little expressions of love every day to survive. The cup of love must constantly be filled; there is never a point where satisfaction leads us to reject love from another.

When Paul wrote the Thessalonians, he reminded them that, although they loved each other, their love needed to increase "more and more" (1 Thessalonians 4:9-10). At the table of the Lamb's wedding feast, there is a constant longing for love—and there is always enough to go around! When Paul lists the fruit of the Spirit, the first one he mentions is love (Galatians 5:22-23). Yet, if love is a fruit, and our life is a tree, then shouldn't our "limbs" be bending under the weight of our produce? Shouldn't our circles of influence—our family, our community, and our church—be able to come to us every day to pick and feed on the love that the Spirit of God is producing in our lives? Maybe for some of us the fruit is sparse, barren, or non-existent. If so, we should turn once again to God and allow him to work in our lives—because we all could use a little more love.

Today, I will... Think of someone I already have a loving relationship with and find a new and exciting way to express my love to them.

THE LOVE OF GOD IS BETTER THAN LIFE

TODAY'S SCRIPTURE: Psalm 63:3-4

Exaggeration is a tool all of us use at times to express our utter disdain or absolute satisfaction in something or someone. My children are masters at exaggeration: "You ALWAYS say no!" and "We NEVER do anything fun!" are ones we occasionally hear. In those moments, my wife and I correct them, trying to help them to see that exaggeration isn't helpful to their case. At other times, however, exaggeration is exactly what is needed to grasp the magnitude of a situation. For example, someone might say to a friend who is considering becoming a Christian, "This is the most important decision of your life"—and truly it is!

In Psalm 63:3 David makes quite an exaggerated claim about the love of God when he writes, "Your steadfast love is better than life." Surely David is going a little overboard in this instance. How can the love of God be better than life itself? Ironically, David penned this Psalm when he was in the wilderness of Judah, most likely running from enemies or even his own son as they attempted to murder him. In this moment, when his life was at its most precarious moment, David confesses, "If I die, I do not lose the love of God; for it is better than life itself." David had an incredible faith.

As we come to taste the sweetness and the glory of God's love in our hearts, we can understand why David would make such a comment. This present life is fleeting, full of pain, struggle, and loss; on the other hand, God's love is eternal, steadfast, and secure. This life may let me down, or may leave me with unmet expectations, but God's love never will; it is always there, always waiting to bless us more today than it did the day before. As we sometimes sing, inspired by Lamentations 3:22, "The steadfast love of the Lord never ceases!" What a wonderful comfort we possess: That God's love, given by the Spirit (Rom. 5:5), is better than all that life has to offer.

Today, I will…Take 5 minutes as I begin my day to think, pray, and sing about the love of God.

THE CHARACTER OF LOVE IN MY LIFE

TODAY'S SCRIPTURE: 1 Corinthians 13

When Paul lists the fruit of the Spirit in Galatians 5:22-23, he does two things: 1) He begins the list with love, making it the foundation for the subsequent virtues 2) He calls it the fruit "of the Spirit" implying that these attributes are simply natural outgrowths of God working in our lives. Therefore, if I am walking in the Spirit, I should expect to grow and mature in love; that is, the longer that you are a Christian, the more loving you should become. Yet, what does this look like?

Defining love in our present climate is quite a difficult task. For many today, love means accepting and affirming any and all choices that someone makes. Lest we be trapped and cheated by the philosophies of men (Colossians 2:8), the Spirit himself defines for us the character of love in 1 Corinthians 13. As we read through this inspired list, a few stand out: that love is patient, kind, and honest (it does not rejoice in evil, v. 6). If these three were the only ones listed, we could spend our entire lives trying to pursue them and still come up short!

Love is patient with the faults and failures of others; it gives time for growth and maturity, offering grace as often as need. This patience comes from reflecting on how patient God has been with us as we fail and fall time and time again. Love is kind and gentle; it offers a word of encouragement, where a word of discouragement might come more naturally. It handles the feelings and convictions of others with respect and caution. Yet love is also honest; it doesn't hold back what it helpful. It recognizes that the best policy is a truthful one—despite the difficulty of practicing such. It understands that the lies and deceptions of Satan are far more harmful than the pain that the truth might initially cause. Yet such honesty is always tempered by gentleness and patience.

Do you witness this type of love in your life? Is God growing this fruit in you?

Today, I will... Say something kind to 5 people I come into contact with today.

BORN AGAIN TO LOVE

TODAY'S SCRIPTURE: 1 Peter 1:22-23

Why did God save you? How would you answer that question? We are used to answering, "How did God save you?" Or maybe, "How did you receive salvation?" Yet I wonder how often we stop to think, "Why did God save me?" One way to answer would be "for the sake of his name" (Rom. 1:5); others might say so that they might go to heaven. Interestingly, Peter informs us that we are born again "for a sincere brotherly love" (1 Peter 1:22). We are reborn, by the water and Spirit, so that we might learn to love.

If that is the case, then my failure to prioritize, pursue, and perfect love in my life is a great mistake. This is why John can make such absolute claims about the love of God being expressed in our lives in 1 John 4:8-ff. To summarize: if you don't know love, then you don't know God. This is a chilling reminder that, if we are lacking love, that we aren't simply deficient in a Christian virtue, but that we are cut off from the very source of our salvation.

As I reflect on my life—my pursuits and priorities as a Christian—I believe an honest evaluation would reveal that I have placed far too little value on love. It's easy to give lip service to love, while lying in your heart. Over the years I heard preachers decry the lack of Biblical knowledge among our people (a serious concern to be sure), yet how often do we mourn the lack of love we sometimes witness in our pews, in our publications, and even online? Of course, as John points out, knowledge of God and a loving heart aren't mutually exclusive—they are codependent.

So, let us pursue love above all else (1 Cor. 14:1). Let us remember why we were saved: to genuinely love. Let us seek, in everything we do, to be the light of love in a world of darkness, holding forth God's lamp of love in culture of hate.

Today, I will... Tell someone that I care about that I love them. Send a card, a text, make a call—or better yet—say it to them in person.

Fruit of the Spirit In My Life:
Joy

JIM GARDNER

JOY IN THE GOOD NEWS

TODAY'S SCRIPTURE: Matthew 13:44

The gospel begins with joy. The angels proclaim to the shepherds "good news of great joy that will be for all the people" (Luke 2:10). When the wise men see the star over where the child lay, "they rejoiced exceedingly with great joy" (Matthew 2:10).

We know nothing of the later lives of the shepherds or the wise men, but they could never have lived unchanged, as though they had not heard a message of surpassing joy offered to us all. Each of them would have had to choose how to respond to that message.

In back-to-back parables in Matthew 13, Jesus likens the kingdom of heaven to buried treasure and a pearl of great value. When a man finds the treasure, "in his joy he goes and sells all that he has" so that he can buy the field where the treasure lies (Matthew 13:44). When the merchant finds the great pearl, he "went and sold all that he had and bought it" (Matthew 13:45).

Following Christ demands that we give up everything, but we do not lose by the transaction. Following Christ, we give up the search for happiness in places where it could have never been found. We spare ourselves the "grievous evil" of "riches...kept by their owner to his hurt" (Ecclesiastes 5:13). We discover that "those who hunger and thirst for righteousness" shall be satisfied and blessed (Matthew 5:6). We find His yoke easy, and His burden light, and rest for our souls laboring for Him (Matthew 11:29-30).

Many people have asked me how they can learn to love God more deeply. I know no better answer than to point to Christ as He is revealed in the Bible, and especially in the gospels. The French writer and skeptic Renan described the book of Luke as the loveliest book in the world. He thought it was too lovely to be true. But it is true, and Christ so surpassingly lovely that to lose ourselves in Him is no loss, but great gain and true joy.

Today, I will... spend more time thinking about some aspect of Christ's character and how I can be more like Him in that specific way.

JOY IN THE WORK OF GRACE

TODAY'S SCRIPTURE: Matthew 5:12

When Christians travel to Israel or to the cities in which Paul taught, they typically do so, not expecting to learn information about places that twenty centuries have inevitably changed almost beyond recognition, but for the emotionally moving experience of walking where Jesus and His apostles once walked. We long for connection. We want their lives somehow to touch ours.

The good news of the gospel partly consists of God's gracious choice to grant that connection. By choosing to make the gospel His power to save, He has chosen to make those who teach the gospel the instruments of His grace. We are not only saved, but given the honor of helping to save others.

Jesus taught that this fellowship in the work of God extends back even before the gospel was proclaimed. To those who suffer persecution for His sake, He says, "Rejoice and be glad, for your reward is great in heaven, for so they persecuted the prophets who were before you" Matthew 5:12).

We often teach evangelism as a duty, and so it is. As Paul tells the Corinthians, "Woe to me if I do not preach the gospel" (1 Corinthians 9:16). But the duty of evangelism is also an honor and privilege. The gospel gives us the opportunity to find meaning in helping to fulfill God's purposes. We are salt and light. What greater honor could we receive than be chosen to "proclaim the excellencies of Him who called you out of darkness into his marvelous light" (1 Peter 2:9)?

And this honor has been given to us despite our obvious failings. It is God's method of grace. He not only spared Rahab the prostitute, but made her the ancestress of Christ. Paul was "a blasphemer, persecutor, and insolent opponent," and "the grace of our Lord overflowed" to make him an apostle and example for us (1 Timothy 1:13-16). We ought joyfully to say with Paul, "To the King of the ages, immortal, invisible, the only God, be honor and glory forever and ever. Amen" (1 Timothy 1:17).

Today, I will... reflect on those who have gone before me in the gospel and purpose to be worthy of their fellowship.

JOY IN TRIALS

TODAY'S SCRIPTURE: James 1:2-4

God has made us so that we cannot become the person He intends us to be except by sustained effort and struggle. Even the most gifted athletes can reach their potential only by years of disciplined training. Even the most brilliant scholars master their field of knowledge only by years of painstaking study. In the same way, even the most devoted Christian has hard work to do in becoming like Christ. The purpose and proof of being born again is the life that follows.

Paul tells the Romans, "Do not be conformed to this world, but be transformed by the renewal of your mind, that by testing you may discern what is the will of God, what is good and acceptable and perfect" (Romans 12:2). Similarly, James exhorts us, "Count it all joy, my brothers, when you meet trials of various kinds, for you know that the testing of your faith produces steadfastness. And let steadfastness have its full effect, that you may be perfect and complete, lacking in nothing" James 1:2-4).

Trials that genuinely test us are certainly not easy or pleasant in themselves, but the path to perfection lies through them. Athletes cannot transform their body's performance except by training that challenges performance. Scholars cannot learn except by going beyond what they have known. Christians must "work out [their] own salvation with fear and trembling" (Philippians 2:12).

But we work out our salvation also with joy, because the reward for endurance is so great. The word used in the Greek New Testament for "save" could also be translated as to heal, to make well. God's will is that we be saved, made well from the sickness of sin. God has promised that if we "let steadfastness have its full effect," we can become "perfect and complete, lacking in nothing" (James 1:4). If enduring sickness in our body can help cure sickness in our soul, if enduring malice and violence can help bring peace that passes understanding, let us joyfully endure.

Today, I will...plan a way to be made better by the most difficult circumstances in my life.

JOY IN OTHER PEOPLE

TODAY'S SCRIPTURE: 3 John 4

In the Sermon on the Mount, Jesus warns us not to store up earthly treasure, and gives two reasons why doing so is foolish. Such treasure is uncertain: "moth and rust destroy and...thieves break in and steal" (Matthew 6:19). Perhaps even more important, such treasures inherently corrupt, "For where your treasure is, there your heart will be also" (Matthew 6:21).

What is a warning about earthly treasures is also a promise about rightly valued treasures. Loving God and other people reinforces itself. As we invest our affections more and more in the lives of others, our heart follows.

Paul's letters record his constant labor in the gospel, and the resulting profound emotional tie between him and those whom he taught. Among many similar passages, he addresses the Philippians as "my brothers, whom I love and long for, my joy and crown...my beloved" (Philippians 4:1). He writes to the Thessalonians, "For what is our hope or joy or crown of boasting before our Lord Jesus at His coming? Is it not you? For you are our glory and joy (1 Thessalonians 2:19-20).

John's letters are even more filled with affection. He says of himself, "I have no greater joy than to hear that my children are walking in the truth" (3 John 4). His statement rings true, because all of his letters reflect the decision to love others at a level the world reserves for family. Young Christians have truly become his children.

Jesus taught the great paradox that the way to find life is to lose it, the way to be fulfilled is to empty oneself in service. Life does work that way. If we think clearly, anything that we have ever done to help eternal beings, made in God's image and beloved by Him, live more happily and securely in His grace is a joy beyond reckoning and that lasts forever.

Today, I will...reach out to someone I know needs encouragement and let myself be encouraged by caring for someone else.

JOY AT THE END

TODAY'S SCRIPTURE: Matthew 25:21

God has made us so that a large measure of human happiness lies in our expectations for the future rather than enjoyment of our present circumstances. Even at the darkest moment of our lives, Christians believe that "the sufferings of this present time are not worth comparing with the glory that is to be revealed to us" (Romans 8:18), and thus can find peace and joy in the midst of severe trials.

What heaven will be like in actual experience is necessarily to a large extent beyond our comprehension. Descriptions of heaven in Revelation and elsewhere in the New Testament are largely metaphorical because they must be. Physical beings can never fully grasp their place in a state of existence that transcends the physical.

We can know it will be glorious. We can know that all evil will be excluded and every tear dried. We can know that we will see God face to face and know Him as He knows us (1 Corinthians 13:12).

Heaven will be a place where other people's judgments and our own sense guilt and self-doubt fade into insignificance. In the parable of the talents, the Master greets each of His faithful servants with the same words: "Well done, good and faithful servant. You have been faithful over a little; I will set you over much. Enter into the joy of your master" (Matthew 25:21,23). Consider what it will mean to have our Creator, whose judgments are true and righteous altogether, approve our service.

We look forward to joy in heaven, and in that hope find joy now. The writer of Hebrews compares the Christian life to running a race. Having described in the previous chapter the heroes of faith who have gone before us, he says that we run the race "surrounded by so great a cloud of witnesses" (Hebrews 12:1). Yet, even in the presence of that mighty company, we focus on "Jesus, the founder and perfecter of our faith," who ran His race "for the joy that was set before Him" (Hebrews 12:2). So we run for the joy set before us.

Today, I will...examine my life and ask what change I need to make now so that I can finish my race with joy.

Fruit of the Spirit In My Life: Peace

MATTHEW SOKOLOSKI

WHAT ARE YOU KNOWN FOR?

TODAY'S SCRIPTURE: Matthew 5:1-11

What are you known for? We have a tendency to categorize and use labels because that makes it easier to identify people. For example, Democrat or Republican, Liberal or Conservative. Do you proudly wear a label? Or perhaps we are known by our passions and interests: one has a love for Disney, while another is a runner. Some pour their hearts into homeschooling, while another into cooking. We may be known by many things but what should we be known as?

In the beatitudes, Jesus teaches, "Blessed are the peacemakers, for they shall be called sons of God" (Matthew 5:9). In a world of divisiveness, labels, sides and polarization are we known for being peacemakers? In our interactions and conversations, both in person and online, are we seeking to make our point, or seeking to make peace? Being a peacemaker is not being quiet, or merely avoiding conflict, but rather bringing reconciliation where there is division, bringing harmony where there is discord. This may require confrontation. You see, Jesus came to restore our relationship with God. He "emptied himself, by taking the form of a servant" (Philippians 2:7), confronted the problem of our sin, and "in every respect has been tempted as we are, yet without sin" so that "we may receive mercy and find grace to help in time of need" (Hebrews 4:15-16). Likewise, we ought to reflect Jesus in our own walk and seek to bring restoration in the relationships around us, to reflect the mercy and grace of God to others. By all means, be politically active and pursue your passions, but first and foremost be known as a peacemaker.

Notice the result of being a peacemaker - we are called "sons of God." To be the son or daughter of your father or mother shows origin and connection. Being sons of God shows the connection to our Father and the source of our peacemaking.

Today, I will...reach out to someone that I can improve my relationship with or make a step in the direction of reconciliation.

THE PEACE OF JESUS

TODAY'S SCRIPTURE: John 13-17

What would be your last words to your family and friends if you knew you only had a few hours left to live? You hear of those who, on their deathbed, are the ones actually offering comfort to the living as their own death approaches. In John chapters 13 through 17, "when Jesus knew that his hour had come to depart out of this world to the Father," he washes his disciples feet, offers them powerful teaching and words of encouragement, and prays for them (and us). In these last hours Jesus tells them "Peace I leave with you; my peace I give to you. Not as the world gives do I give to you. Let not your hearts be troubled, neither let them be afraid" (John 14:27).

Shortly after these words Jesus will be arrested, placed on trial, and crucified. The disciples will abandon him and scatter as cowards. And yet, three days later Jesus is raised. These disciples will be transformed into bold proclaimers of the Gospel, and will endure suffering, persecution, and even death for the sake of Christ. What brought about this change? It was the reality of the resurrection and its implications. The disciples did not fear death because of the peace Jesus had given them. This was not the peace of the world - no in fact, far from it. Life was not comfortable and free of concern and conflict, but rather one of challenging and fulfilling work in the kingdom that came with suffering and persecution. And yet, these disciples had peace and their hearts were not troubled.

Do you have peace, or is your heart troubled? Instead of facing life with fear, can you allow your conviction and trust in Jesus to transform you into a fearless proclaimer of the Good News? Allow the peace that Jesus gives us to settle your heart in the face of whatever challenges may come from the world.

Today, I will...write down my fears, lay them before God in prayer, and then tear them up and discard them.

THE STRUGGLE IS REAL

TODAY'S SCRIPTURE: Romans 6-8

What is it that you do, even though you know you ought not do it? Is it the lack of control you give in to when your sweet tooth strikes? Is it the words you say about another behind his back? Is it an addiction of some sort - to alcohol, pain killers, or pornography? The struggle is real, but the chains of sin can be broken.

Paul writes, "There is therefore no condemnation for those who are in Christ Jesus. For the law of the Spirit of life has set you free in Christ Jesus from the law of sin and death" (Romans 8:1). Jesus said, "Truly, truly, I saw to you, whoever hears my word and believes him who sent me has eternal life. He does not come into judgement but has passed from death to life" (John 5:24). Paul continues, "For those who live according to the flesh set their minds on the things of the flesh, but those who live according to the Spirit set their minds on the things of the Spirit. For to set the mind on the flesh is death, but to set the mind on the Spirit is life and peace" (Romans 8:5-6).

As Christians, we ought to have the fruit of the spirit evident in our lives. The struggle is real, but the Spirit enables us and we are no longer bound to sin and death. I may not initially want to forgive an atrocity, but it is the power of Christ in me and the fruit of the Spirit manifest in my life that enables me to forgive because God first forgave me. Instead of clinging to bitterness and hurt, we offer forgiveness and find healing. We no longer cling to the tendencies of the flesh, but rather set our minds on the things of the Spirit and find life and peace. Instead of being broken and sinful, we are whole and holy.

Today, I will...share a struggle with a fellow Christian to seek encouragement, and to turn my mind away from the flesh and toward the Spirit.

BARRIER BREAKER

TODAY'S SCRIPTURE: Ephesians 2:11-22

Montagues and Capulets; the Sharks and the Jets; team Edward and team Jacob. There are divides in every generation - some silly, some serious. Black and white; Hutus and Tutsis; Jew and Gentile. Who is the "other" in your life? Who is the "them" that opposes your "us"? Jesus comes to break down all barriers. Not only does Jesus remove the divide between us and God, Jesus gives every relationship the possibility to be made whole.

Paul writes to the Ephesians and calls to mind the divide that had been between the Jew and the Gentile, "but now in Christ Jesus you who once were far off have been brought near by the blood of Christ. For he himself is our peace, who has made us both one and has broken down in his flesh the dividing wall of hostility by abolishing the law of commandments expressed in ordinances, that he might create in himself one new man in place of the two, so making peace, and might reconcile us both to God in one body through the cross, thereby killing the hostility" (Ephesians 2:11-16).

The Gentile who was not part of God's chosen people, is welcome and can enjoy all the promises and blessings to be found in God. No longer foreigners, we are now fellow citizens. Not only are we now unified in one spirit and one Father, but we are being built together into a holy temple. We are living stones, a royal priesthood (I Peter 2:5) - serving a living God. This is peace, this is unity, this is being made whole together, but it is only founded on Christ Jesus as our cornerstone. Who are we to divide, when Christ has given us the ministry of reconciliation (2 Corinthians 5:18)? May we extend the peace Christ has provided us to others.

Today, I will...connect with a friend, an acquaintance, or even someone I don't like, who is not a Christian, and offer them encouragement in hopes that they too would come to know the peace of God.

THE PEACE OF THE CROSS
TODAY'S SCRIPTURE: Colossians 1:15-23

It is a pivotal moment in the gospel account when Peter confesses that Jesus is the Christ (Mark 8:29). After this confession Jesus "began to teach them that the Son of Man must suffer many things," be rejected, killed, and after three days rise again. Peter takes Jesus aside to rebuke him, to which Jesus responds, "Get behind me, Satan!" (Mark 8:31-33). This gives us, as the reader, whiplash as we move from Peter's confession, to Jesus' rebuking of Peter. So what gives?

You see, the disciples were looking for a Messiah, but their concept was too small and earthly. They wanted a political leader that would deliver them from the Romans and set up a new kingdom. Peter has just confessed Jesus as the Christ, and now Jesus is telling Peter that He must suffer and die. This was not Peter's concept of a Messiah; thus Peter felt the need to rebuke Jesus. (Perhaps Peter was so focused on the suffering, rejection, and killing, that he missed that Jesus would rise again.) Jesus rebukes Peter, because in his misunderstanding, Peter is being an adversary to the mission that Jesus must accomplish. Jesus came, not as a victorious political leader to establish an earthly kingdom, but rather as a suffering servant, come to die as a sacrificial lamb and to establish a heavenly kingdom that will never fail.

Paul writes to the Colossians, "For in him all the fullness of God was pleased to dwell, and through him to reconcile to himself all things, whether on earth or in heaven, making peace by the blood of the cross" (1:19-20). This is why Jesus brings us peace, not peace that the world can offer - shallow, temporary, and on certain terms - but instead deep, abiding, and everlasting peace. John records for us that on the evening of the day of his resurrection, when Jesus appears and stands among his disciples, he says to them, "Peace be with you" (20:19).

Today, I will...thank God for Christ's sacrifice and find comfort in the peace of the Savior.

Fruit of the Spirit In My Life: Patience

BART WARREN

DIFFERENT

TODAY'S SCRIPTURE: Galatians 5:22

"But the fruit of the Spirit is...patience..." (Galatians 5:22).

One definition of patience is "the capacity to accept or tolerate delay, trouble, or suffering without getting angry or upset." This is a rare quality among our fellow human beings. We have come to expect instant outrage at even the most modest of inconveniences or disagreements. If we are not careful, we can become accustomed to the immediate animosity and fall into the trap of being routinely angry and impatient with those around us.

There are a number of very stark and very clear distinctions between the works of the flesh and the fruit of the Spirit as described in Galatians 5. Consider the actions and attitudes that are labeled enmity, strife, jealousy, fits of anger, rivalries, dissentions, divisions, and envy (cf. Galatians 5:20-21). This is the norm and status quo for the world. For those who do not know what it means to be filled with the Spirit, to emulate Jesus, and to be part of a Christian community, the bar is set pretty low for what is expected as far as interaction with others goes.

Not so for the Christian. We are to be different. What could be more easily identifiable as being different than being patient? We are to be known by our love (John 13:35), and love is patient (1 Corinthians 13:4)! Want to stand out as being different? Demonstrate patience.

Ugliness like strife, jealousy, divisions, etc. would dissipate if we exhibited righteous patience with each other. Fights would be diffused and arguments would be reconciled if we would accept misfortune without unbridled fits of anger.

Be patient with the waiter/waitress at the restaurant. Be patient with teller at the bank. Be patient with the person in the car in front of you. Be patient with your boss or subordinates. Be patient with your spouse and children.

Today, I will...make a concerted effort to give others the benefit of the doubt. I will demonstrate patience by assuming the best about others and giving them plenty of time and space to express themselves without my getting upset and giving in to a "fit of anger."

HOW TO GET THE CHICKEN

TODAY'S SCRIPTURE: Proverbs 14:29

Someone once said: "The key to everything is patience. You get the chicken by hatching the egg, not smashing it."

So many aspects of our lives are disrupted and destroyed due to impatience. We grow weary of waiting, smash the egg, and then complain that we have no baby chickens. Consider a few biblical passages about the necessity of patience:

> "Whoever is slow to anger (i.e., the patient person) is better than the mighty, and he who rules his spirit than he who takes a city" (Proverbs 16:32).

> "Whoever is slow to anger (the patient person) has great understanding, but he who has a hasty temper exalts folly" (Proverbs 14:29).

> "Love is patient and kind..." (1 Corinthians 13:4).

Obviously, we are facing unusual times thanks to the pandemic and social unrest in our country. School administrators and teachers are doing their very best for our children. Let's be patient with them. The pandemic may have you confined to your house, you are working from home, not used to being around your family this much. You might even be conducting school from your home for the first time ever. Let's be patient with each other. The shepherds / elders at your local congregation always carry a heavy weight due to the gravity and magnitude of their job and responsibilities. This has been amplified during the pandemic. Most likely your shepherds have lost sleep in recent months as they pursued the optimal ways to keep the flock safe both spiritually as well as physically. Let's be patient with them.

The sad irony is that so many of us are upset that we don't have any baby chicks...but we are the very ones who could not be bothered to wait for them to hatch. Whether we want to raise baby chicks, or we want to live the good life...the key is patience.

Today, I will...demonstrate my desire to be more patient by refusing to gripe and complain.

BEING PATIENT WITH GOD

TODAY'S SCRIPTURE: James 5:7-11

Sadly, when times are difficult, God is often the first one we question and become frustrated with. Questions like, "Where was God when...?" or "Why would God allow...?" may well be legitimate. However, queries like these are often asked much too soon. The Lord is not given proper place of reverence and His will and word are not appropriately considered or consulted. Additionally, such questions are often asked without caution or much self-reflection.

What about questions like, "What is God trying to teach me here?" or "What do I learn about God in this type of situation?" or "What do I learn about myself and my own faith when I'm presented with these choices and circumstances?"

Has it not occurred to us that maybe we should be asking these types of questions right here, right now? James refers to the patience (or steadfastness) of Job (James 5:11). Much of the book of Job is about wrestling with the question: "Can God be trusted?" It seems that Job's wife had come to believe that God had proven Himself to be untrustworthy. She wondered why her husband kept hanging on in spite of all the pain and misfortune. She wondered aloud why he remained patient with God. In Job 2:9 it is recorded that she asked, "Do you still hold fast your integrity? Curse God and die." Her patience with God seems to have run out.

We learn from James 5:7-9 that the return of the Lord is certain (though the time is unknown). Additionally, we learn from verse 11 that He is coming back on His own time and He has a purpose / plan for each one of us. While the reasons for our specific instances of suffering may remain a mystery to us (as it apparently did to Job), we can know that God – in His infinite wisdom – has a plan.

We must be patient with God. He knows what He is doing. He knows what needs to be done. May we join with Job and say, "Though He slay me, I will hope in Him" (13:15), and, "I know that my Redeemer lives" (19:25). May we join with Jesus Himself and say, "Not as I will, but as you will" (Matthew 26:39).

Today, I will...be careful and more thoughtful about the questions I ask God. Though it will not be easy, I will look for ways to grow in my faith in the midst of my suffering. I will be patient with God.

DIVINE PATIENCE

TODAY'S SCRIPTURE: 2 Peter 3:9

"The Lord is not slow to fulfill His promise as some count slowness, but is patient toward you, not wishing that any should perish, but that all should reach repentance." I am so thankful that the Lord is patient!

What if we were never given an opportunity to repent? What if we were never given the opportunity to go home after embarrassing and damaging mistakes? The world would be bleak and hopeless. But that is not the way it is! Our God is rich in mercy (Ephesians 2:4). We are to "...count the patience of our Lord as salvation..." (2 Peter 3:15). Paul asked the Christians in Rome, "Or do you presume on the riches of His kindness and forbearance and patience, not knowing that God's kindness is meant to lead you to repentance?" (Romans 2:4). God is patient with us and for that we should be thankful. However, we should also be aware that God has expectations that we will imitate Him (Ephesians 5:1). Patience is a divine characteristic that God expects us to share with Him. Consider:

"And we urge you, brothers, admonish the idle, encourage the fainthearted, help the weak, be patient with them all" (1 Thessalonians 5:14). God has been patient with us, now He demands we be patient with others.

"Rejoice in hope, be patient in tribulation, be constant in prayer" (Romans 12:12). We are to rejoice that we are as blessed as we are – we are children of God! When we face our trials and times of suffering, we are to communicate all our concerns and fears to the Lord.

"But if we hope for what we do not see, we wait for it with patience" (Romans 8:25). While the context of this passage is about ultimate resurrection and renewal, application can surely be made to our present circumstances. We don't know for sure what "normal life" will look like on the other side of the pandemic, but through faith we can bear up and wait for the plan of God to unfold.

Today, I will...meditate upon the awesome blessing of divine patience. I will communicate to God that I am thankful for His patience with me by (1) telling Him I'm thankful in prayer and (2) showing Him by being patient with those I interact with today.

DEVELOPING PATIENCE

TODAY'S SCRIPTURE: James 1:2-3

"Count it all joy, my brothers, when you meet trials of various kinds, for you know that the testing of your faith produces steadfastness." If you are like me, you really love being around patient people. They make life more pleasant. They make life sweeter. They make it easier to be yourself and, more than that, to flourish and become an even better version of yourself. But, again, if you are like me, when it comes to showing patience, you could stand to grow and improve a bit in that department. How do we develop patience? Here are two ideas to get you started.

First, don't run from trials but seek to learn from them. According to the book of James, it is when we have been tested and tried that our faith grows stronger. Patience is developed by facing, enduring, and (with the help of God) coming out victorious on the other side. Going through something difficult, even awful, and surviving is not only educational, it is empowering. We learn a number of things about God and self in a time of suffering. Paul shared divine insight that was also born of personal experience when he wrote Philippians 4:4-13. He could be patient and content with his circumstances (even in chains!) because he knew that the Lord was at hand.

Second, keep the big picture or grand scheme of things in mind. Instead of getting bogged down in the little insignificant matters that pop up each day (flat tires, stubbed toes, misplaced car keys, et. al.), try to think from an eternal perspective. In part, that means not to become consumed with what your neighbor is doing but focus on what God is doing with you!

"Be still before the LORD and wait patiently for Him; fret not yourself over the one who prospers in his way, over the man who carries out evil devices! Refrain from anger, and forsake wrath! Fret not yourself; it tends only to evil. For evildoers shall be cut off, but those who wait for the LORD shall inherit the land" (Psalm 37:7-9).

Our situation is not determined by what our neighbor is doing! We are blessed for our faithfulness – our commitment to the LORD, not our ability to keep up with the Joneses. We must not determine what we will do based upon what we see others doing. We are to listen to and patiently follow the LORD.

Today, I will...be mindful of growing in patience. I will actively seek to be a more patient person. I will pray and ask the Lord for help – fully aware of the fact that He may well send me "trials of various kinds" in order that I might become more steadfast!

Fruit of the Spirit In My Life: Goodness

CHUCK MONAN

FOR GOODNESS' SAKE

TODAY'S SCRIPTURE: Galatians 5:22-23

When addressed as "Good Teacher," Jesus responded "Why do you call me good? No one is good except God alone" (Mark 10:18).

Our self-righteous world with its "cancel culture" and "virtue signaling" would do well to remember that goodness derives from God, not social media warriors. God is the essence of good. His being is one of moral perfection, and any time the Bible applies the word to people, it is only as imitators of God's character that it applies.

Strong's notes, "The neuter of the adjective with the definite article signifies that which is good or literally 'the good' as being morally honorable, pleasing to God, and therefore beneficial. Christians are to prove it (Romans 12:2), to cleave to it (Romans 12:9), to do it (Galatians 6:10), to imitate it (3 John 1:11), and to overcome evil with it (Romans 12:21)."

People who live this way will be following Peter's admonition to live such good lives among the pagans that they will stand out. Such goodness is interpreted these days as intolerant, judgmental, and bigoted. No matter; "For everyone who does wicked things hates the light and does not come to the light" (John 3:20). The Christian who lives for God will pursue and practice goodness: "Whatever is true, whatever is honorable, whatever is just, whatever is pure, whatever is lovely, whatever is commendable, if there is any excellence...think about these things" (Philippians 4:8). This is a call to arms for a life of goodness.

> Genuine goodness is a matter of habitually acting and responding appropriately in each situation as it arises, moved always by the desire to please God.
> -The Cloud of Unknowing

Today, I will...love and trust in the Lord because He is good, and His love endures forever.

GOODNESS LOVES THE TRUTH

TODAY'S SCRIPTURE: Luke 4:16-21

In the film The Gospel According to Luke when Jesus prepares to read from the prophecy of Isaiah in the synagogue in Nazareth, he picks up the scroll and kisses it. Whether that happened or not, is there any doubt that Jesus loved God's word? "Sanctify them in the truth; your word is truth" (John 17:17).

In 2020, Churches of Christ said farewell to two towering figures whose influence derived from their love of God and His word. Stafford North and Jimmy Allen filled their ninety years with a relentless devotion to the truth of God.

Stafford's love for Scripture dated back to his childhood when he slept with his Bible. Through a lifetime as a preacher, professor, college administrator, elder, and author, his North Star was always the word of God. He never lost his desire to know God and His truth, and to share it with young and old. A lifetime searching the Scriptures enabled him to explain difficult passages in such a way that even the novice could understand and benefit. His teaching influenced thousands of Christians and congregations.

Jimmy's introduction to God's Word came later, but as soon as he was baptized into Christ he immediately made up for lost time. The combination of a sharp mind and an intense personality produced a preacher unlike any in the brotherhood. He was in demand to preach Gospel Meetings which soon grew into massive gatherings across the country. It is estimated that 15,000 were baptized from his preaching. Yet even after the era of those meetings slowed, Allen continued to dig and study to understand more of the Bible such as the book of Romans. "If you get Romans, God gets you," he said.

It is surely no coincidence that two of the greatest influences of my life shared a deep love and reverence for God's Word. May the Lord raise up more men like Stafford North and Jimmy Allen.

Today, I will...pledge anew to search the Scriptures and let them be the guiding light of my life.

GOODNESS INSPIRES COMPASSION

TODAY'S SCRIPTURE: Matthew 9:35-38

In 1997 Canadian singer Sarah McLachlan released a hauntingly beautiful ballad titled "Angel". And decades later, whenever its first notes are heard on TV, millions immediately change the channel. The quicker the better to avoid those images of sad, neglected little dogs the ASPCA is trying to save.

I cannot watch them. They leave me gutted. If I could rescue all of them, I would.

Jesus was moved with compassion when he saw the crowds. They were harassed and helpless. They were prisoners in their own land to the brutal occupying Romans. There were up against it economically, trying to eke out a meager living in a poor country. They were in constant fear of the sickness and disease that lurked in the shadows.

And they were brutalized by a religious establishment that did nothing to give them hope or direction as they searched to find purpose and meaning: "Woe to you lawyers also! For you load people with burdens hard to bear, and you yourselves do not touch the burdens with one of your fingers" (Luke 11:46). So it remains today. Millions are shackled by false religions and man-made doctrines and are kept from the true freedom only found in Christ (John 8:32). If they do not hear the life-giving Gospel, they will remain harassed and helpless, like sheep without a shepherd.

This is where we come in. We can help the Lord of the harvest by being workers in his field. We can share the Good News of Jesus with the lost.

> I look upon all the world as my parish...in whatever
> part of it I am, I judge it meet, right and my
> bounden duty to declare unto all that are willing
> to hear, the glad tidings of salvation.
> -John Wesley

Today, I will...see people with compassion as Jesus sees them and do my part to share the Living Water.

GOODNESS FOLLOWS THE APOSTLES' TEACHING

TODAY'S SCRIPTURE: 2 Timothy 4:2-4

It is instructive that the first verse describing the fledgling church which began on Pentecost reads, "And they devoted themselves to the apostles' teaching and the fellowship, to the breaking of bread and the prayers" (Acts 2:42). These first Christians weren't making it up as they went along; they were committed to following without deviation that body of teaching given them by Jesus' inspired apostles. (John 16:13)

Two millennia later the church is afflicted with leaders whose egos have led them to believe that their genius offers a better way forward than the God-breathed instruction of Scripture. These change agents state that if churches of Christ will not adopt female leadership and instrumental music, they will not survive. They alone, they tell us, hold the key to the church's future.

Nonsense. The church founded by Christ derives, thrives, and survives because of its source – Jesus of Nazareth, God's Son – not because of man-made doctrines and so-called innovations. The apostle Paul warned Timothy, "Keep a close watch on yourself and on the teaching. Persist in this, for by so doing you will save both yourself and your hearers" (1 Timothy 4:16).

The survival of the church does not rest with teachers who distort the truth to attract crowds and imitate the denominations. It does rest on faithfulness to God and His Word. The heart motivated by God's love will never turn away from the truth to myths. It would never assume that the teachings of men are of equal importance to the apostles' teachings.

Jesus warns, "Not everyone who says to me, 'Lord, Lord,' will enter the kingdom of heaven, but the one who does the will of my Father who is in heaven. On that day many will say to me, 'Lord, Lord, did we not prophesy in your name, and cast out demons in our name, and do many mighty works in your name?' And then I will declare to them, 'I never knew you; depart from me, you workers of lawlessness.'" (Matthew 7:21-24).

Today, I will...follow the apostles' teaching and refuse to substitute them for doctrines derived from men.

GOODNESS BUILDS INTEGRITY

TODAY'S SCRIPTURE: Acts 10:34-36

Roman soldiers in first -century Judea were a menacing, unwanted presence. But Cornelius was different. He was devout, God-fearing, generous, and kind to all. When the apostle Peter was summoned to his house through divine intervention, he would learn an important lesson: God loves and accepts all people who fear him and do what is right. Cornelius was a good man and his integrity led all people to give him a hearing.

The tendency of people to favor their own group while disdaining "the other" is as old as time and as difficult to eradicate as cockroaches. Racism is alive and well and is difficult to root out. Perhaps a way forward is found in the example of Cornelius and the words of John Henry Newman: "It is as absurd to argue men, as to torture them, into believing." A good example is always more convincing than a good speech.

Such an effect was seen half a century ago in the life of Willie Mays.

Possibly the greatest all-around baseball player who ever lived, Mays grew up in the Jim Crow South. Yet racism also awaited Mays in the northern city of Trenton, N.J., and in the west coast enclave of San Francisco. Mays always kept his head, his honor, and his dignity. He won people over with his irrepressible personality, enthusiasm, work ethic, grace, and sheer brilliance as an athlete. He treated everyone well, regardless of how he was treated.

> There are very few paths when words can be used to change people's minds. Once in a while, someone does that. But indelible images can do that. Every time he took the field and played his heart out...he was making a statement. Because of the way he played and conducted himself, Willie Mays made it absurd to be a racist.
> -Bill Clinton

Goodness informs integrity, and integrity nearly always speaks much louder than words. How we live always matters, and can win over our enemies.

Today, I will...live in such a way that friends and foes alike will notice and give thanks to God.

Fruit of the Spirit In My Life: Kindness

RALPH GILMORE

A NEED FOR KINDNESS

TODAY'S SCRIPTURE: Proverbs 21:21; 31:26

Have you noticed that cultural graciousness seems to be on the decline? In some parts of our world, people still say "Ma'am" and "Sir," but it occurs more rarely. During the time of the pandemic of 2020, though, I noticed that more people were holding the doors open for each other. Yet the world as a whole still desperately needs acts of kindness bestowed on each other. Lives have been lost, jobs were lost or altered, and the "new normal" was nothing like we envisioned. We were wearing masks, having our temperatures taken, standing with plexiglass barriers between us, and hand sanitizer dispensers proliferated apparently overnight. It would be difficult to imagine a time when kindness was more needed than now.

According to John Gottman and Robert Levenson, who closely studied the effects of negativity within couples, the suggested ratio for positive personal encounters needed to overcome negative personal encounters is 5:1.** Anecdotally, we know that the ratio is great although probably the exact percentage is unknown. So, as individuals and communities, we must be intentional about showing kindness. On a given day, you may have a hundred people who are kind to you and one person who is really the opposite. Which one do you remember when someone asks you how your day went?

The need for kindness was also great in Solomon's day. Thus, he describes the pursuit of righteousness and kindness as resulting in life, righteousness and honor (Proverbs 21:21). Solomon also portrays the virtuous woman (women) as having kindness on her tongue (Proverbs 31:26). The Hebrew word for "kindness" is usually rendered "loving kindness." It is a word that is rich in meaning. We will study the word further in the next devo. At this point, suffice it to say that the word has to do with God's faithfulness to His word. If you are starving for kindness from those around you, why not "try a little kindness to overlook the blindness of narrow-minded people on the narrow-minded streets."***

Today, I will...intentionally try to be kind to all people, but especially to those people to whom my first inclination is not to be kind.

**collectivehub.com; May 2017
***lyric from 'Try a Little Kindness' by Glen Campbell

A MIND OF KINDNESS

TODAY'S SCRIPTURE: Ruth 3:10; Romans 2:4

Since the seat of kindness is the mind, today we will try to understand kindness better as it relates to God. As mentioned in yesterday's devo, the Hebrew word most often used for kindness is *chesed*. The word is often rendered as "loving kindness" because this is the proper outcome of being loyal to a covenant while having a heart of compassion. Therefore, the word is difficult to translate in English.

Naomi responded to her daughter-in-law with this very type of kindness when Ruth decided to follow Naomi after the death of her husband. Naomi proclaims to Ruth the general principle, "And Naomi said to her daughter-in-law, "May he be blessed by the Lord, whose kindness has not forsaken the living or the dead!" (Ruth 2:20). And to imagine—this kindness shown to Naomi came from a Moabite woman.

In the New Testament, kindness has prompted God to provide the gospel as His hand leading us to repentance (Romans 2:4). How blessed we are that God's has been kind to each of us. In Ephesians 2:7, we learn that God's kindness, to be embodied in the person of Jesus, was in the eternal mind of God. The Holy Spirit is also involved in showing kindness to us in that kindness is a fruit from the Spirit that lives in us (Galatians 6:22). So, the entire Godhead is committed to showing you their kindness. You are loved by all three members of the one true and living God! The loving-kindness of God our Savior has appeared to all people through the giving of the the good news for all of us (Titus 3:4).

The mind of kindness begins with understanding the kindness of God, as we have briefly outlined. Then, as we have received the kindness of the gospel in our hearts, we are admonished to put on this same kindness as God works in our lives (Colossians 3:12).

Today, I will...be more intentional in seeking understanding about how kindness, as well as other attributes, lead God to reach out to me so that I may live.

A TALK OF KINDNESS

TODAY'S SCRIPTURE: Zechariah 7:9; Ephesians 4:32

Talking your walk is so much easier than walking it. However, let us not underestimate the importance of talking it. Today we will address a talk of kindness. There are people who are not kind who learn to talk that way out of vested interests, but generally there are no kind people who do not talk that way.

How important is a talk of kindness? "Kindness builds trust and creates a safety net for all types of relationships."** Isn't it odd that at our places of employment we can talk kindly to almost anyone because we are trained to do so. Why, then, is it so difficult to be kind to those closest to us? Included in this concept is not only how we speak to each other but how we speak about each other to other people. A sign of a mature relationship is consistency between how we speak to each other and how we speak about each other.

If one is consistently kind to another, then trust is built up over time. This is essential if trust has ever been broken. I may feel entitled to speak harshly to someone who has hurt me. Yet, if trust is ever to be restored, kindness needs to characterize our communication patterns. How many church divisions could have been avoided if more kindness had been utilized. Zechariah encouraged his audience to "render true judgments" and to "show kindness and mercy to one another" (7:9), and Paul directs Christians to be kind one to another (Ephesians 4:32).

What if kindness is not representative of our communication with each other? The absence of kind speaking can lead to anger, distrust, insecurity, and other forms of dysfunctional interactions. A fellow faculty member several years ago offered me some sound advice concerning how I should conduct the Open Forum, a part of the FHU Bible Lectureship for many years. He told me simply, "Be gracious." I remembered those words, and there were multiple occasions when they paid positive dividends.

Today, I will...identify two times today where I can apply more kindness to my speech.

**therelationprotocol.com

A WALK OF KINDNESS

TODAY'S SCRIPTURE: Micah 6:8; James 3:9

In the previous devo, we spoke of a "talk" of kindness. Now we will address a walk that should accompany our talk. Those who are millennials and Gen Z have several points of connection, but one of them is an adoration for kindness under display. Toms shoes thrive by selling canvas shoes to the younger generations largely because they give away a pair of shoes to the needy for every pair sold. Tacos4Life gives tacos away to the hungry when you buy their tacos. The story is often repeated in our culture—kindness is a much-appreciated but seldom seen virtue. So, how do we demonstrate that our walk is fueled by kindness?

When Micah summarizes the life that God asks of us, he tells us to "do justice, love kindness, and *walk* (emp. mine) humbly with our God" (6:8). It is a Christian attribute, a way of life, that must be added to our lives in word and deed (2 Peter 1:5-7). Paul affirms that love is kind (1 Corinthians 13:4).

Walking in kindness is one of the ways Paul identifies the walk of Jesus followers (Ephesians 4:1; 32). In reality, kindness in our walk has the DNA of Jesus in several ways one of which is respect. When I walk in kindness, I should respect the humanity of everyone because we are all in the image of God. James sheds light on this idea by noting the impossibility of loving God and cursing others who are also in His image (3:9). Quickly in your mind survey some of the major issues dividing our societies today: which ones could not be improved by mutual respect?

When I learn to respect all humanity, one concomitant result will be that I will recognize the rights that all people have because of their heritage of the divine. This does not mean that there is no truth and that all are equally right. But even Jefferson as a humanist knew that the Creator vested us with rights, like life, liberty, and the pursuit of happiness, from which we should not be alienated. Respect and rights could improve our congregations, our homes, our societies, and even our own self-images.

Today, I will...show respect for everyone I meet by walking in kindness.

A BALANCED VIEW OF KINDNESS

TODAY'S SCRIPTURE: Romans 11:22; Matthew 23

I love Jesus and I believe that millions do. To do so often means that I need to use my faith in the importance of kindness in a general sense to seek understanding of the kindness motif in a specific sense. What was Jesus like on an average day in His ministry to others? Was he always kind? Obviously, there are times that Jesus was incredibly frank and even at times a little harsh. In Matthew 23, there is the list of "Woes" that Jesus leveled against the Pharisees. If one examined only this passage, it would be misrepresentative because Jesus has battled the Pharisees and their misconceptions of the Gospel for nearly three and one-half years. Jesus was not customarily unkind to anyone or any group of people. However, the hardness of the hearts of the Pharisees should have been evident to every disciple of Jesus. Besides, Jesus knew that his mission to the earth included his sacrificial death and the Pharisees would contribute to this end.

Romans 11:22 reveals this balanced side of God where kindness and severity seem juxtaposed. However, they are not at odds with each other. In a series of questions that Paul addresses in Romans 9-11, God's interaction with the Jews and the Gentiles relative to kingdom issues is the integral topic. Paul's unabashed humility in the face of such difficult ideas is portrayed in Romans 11:33 where he concludes that in some ways God's ways are above our absolute scrutiny (cf. Isaiah 55:11-12).

I believe the balance in kindness and severity is best understood in view of one's primary attitude or customary approach in human connections. Like Jesus, on an average day our relationships with others should be kind. It is the "default position" for every Christian. We cannot properly meme Christ with meanness, harsh words, and anger. There may come a time when we need to resort to another type of response to others, but that should not be our first reaction. Jesus, as Paul says, wants us to live peaceably with all if it is at all possible (Romans 12:18).

Today, I will...be kind to everyone I encounter, as much as is possible.

Fruit of the Spirit In My Life: Gentleness

DON DELUKIE

MOUNTAIN MAN GENTLENESS

TODAY'S SCRIPTURE: Galatians 5:22, 23

While traveling through the mountains of north Arkansas with a man many deemed a "mountain man", a rugged individual who was "rough and tumble", the mountain man was asked. Can you give a definition of gentleness? His answer was amazing. He said - "a four year old with a kitten." Think about that for a minute. Two year olds may try to pick up a kitten on the wrong end, not knowing any better and not meaning any harm. Isn't it interesting how cats will be so patient with a child? Although they will run and hide if they see that two year heading their way again! But a four year old has learned the "need" and the "how" to be gentle. (For an interesting extra, google "Koko and the kitten" to see how a huge gorilla handled a kitten).

With so many graces lost in today's super-charged society, we observe people screaming at those who hold a different opinion. As christians we must learn the "need" and the "how" to be gentle. Proverbs 15:1 A soft answer turns away wrath, but a harsh word stirs up anger.

As we move from babes in Christ to mature servants we learn to not upend people, or shout them down, but to be as gentle as a four year old with a kitten. Someone said "meekness is not weakness." It often requires much more bravery and inner strength to be meek and gentle than aggressive and assertive.

Try this with your family, church members, people at work, your boss, etc, the next time some situation gets "charged," try being the one who is gentle. It works because it is a christian principle. Our Lord Jesus was a gentle man. If we can't speak gently, we can act gentle and be that light in someone's life who doesn't ignite fuses, but defuses situations. To know the "secret" of why some are so respected and so effective, look for this trait.

Today, I will...try a little tenderness to be more like our Lord.

GENTLENESS AMONG GOD'S PEOPLE

TODAY'S SCRIPTURE: James 3:17

A sad thing in many churches today is the constant bickering that goes on, both on the forefront and behind the scenes. I must not be a part of that. No, no. Oh, I stand for doctrinal truths, but petty matters only cause schism and division. Our freedom in a physical realm may give us the urge to demand certain things in the spiritual realm. Old timers always said, "beggars can't be choosers".

Today there are many who are always demanding things. Since these things are rarely biblical or spiritual matters, the result can be strife, envy, confusion, and downright evil. Usually the perpetrators insist that their case is a spiritual one when it's rooted in what is wanted or demanded. James braces this with these words, "But if you have bitter jealousy and selfish ambition in your hearts, do not boast and be false to the truth" (James 3:14). How often have you seen people demanding certain things be gentle about it? They push, they stir, they aggressively agitate! If in the midst of chaos, moderation is sought, whom do we seek? A wise one, right?

Consider these words, "Who is wise and understanding among you? By his good conduct let him show his works in the meekness of wisdom. (James 3:13). All the movers and shakers do is move people to other congregations and shake people up, and create confusion. Notice, James 3:16 "For where jealousy and selfish ambition exist, there will be disorder and every vile practice." We ask ourselves, am I part of the of the cure? Can I help gently settle people and matters, and not stir them up. Summarizing we notice James's admonition - James 3:17 "But the wisdom from above is first pure, then peaceable, gentle, open to reason, full of mercy and good fruits, impartial and sincere."

Today, I will... be a gentle peacemaker for then I have God's greatest of blessings.

GENTLE CROCODILES

TODAY'S SCRIPTURE: 2 Corinthians 10:1

One of the most ferocious beasts and deadliest of predators is the crocodile. Stories from every place they are known to exist include tales of horror. Not only to the usual prey, but to human beings as well. The largest ever recorded was just over 20 feet long! While appearing to be lethargic, crocodiles can move with much speed on land and in the water! Now add in the most powerful biting force in nature at 3,700 pounds per square inch! Humans have about 150 psi, hyenas, tigers, and lions about 1,000 psi, and sharks (depending on size) about 1,300 psi.

They remind me of Satan. As beasts migrate and cross rivers, the Crocs slaughter them mercilessly. As we journey toward the prize of life we have many obstacles and the Devil is seeking whom he may devour (1 Peter 5:8) However the intimidating, reckless, destructive crocodile with it's unimaginable bite force can be one of the gentlest of all creatures! When crocodile eggs hatch the newborn start making croaking noises so the mother will hear them. Other crocs hear them also and often cannibalize their own helpless kind. The mother hurries to the nest site and starts gathering babies in her mouth, and gently takes them to the relative safety of the river. Her bite force is throttled for her babies' lives are at stake. If such a river monster can curtail it's wildness, so we can control our tongue when dealing with those not as mature.

Today let us not "bite and devour" one another (Galatians 5:15) as we injure and harm our own kind. Jesus never did this. Ephesians 4:32 reminds us to "Be kind to one another, tenderhearted, forgiving one another, as God in Christ forgave you".

Today, I will... not lead without gentleness of action and mouth.

GENTLENESS WORKS

TODAY'S SCRIPTURE: Philippians 2:3

A beautiful horse spent all it's adult life in a pen about half an acre. It was well kept, well fed, and allowed freedom within it's boundaries. It was a beautiful golden palomino. The horse was no danger to anyone and enjoyed those sugar cubes some gave him through the fence. He seemed to delight in children. The horse was sold. The new owners came to move him. Bear in mind that this horse had never been out of his enclosure his entire adult life. The new owners were loud boisterous, and frightening. There was a bank on one side of the lot and they backed a trailer up to the fence there to load the animal. They cut the wire in the fence at this point and proceeded to try and get a rope on the horse and get him in the trailer. Unfamiliar with a rope or bridle he ran from them. They finally got a rope on him and attempted to get him to the trailer. He refused. That's when they started cursing him, jerking on the rope, and shoving him to no avail. Then they started beating him. They beat him until blood was dripping off his wonderful coat! But, he would not budge. They sent for a genuine cowboy. He asked them to leave. He talked gently to the horse, rubbed his neck and muzzle, took off the rope, and after about thirty minutes of working with him led him right into the trailer!

There are people with confined thinking. They are secure where they are and happy with life. In our attempts to move them to Christ we must not torment them, belittle them, or beat them up verbally. But with gentleness of word and action we can calm them and open up many opportunities. To be like Christ is to be gentle.

Today, I will... be gentle to all God's creation, especially people He created.

GENTLENESS INVOLVES LAWFULNESS

TODAY'S SCRIPTURE: Titus 3:1,2

In today's text, Paul charges young men and old, older women and younger, servants and those walking with Christ toward eternity to do their respective duties. Paul then urges them to submit to government authorities. Some people it seems, feel above the law, "And especially those who indulge in the lust of defiling passion and despise authority" (2 Peter 2:10).

There is something missing because they are driven by what they want, the way they want it, with no repercussions. Whether police officers, military servicemen, or elected government officials who are expected to responsibly serve citizens. They lead police on long, dangerous pursuits that often have a fiery ending. They refuse to obey commands and resist in every way they can. Why? It is true there are some in these positions that fail in their service. It's rare. But, the real reason is that some individuals are driven with false pride and zeal that causes them to resist. The one thing they are not is gentle. If they were living out the fruit of the spirit and the example of Jesus, they would possess gentle humility.

Our text (Titus 3:1,2) calls us to be obedient to civil authorities as well as to the Lord—an indictment against those who refuse to live with gentleness. This obedience isn't that of worshiping, but of cooperating, as Paul explains in Romans 13:1-3. Please take a minute read these verses and imagine how our society would improve if we practiced gentleness.

Today, I will... show my gentleness to all demonstrating God's authority.

Fruit of the Spirit In My Life: Self-Control

DAVID SPROULE

SELF-CONTROL IS ESSENTIAL TO GO TO HEAVEN

TODAY'S SCRIPTURE: 1 Corinthians 9:27

"I can't help myself—that's just the way I am." How often do we lose our temper? How often do we say things that we shouldn't say? How often do we think things we shouldn't think? How often do we long for things that we shouldn't desire? How often do we react in ways that we shouldn't react? Is it a legitimate response to merely say, "I can't help myself—that's just the way that I am"?

God's Word clearly teaches that I don't get a pass because I think that I don't have the willpower to control myself. In fact, Scripture emphatically teaches just the opposite.

Jesus called the people to Himself, in Mark 8:34, and said to them, "If anyone would come after me, let him deny himself..." To "deny" self literally has the idea to say "No!" to yourself—forgetting yourself and your own interests. In order to "follow" Christ, my Lord has given me the ability to "help myself" and change "the way that I am." I cannot legitimately use that as an excuse!

In both (1) the identifying of the fruit of the Spirit (Galatians 5:22-23) and (2) the essential qualities (sometimes called "Christian graces") that we must supply to our faith (2 Peter 1:5-7), the inspired apostles included "self-control." The Greek word used in these verses literally involves "holding one's self in," and it distinguishes one who restrains his passions, desires and behavior. Seeing that self-control is a requirement in these texts, it is obvious that our Lord would not require something of us that we could not properly and acceptably obey.

Is self-control a big deal...eternally-speaking? Consider Paul's determination: "I discipline my body and keep it under control, lest after preaching to others I myself should be disqualified" (1 Corinthians 9:27). Failing to keep my body "under control" can ultimately lead me to be "disqualified," in the sight of God, to dwell with Him eternally. This is such a critical matter!

Today, I will... Pray to God and ask Him to help me to "be all the more diligent" to "practice" self-control, in order that I might "be richly provided...an entrance into the eternal kingdom" (2 Peter 1:10-11).

CONTROLLING MY INPUTS AND ENVIRONMENT

TODAY'S SCRIPTURE: Mark 7:21-23

Every Christian has the responsibility to master his passions and practice self-control (Galatians 5:22-23; 2 Peter 1:5-7). There is no doubt (Scripturally) about that. And, surely, every faithful Christian truly has a desire to do just that. So, how can I? How can I master my passions and practice self-control? What does the Bible teach me about that?

God's Word teaches that, in order to control myself, I must effectively control those things that I allow into my heart. That is the critical place to start.

In the early days of computers, it was noted that the "outputs" of a computer program were tied directly to the "inputs" of that computer program. A phrase was coined in 1957, "Garbage in, garbage out." If garbage was coming out, it was because garbage was going in. If you wanted to alter the output, you needed to alter the input.

Of course, what was learned about computers in the mid-twentieth century has been true of humans since their creation. The Creator of humans stated, "For from within, out of the heart of man, come evil...All these evil things come from within..." (Mark 7:21-23). In order for evil to come out of the heart, it must have first entered into the heart (7:19). If we can keep the evil/garbage from going in, we can keep the evil/garbage from coming out!

Therefore, as Christians, we must learn to control our inputs. If we watch television and movies with foul language, that gets into our hearts and that's what will come out. If we allow our eyes to view nudity and pornographic material, that gets into our hearts and will influence our desires and behavior. If we hang around ungodly individuals, their conduct gets into our hearts and will influence our conduct. That's why God tells us to "not be deceived" (Galatians 6:7), to monitor our "company" (1 Corinthians 15:33), and to "abstain from passions of the flesh, which wage war against your soul" (1 Peter 2:11). To better control ourselves, we must control our inputs.

Today, I will... Pray to God and ask Him to give me the strength to "abstain from all appearance of evil" (1 Thessalonians 5:22, KJV).

CONTROLLING MY THOUGHTS

TODAY'S SCRIPTURE: Philippians 4:8

Even Christians struggle with self-control. We struggle with our attitudes, our tempers, our tongues, our desires, our lusts, our reactions, etc. When we fail to exercise self-control, we feel guilty and defeated. What can we do to better discipline our bodies and bring them into subjection?

The wise man wrote, "For as he thinks in his heart, so is he" (Proverbs 23:7, NKJV). Who we are and how we behave is tied directly to what we think. Therefore, if we are going to be faithful followers of Christ, we must "take every thought captive to obey Christ" (2 Corinthians 10:5). What vivid terminology! As one might capture a felon, bind him with restraints and lock him in a prison cell, that's what we must do with our thoughts—capture them before they can lead to sinful action, bind them with the restraints of Christ and cast them into a bottomless prison where they can no longer harm us.

Capturing our thoughts requires curbing our opinion about ourselves. We must never "think of [ourselves] more highly than [we] ought to think" or to "be wise in [our] own sight" (Romans 12:3, 16). A sense of entitlement will lead us to lose our temper and to look like the world, rather than to "gain Christ" (Philippians 3:8) and to look like Him!

Capturing our thoughts requires curbing our material desires and learning to "be content with what [we] have" (Hebrews 13:5). It requires curbing our fleshly desires and learning to "flee" from lustful and tempting situations (1 Corinthians 6:18), rather than letting our "heart turn aside" and see how "near" we can get to the "paths" of immorality (Proverbs 7:25; 5:8).

Capturing our thoughts requires curbing any "bitter envy and self-seeking" in our hearts (James 3:14), and, rather than harbor grudges and "count up wrongdoing" (1 Corinthians 13:5, ESV footnote), working on developing a heart that favors forgiving others (Ephesians 4:31-32).

Capturing our thoughts requires focusing our minds upon positive and righteous thoughts and meditating upon "whatever" things are "true...honorable...just...pure...lovely... [and] commendable" (Philippians 4:8).

Today, I will... Pray to God and ask Him to give me the strength to stop, to "think on my ways" and to "turn my feet to [His] testimonies" (Psalm 119:59).

CONTROLLING MY WORDS

TODAY'S SCRIPTURE: James 1:19, 26

One of the greatest challenges that a Christian faces is in trying to "not stumble in what he says" and in keeping his tongue from "setting on fire the entire course of life" (James 3:2, 6). Some first-century Christians found themselves "saying what they should not" (1 Timothy 5:13), which remains a struggle in our present day. How can we learn to control our tongues?

First, we must learn to listen. "If one gives an answer before he hears, it is his folly and shame" (Proverbs 18:13).

Second, we must take time to think. "The heart of the righteous ponders how to answer" (Proverbs 15:28).

Third, we must train ourselves to pause before we speak. "Do you see a man who is hasty in his words? There is more hope for a fool than for him" (Proverbs 29:20).

Fourth, we must use our words sparingly and restrain ourselves from saying everything we are thinking. "When words are many, transgression is not lacking, but whoever restrains his lips is prudent" (Proverbs 10:19). "A fool vents all his feelings, but a wise man holds them back" (Proverbs 29:11, NKJV; cf. Proverbs 11:12; 13:3; 21:23).

Fifth, we must watch our tone. "A soft answer turns away wrath, but a harsh word stirs up anger" (Proverbs 15:1). "There is one whose rash words are like sword thrusts, but the tongue of the wise brings healing" (Proverbs 12:18; cf. 17:27; 16:24). The right words with the wrong tone become the wrong words.

Finally, after taking all of the above precautions first, then we need to watch the words that we actually speak. "Let no unwholesome word proceed from your mouth" (Ephesians 4:29, NASB). Put away "obscene talk from your mouth" (Colossians 3:9). "Do not speak evil against one another" (James 4:11). Is what I am going to say true? Is it nice? Is it necessary? What ultimate purpose does it serve? Could it be misunderstood? Would it be better to not say it at all?

Today, I will... Pray to God and ask Him to give me the strength to "bridle" my tongue and to "be quick to hear, slow to speak" (James 1:26, 19).

FRIDAY

FOLLOWING THE EXAMPLE OF JESUS

TODAY'S SCRIPTURE: Hebrews 4:15

The Bible says that Jesus was "one who in every respect has been tempted as we are, yet without sin" (Hebrews 4:15). Thus, we find in Jesus one who controlled His inputs and environment, one who controlled His thoughts, one who controlled His words, and one who controlled His temper and reactions. How did He do it?

Consider the extensive maltreatment that Jesus endured—He was despised, rejected, afflicted, betrayed, arrested, bound, mocked, lied about, spit upon, beaten, crowned with thorns, scourged, reviled, blasphemed and crucified. How would you have responded to any or all of that? We are charged to "follow in His steps," as we are reminded, "When He was reviled, He did not revile in return; when He suffered, He did not threaten" (1 Peter 2:21-23). How was He able to control His temper and not react sinfully?

First of all, we know that Jesus memorized Scripture. To each of the devil's temptations, He quoted Scripture (Matthew 4:1-11). If I want to overcome temptation and control my reactions, I must store up God's "word in my heart, that I might not sin against [Him]" (Psalm 119:11). Writing God's Word on our hearts is a Jesus-proven way to control ourselves and to keep from sinning.

Additionally, we recognize that Jesus "continued entrusting Himself to Him who judges justly" (1 Peter 2:23). Jesus kept on turning to His Father, and He kept on trusting in His Father and relying on His Father (Matthew 18:35; 26:39, 42, 53; Luke 23:34, 46; John 8:29; 15:10). If Jesus needed His Father, how much more do we need to continually entrust ourselves to our heavenly Father and beg for His strength?

The One who overcame will give us the strength to overcome (John 16:33; 1 John 4:4). The One who controlled Himself "is able to help those who are being tempted" to overcome (Hebrews 2:18). The One who resisted the devil will empower us to resist steadfastly (James 4:7; 1 Peter 5:8-9; 2:11-12).

Today, I will... Pray to God and ask Him to give me the strength to "imitate Christ" (1 Corinthians 11:1, NKJV), and with His help, to "discipline my body and keep it under control" (1 Corinthians 9:27).

OTHER TITLES AVAILABLE

To order, visit **thejenkinsinstitute.com/shop**

Made in USA - Kendallville, IN
1217190_9798554042485
01.05.2021 1153